EXAMINATION SECTION

EXAMINATION SECTION

TEST 1

DIRECTIONS: Each question or incomplete statement is followed by several suggested answers or completions. Select the one that BEST answers the question or completes the statement. *PRINT THE LETTER OF THE CORRECT ANSWER IN THE SPACE AT THE RIGHT.*

1. Upon arriving at the scene of an accident in which a pedestrian was struck and killed by an automobile, an officer's first action was to clear the scene of spectators.
   Of the following, the PRINCIPAL reason for this action is that
   A. important evidence may be inadvertently destroyed by the crowd
   B. this is a fundamental procedure in first aid work
   C. the operator of the vehicle may escape in the crowd
   D. witnesses will speak more freely if other persons are not present

   1.____

2. In questioning witnesses, an officer is instructed to avoid leading questions or questions that will suggest the answer.
   Accordingly, when questioning a witness about the appearance of a suspect, it would be BEST for him to ask:
   A. What kind of hat did he wear?
   B. Did he wear a felt hat?
   C. What did he wear?
   D. Didn't he wear a hat?

   2.____

3. The only personal description the police have of a particular criminal was made several years ago.
   Of the following, the item in the description that will be MOST useful in identifying him at the present time is the
   A. color of his eyes
   B. color of his hair
   C. number of teeth
   D. weight

   3.____

4. Crime statistics indicate that property crimes such as larceny, burglary, and robbery are more numerous during winter months than in summer.
   The one of the following explanations that MOST adequately accounts for this situation is that
   A. human needs, such as clothing, food, heat, and shelter, are greater in winter
   B. criminal tendencies are aggravated by climatic changes
   C. there are more hours of darkness in winter and such crimes are usually committed under cover of darkness
   D. urban areas are more densely populated during winter months, affording greater opportunity for such crimes

   4.____

5. When automobile tire tracks are to be used as evidence, a plaster cast is made of them.
   Of the following, the MOST probable reason for taking a photograph is that
   A. photographs can be duplicated more easily than castings
   B. less skill is required for photographing than casting
   C. the tracks may be damaged in the casting process
   D. photographs are more easily transported than castings

6. It is generally recommended that an officer, in lifting a revolver that is to be sent to the police laboratory for ballistics tests and fingerprint examination, do so by insetting a pencil through the trigger guard rather than into the barrel of the weapon.
   The reason for preferring this procedure is that
   A. every precaution must be taken not to eliminate fingerprints on the weapon
   B. there is a danger of accidentally discharging the weapon by placing the pencil in the barrel
   C. the pencil may make scratches inside the barrel that will interfere with the ballistics tests
   D. a weapon can more easily be lifted by the trigger guard

7. PHYSICIAN is to PATIENT as ATTORNEY is to
   A. court   B. client   C. counsel   D. judge

8. JUDGE is to SENTENCE as JURY is to
   A. court   B. foreman   C. defendant   D. verdict

9. REVERSAL is to AFFIRMANCE as CONVICTION is to
   A. appeal   B. acquittal   C. error   D. mistrial

10. GENUINE is to TRUE as SPURIOUS is to
    A. correct   B. conceived   C. false   D. speculative

11. ALLEGIANCE is to LOYALTY as TREASON is to
    A. felony   B. faithful   C. obedience   D. rebellion

12. CONCUR is to AGREE as DIFFER is to
    A. coincide   B. dispute   C. join   D. repeal

13. A person who has an uncontrollable desire to steal without need is called a
    A. dipsomaniac   B. kleptomaniac
    C. monomaniac   D. pyromaniac

14. In the sentence, "The placing of any inflammable substance in any building or the placing of any device or contrivence capable of producing fire, for the purpose of causing a fire is an attempt to burn," the MISSPELLED word is
    A. inflammable   B. substance   C. device   D. contrivence

15. In the sentence, "The word 'break' also means obtaining an entrance into a building by any artifice used for that purpose, or by colussion with any person therein," the MISSPELLED word is
    A. obtaining   B. entrance   C. artifice   D. colussion

    15.____

16. In the sentence, "Any person who with intent to provoke a breech of the peace causes a disturbance or is offensive to others may be deemed to have committed disorderly conduct," the MISSPELLED word is
    A. breech   B. disturbance   C. offensive   D. committed

    16.____

17. In the sentence, "When the offender inflicts a grevious harm upon the person from whose possession, or in his presence, property is taken, he is guilty of robbery, the MISSPELLED word is
    A. offender   B. grevious   C. possession   D. presence

    17.____

18. In the sentence, "A person who wilfully encourages or advises another person in attempting to take the latter's life is guilty of a felony," the MISSPELLED word is
    A. wilfully   B. encourages   C. advises   D. attempting

    18.____

19. The treatment to be given the offender cannot alter the fact of his offense; but we can take measures to reduce the chances of similar acts in the future. We should banish the criminal, not in order to exact revenge nor directly to encourage reform, but to deter him and others from further illegal attacks on society.
    According to this paragraph, the PRINCIPAL reason for punishing criminals is to
    A. prevent the commission of future crimes
    B. remove them safely from society
    C. avenge society
    D. teach them that crime does not pay

    19.____

20. Even the most comprehensive and best substantiated summaries of the total volume of criminal acts would not contribute greatly to an understanding of the varied social and biological factors which are sometimes assumed to enter into crime causation, nor would they indicate with any degree of precision the needs of police forces in combating crime.
    According to this statement,
    A. crime statistics alone do not determine the needs of police forces in combating crime
    B. crime statistics are essential to a proper understanding of the social factors of crime
    C. social and biological factor which enter the crime causation have little bearing on police needs
    D. a knowledge of the social and biological factors of crime is essential to a proper understanding of crime statistics

    20.____

21. The police officer's art consists in applying and enforcing a multitude of laws and ordinances in such degree or proportion and in such manner that the greatest degree of social protection will be secured. The degree of enforcement and the method of application will vary with each neighborhood and community.
According to the foregoing paragraph,
    A. each neighborhood or community must judge for itself to what extent the law is to be enforced
    B. a police officer should only enforce those laws which are designed to give the greatest degree of social protection
    C. the manner and intensity of law enforcement is not necessarily the same in all communities
    D. all laws and ordinances must be enforced in a community with the same degree of intensity

22. Police control in the sense of regulating the details of police operations involves such matters as the technical means for so organizing the available personnel that competent police leadership, when secured, can operate effectively. It is concerned not so much with the extent to which popular controls can be trusted to guide and direct the course of police protection a with the administrative relationships which should exist between the component parts of the police organism.
According to the foregoing statement, police control is
    A. solely a matter of proper personnel assignment
    B. the means employed to guide and direct the course of police protection
    C. principally concerned with the administrative relationships between units of a police organization
    D. the sum total of means employed in rendering police protection

23. Two patrol cars hurry to the scene of an accident from different directions. The first proceeds at the rate of 45 miles per hour and arrives in four minutes. Although the second car travels over a route which is three-fourths of a mile longer, it arrives at the scene only a half-minute later.
The speed of the second car, expressed in miles per hour, is
    A. 50   B. 55   C. 60   D. 65

24. A motorcycle officer issued 72 traffic summonses in January, 60 in February and 83 in March.
In order to average 75 summonses per month for the four months of January, February, March, and April, during April he will have to issue _____ summonses.
    A. 80   B. 85   C. 90   D. 95

25. In a unit of the Police Department to which 40 officers are assigned, the sick report record during 2022 was as follows: 1 was absent 8 days, 5 were absent 3 days each, 4 were absent 5 days each, 10 were absent 2 days each, 8 were absent 4 days each, 5 were absent 1 day each.
The average number of days on sick report for all the members of this unit is MOST NEARLY
    A. ½   B. 1   C. 2 ½   D. 3

Questions 26-30.

DIRECTIONS: Column I lists various statements of fact. Column II is a list of crimes. Next to the numbers corresponding to the number preceding the statements of fact in Column I, place the letter preceding the crime listed in Column II with which Jones should be charged. In answering these questions, the following definitions of crimes should be applied, bearing in mind that ALL elements contained in the definitions must be present in order to charge a person with that crime.

BURGLARY is breaking and entering a building with intent to commit some crime therein. EMBEZZLEMENT is the appropriation to one's use of another's property which has been entrusted to one's care or which has come lawfully into one's possession. EXTORTION is taking or obtaining property from another with his consent, induced by a wrongful use of force or fear. LARCENY is taking and carrying away the personal property of another with intent to deprive or defraud the true owner of the use and benefit of such property. ROBBERY is the unlawful taking of the personal property of another from his person or in his presence by force or violence, or fear of injury.

COLUMN I

26. Jones, believing Smith had induced his wife to leave him, went to Smith's home armed with a knife with which he intended to assault Smith. When his knock was unanswered, he forced open the door of Smith's home and entered but, finding the house empty, he threw away the knife and left.

27. Jones was employed as a collection agent by Smith. When Smith refused to reimburse him for certain expenses he claimed to have incurred in connection with his work, Jones deducted this amount from sums he had collected for Smith.

28. Jones spent the night in a hotel. During the night he left his room, went downstairs to the desk, stole money and returned to his room.

29. Jones, a building inspector, found that the elevators in Smith's building were being operated without a permit. He threatened to report the matter and have the elevators shut down unless Smith paid him a sum of money. Smith paid the amount demanded

30. Jones held-up Smith on the street and, pointing a revolve at him, demanded his money. Smith, without resisting, handed Jones his money. When Jones was apprehended, it was discovered that the revolver was a toy.

COLUMN II

A. burglary
B. embezzlement
C. extortion
D. larceny
E. robbery
F. no crime

26._____
27._____
28._____
29._____
30._____

Questions 31-40.

DIRECTIONS: Questions 31 through 40 consist of statements from which a term is missing. Each of these statements can be completed correctly with one of the terms in the following list. In the space opposite the number corresponding to the number of the question, place the LETTER preceding the term in the following list which MOST accurately completes the statement.

- A. affidavit
- B. appeal
- C. arraignment
- D. arrest
- E. bench warrant
- F. habeas corpus
- G. indictment
- H. injunction
- I. sentence
- J. subpoena

31. A _____ is a writ calling witnesses to court. 31._____

32. _____ is a method used to obtain a review of a case in court of superior jurisdiction. 32._____

33. A judgment passed by a court on a person on trial as a criminal offender is called a _____. 33._____

34. _____ is a writ or order requiring a person to refrain from a particular act. 34._____

35. _____ is the name given to a writ commanding the bringing of the body of a certain person before a certain court. 35._____

36. A _____ is a court order directing that an offender be brought into court. 36._____

37. The calling of a defendant before the court to answer an accusation is called _____. 37._____

38. The accusation in writing, presented by the grand jury to a competent court charging a person with a public offense is an _____. 38._____

39. A sworn declaration in writing is an _____. 39._____

40. _____ is the taking of a person into custody for the purpose of holding him to answer a criminal charge. 40._____

Questions 41-55.

DIRECTIONS: Questions 41 through 55 consist of statements from which a term is missing. Each of these statements can be completed correctly with one of the terms in the following list. In the space opposite the number corresponding to the number of the question, place the LETTER preceding the term in the following list which MOST accurately completes the statement.

A. accessory   B. accomplice   C. alibi
D. autopsy   E. ballistics   F. capital
G. confidence man   H. commission   I. conspiracy
J. corroborated   K. grand jury   L. homicide
M. misdemeanors   N. penology   O. perjury

41. _____ is the dissection of a dead human body to determine the cause of death. 41._____

42. The general term which mean the killing of one person by another is _____. 42._____

43. _____ is the science of the punishment of crime. 43._____

44. False swearing constitutes the crime of _____. 44._____

45. A combination of two or more persons to accomplish a criminal or unlawful act is called _____. 45._____

46. By _____ is meant evidence showing that a defendant was in another place when the crime was committed. 46._____

47. _____ is a term frequently used to describe a person engaged in a kind of swindling operation. 47._____

48. A _____ offense is one for which a life sentence or death penalty is prescribed by law. 48._____

49. A violation of a law may be either an act of omission or an act of _____. 49._____

50. An _____ is a person who is liable to prosecution for the identical offense charged against a defendant on trial. 50._____

51. A person would be an _____ who after the commission of a crime aided in the escape of one he knew to be an offender. 51._____

52. An official body called to hear complaints and to determine whether there is ground for criminal prosecution is known as the _____. 52._____

53. Crimes are generally divided into two classes, namely felonies and _____. 53._____

54. _____ is the science of the motion of projectiles. 54._____

55. Testimony of a witness which is confirmed by another witness is _____. 55._____

Questions 56-60.

DIRECTIONS: Next to the question number which corresponds with the number of each item in Column I, place the letter preceding the adjective in Column II which BEST describes the persons in Column I.

COLUMN I		COLUMN II	
56.	A talkative woman	A. abstemious	56._____
		B. pompous	
57.	A person on a reducing diet	C. erudite	57._____
		D. benevolent	
58.	A scholarly professor	E. docile	58._____
		F. loquacious	
59.	A man who seldom speaks	G. indefatigable	59._____
		H. taciturn	
60.	A charitable person		60._____

Questions 61-65.

DIRECTIONS: Next to the question number which corresponds with the number preceding each profession in Column I, place the letter preceding the word in Column II which BEST explains the subject of that profession.

COLUMN I		COLUMN II	
61.	Geologist	A. animals	61._____
		B. eyes	
62.	Oculist	C. feet	62._____
		D. fortune-telling	
63.	Podiatrist	E. language	63._____
		F. rocks	
64.	Palmist	G. stamps	64._____
		H. woman	
65.	Zoologist		65._____

Questions 66-70.

DIRECTIONS: Next to the question number corresponding to the number of each of the words in Column I, place the letter preceding the word in Column II that is MOST NEARLY OPPOSITE to it in meaning.

COLUMN I		COLUMN II	
66.	comely	A. beautiful	66._____
		B. cowardly	
67.	eminent	C. kind	67._____
		D. sedate	
68.	frugal	E. shrewd	68._____
		F. ugly	
69.	gullible	G. unknown	69._____
		H. wasteful	
70.	valiant		70._____

KEY (CORRECT ANSWERS)

1.	A	16.	A	31.	J	46.	C	61.	F
2.	C	17.	B	32.	B	47.	G	62.	B
3.	A	18.	A	33.	I	48.	F	63.	C
4.	C	19.	A	34.	H	49.	H	64.	D
5.	C	20.	A	35.	F	50.	B	65.	A
6.	C	21.	C	36.	E	51.	A	66.	F
7.	B	22.	C	37.	C	52.	L	67.	G
8.	D	23.	A	38.	G	53.	N	68.	H
9.	B	24.	B	39.	A	54.	E	69.	E
10.	C	25.	C	40.	D	55.	K	70.	B
11.	D	26.	A	41.	D	56.	F		
12.	B	27.	B	42.	M	57.	A		
13.	B	28.	D	43.	O	58.	C		
14.	D	29.	C	44.	P	59.	H		
15.	D	30.	E	45.	J	60.	D		

EXAMINATION SECTION
TEST 1

DIRECTIONS: Each question or incomplete statement is followed by several suggested answers or completions. Select the one that BEST answers the question or completes the statement. *PRINT THE LETTER OF THE CORRECT ANSWER IN THE SPACE AT THE RIGHT.*

1. Which of the following is the LEAST important factor to consider in surveying the physical layout of a building for traffic flow?

    A. Location of windows
    B. Number of entrances
    C. Number of exits
    D. Location of first aid rooms

2. The major purpose of any security program in a large organization is to prevent unlawful acts.
   If adequate patrol coverage is provided at a given location, it is MOST likely that

    A. crimes will not be committed
    B. undesirables will not enter the building
    C. unlawful acts will increase in the long run
    D. there will be less opportunity to commit a crime

3. The MOST frequent cause of fires in public facilities is

    A. incinerators   B. vandalism
    C. electrical sources   D. smoking on the job

4. After bomb threats are received, it is sometimes necessary to evacuate a facility. How long BEFORE the threatened time of explosion should a facility be evacuated?
   At least _____ minutes.

    A. 15   B. 25   C. 50   D. 60

5. Once a facility is evacuated because of a bomb threat, how much time should pass before the public and employees are allowed to enter the building?
   _____ minutes.

    A. 10   B. 20   C. 40   D. 60

6. Of the following locations in public buildings, the one which is the LEAST likely place for bombs to be planted is in

    A. storerooms   B. bathrooms
    C. cafeterias   D. waste receptacles

7. The one of the following that is the surest means of establishing positive identification of someone entering a facility is by

    A. personal recognition   B. I.D. badge
    C. social security card   D. driver's license

8. The one of the following which most probably would NOT be included in a police record report concerning an incident at a facility is the

   A. name of complainant or injured party
   B. name of the investigating officer
   C. statement of each witness
   D. religion of complainant or injured party

9. Preventing trouble is one of the primary concerns of special officers.
   When dealing with unruly groups of people who threaten to become violent, which of the following is a measure which should NOT be taken?

   A. Maintain close surveillance of such groups
   B. Try to contact the leaders of the group regardless of their militancy
   C. Keep the officer force alerted
   D. Have the officer force deal aggressively with provocations

10. Of the following, the MOST important factor to consider in the deployment of officers dealing with a client population is the officers' ability to

    A. remain calm
    B. look stern
    C. evaluate personality
    D. take a firm stand

11. Assume that an offender is struggling with a group of officers who are trying to arrest him.
    What force, if any, can be used to overcome this resistance?

    A. The amount of force acceptable to the public
    B. The amount of force necessary to restrain the offender and protect the officers
    C. Any amount of force that is acceptable to the officers at the scene
    D. No force may be used until the police arrive

12. Assume that a fire is discovered at your work location. The one of the following actions which would be INAPPROPRIATE for you to take is to

    A. notify the telephone operator
    B. station a reliable person at the entrance
    C. open all windows and doors in the area
    D. start evacuating the area

13. If a person has an object caught in his throat or air passage but is breathing adequately, which one of the following should you do?

    A. Probe for the object
    B. Force him to drink water
    C. Lay him over your arm and slap him between the shoulder blades
    D. Allow him to cough and to assume the position he finds most comfortable

14. The one of the following methods which should NOT be used to report a fire is to

    A. call 911
    B. pull the handle in the red box on the street corner
    C. call the fire department county numbers listed in each county directory
    D. call 411

15. Assume that an officer, alone in a building at night, smells the strong odor of cooking or heating gas. In addition to airing the building and making sure that he is not overcome, it would be BEST for the officer to call

    A. his superior at his home and ask for instructions
    B. for a plumber from the department of public works
    C. 911 for police and fire help
    D. the emergency number at Con Edison

16. Of the following situations, the one that is MOST dangerous for an officer is when he

    A. investigates suspicious persons and circumstances
    B. finds a burglary in progress or pursues burglary suspects
    C. attempts an arrest or finds a robbery in progress
    D. patrols on the overnight shift

17. An officer on security patrol generally should spend MOST of his time

    A. checking doors and locks
    B. helping the public and answering questions
    C. chasing criminals and looking for clues
    D. writing reports on unusual incidents

18. The one of the following that is an ACCEPTABLE way to arrest a person is to

    A. tell him to report to the nearest police precinct
    B. send a summons to his permanent address
    C. tell him in person that he is under arrest
    D. show him handcuffs and ask him to come along

19. A carbon dioxide fire extinguisher is BEST suited for extinguishing _____ fires.

    A. paper   B. rag   C. rubbish   D. grease

20. A pressurized water or soda-acid fire extinguisher is BEST suited for extinguishing _____ fires.

    A. wood   B. gasoline
    C. electrical   D. magnesium

21. The one of the following statements that does NOT apply to the use of handcuffs is that they

    A. are used as temporary restraining devices
    B. eliminate the need for vigilance
    C. cannot be opened without keys
    D. are used to secure a violent person

22. The one of the following that is GENERALLY a crime against the person is

    A. trespass   B. burglary   C. robbery   D. arson

23. Of the following, the SAFEST way of escape from an office in a burning building is generally the

    A. stairway
    B. rooftop
    C. passenger elevator
    D. freight elevator

24. In attempting to control a possible riot situation, an officer pushed his way into a crowd gathered outside the building and tried to cause confusion by arguing with members of the group.
    This procedure NORMALLY is considered

    A. *desirable;* any violence that occurs will remain outside the building
    B. *desirable;* the crowd will break into smaller groups and disperse
    C. *undesirable;* to maintain control of the situation, the officer must not become part of the crowd
    D. *undesirable;* the supervisor should stay clear of the scene

25. Which one of the following is MOST effective in making officers more safety-minded?

    A. Maintaining an up-to-date library of the latest safety literature
    B. Reading daily safety bulletins at roll-call
    C. Holding informal group safety meetings periodically
    D. Offering prizes for good safety slogans and displays

KEY (CORRECT ANSWERS)

1. A	11. B
2. D	12. C
3. C	13. D
4. A	14. D
5. D	15. D
6. C	16. C
7. A	17. A
8. D	18. C
9. D	19. D
10. A	20. A

21. B
22. C
23. A
24. C
25. C

TEST 2

DIRECTIONS: Each question or incomplete statement is followed by several suggested answers or completions. Select the one that BEST answers the question or completes the statement. *PRINT THE LETTER OF THE CORRECT ANSWER IN THE SPACE AT THE RIGHT.*

1. Assume that an angry crowd of some 75 to 100 people has built up in one of the hallways of a center and that only one superior officer and two subordinate officers are on duty in the building. A glass panel in one of the stairway doors has just been broken under the pressure of the crowd and a bench has been hurled down a flight of stairs. The one of the following actions that the superior officer SHOULD take in this situation is to

    A. push his way into the crowd and try to reason with them
    B. order the two other officers to try to quiet the crowd
    C. call the police on 911 and meet them outside the building
    D. do nothing at this point in order to avoid a riot

2. One of the duties and responsibilities of a supervisor is to test the knowledge of the officers concerning their post conditions.
   This should be done if the officer's assignment is

    A. fixed only
    B. roving only
    C. roving only in a troublesome spot
    D. either fixed or roving

3. An officer discovers early one morning that an office in the building he guards has been burglarized.
   Of the following, it is important for the officer to FIRST

    A. go through the building and look for suspects
    B. call the police and protect the area and whatever evidence exists until they arrive
    C. allow people into their offices as they come to work
    D. examine, sort, and handle all evidence before the police get there

4. Assume that two officers are interrogating one suspect. How should these officers position themselves during the interrogation?

    A. One officer should stand on either side of the suspect.
    B. One officer should stand to the right of the suspect, and the other officer should stand behind the suspect.
    C. Both officers should stand to the right of the suspect.
    D. One officer should stand to the right of the suspect, and the other officer should stand in front of the suspect.

5. A witness who takes an oath to testify truly and who states as true any matter which he knows to be false is guilty of

    A. perjury   B. libel   C. slander   D. fraud

6. An officer checking a substance suspected of containing narcotics should GENERALLY

   A. taste it in small amounts
   B. send it to a laboratory for analysis
   C. smell it for its distinctive odor
   D. examine it for its unusual texture

7. A certain center is situated in an area where frequent outbreaks of hostilities seem to be focused on the center itself.
   Which of the following BEST explains why the center may be a target for hostile acts?
   It

   A. serves community needs
   B. represents governmental authority
   C. represents all ethnic groups
   D. serves as a neutral battlefield

8. An officer often deals with people who might be addicted to drugs.
   The one of the following symptoms which is NOT generally an indication of drug addiction is

   A. dilation of the eye pupils
   B. frequent yawning and sneezing
   C. a deep, rasping cough
   D. continual itching of the arms and legs

9. In emergency situations, panic will MOST probably occur when people are

   A. unexpectedly confronted with a terrorizing condition from which there appears to be no escape
   B. angry and violent
   C. anxious about circumstances which are not obvious, easily visible or within the immediate area
   D. familiar with the effects of the emergency

10. The one of the following actions on the part of a person that would NOT be considered *resisting arrest* is

    A. retreating and running away
    B. saying, *You can't arrest me*
    C. pushing the officer aside
    D. pulling away from an officer's grasp

11. Which of the following items would NOT be considered an APPROPRIATE item of uniform for an officer to wear while on duty?

    A. Reefer type overcoat
    B. Leather laced shoes with flat soles
    C. White socks
    D. Cap cover with cap device displayed

12. What can happen to an officer if the leather thong on his night stick is NOT twisted correctly?
    The

    A. baton may be taken out of the officer's hand
    B. officer's wrist may be broken
    C. leather will tear more easily
    D. officer's arm may be injured

13. The one of the following kinds of information which SHOULD be included in the log book is

    A. any important matter of police information
    B. an item noted in Standard Operating Procedures only
    C. everything of general interest
    D. a crime or offense only

14. While on patrol at your work location, you receive a call that an assault has taken place. Upon your arrival at the scene, the victim, who has severe lacerations, informs you that the assailant ran into a nearby basement.
    After apprehending the suspect, the type of search you should conduct is a _____ search.

    A. wall   B. frisk   C. body   D. strip

15. A tactical force is valuable in MOST emergency situations PRIMARILY because of its

    A. location   B. morale
    C. flexibility   D. size

16. An officer should be encouraged to talk easily and frankly when he is dealing with his superior.
    In order to encourage such free communication, it would be MOST appropriate for a superior to behave in a(n)

    A. *sincere* manner; assure the officer that you will deal with him honestly and openly
    B. *official* manner; you are a superior officer and must always act formally with subordinates
    C. *investigative* manner; you must probe and question to get to a basis of trust
    D. *unemotional* manner; the officer's emotions and background should play no part in your dealings with him

17. Research findings show that an increase in free communication within an agency GENERALLY results in which one of the following?

    A. Improved morale and productivity
    B. Increased promotional opportunities
    C. An increase in authority
    D. A spirit of honesty

18. Assume that you are a superior officer and your superiors have given you a new arrest procedure to be followed. Before passing this information on to your subordinates, the one of the following actions that you should take FIRST is to

    A. ask your superiors to send out a memorandum to the entire staff
    B. clarify the procedure in your own mind
    C. set up a training course to provide instructions on the new procedure
    D. write a memorandum to your subordinates

18._____

19. Communication is necessary for an organization to be effective.
    The one of the following which is LEAST important for most communication systems is that

    A. messages are sent quickly and directly to the person who needs them to operate
    B. information should be conveyed understandably and accurately
    C. the method used to transmit information should be kept secret so that security can be maintained
    D. senders of messages must know how their messages were received and acted upon

19._____

20. Which one of the following is the CHIEF advantage of listening willingly to subordinate officers and encouraging them to talk freely and honestly?
    It

    A. reveals to superiors the degree to which ideas that are passed down are accepted by subordinates
    B. reduces the participation of subordinates in the operation of the department
    C. encourages officers to try for promotion
    D. enables officers to learn about security leaks on the part of officials

20._____

21. A superior may be informed through either oral or written reports.
    Which one of the following is an ADVANTAGE of using oral reports?

    A. There is no need for a formal record of the report.
    B. An exact duplicate of the report is not easily transmitted to others.
    C. A good oral report requires little time for preparation.
    D. An oral report involves two-way communication between a subordinate and his superior.

21._____

22. Of the following, the MOST important reason why officers should communicate effectively with the public is to

    A. improve the public's understanding of information that is important for them to know
    B. establish a friendly relationship
    C. obtain information about the kinds of people who come to the center
    D. convince the public that services are adequate

22._____

23. Officers should generally NOT use phrases like *too hard, too easy,* and *a lot* principally because such phrases

    A. may be offensive to some minority groups
    B. are too informal

23._____

C. mean different things to different people
D. are difficult to remember

24. The ability to communicate clearly and concisely is an important element in effective leadership.
   Which of the following statements about oral and written communication is GENERALLY true?

   A. Oral communication is more time-consuming.
   B. Written communication is more likely to be misinterpreted.
   C. Oral communication is useful only in emergencies.
   D. Written communication is useful mainly when giving information to fewer than twenty people.

25. Rumors can often have harmful and disruptive effects on an organization.
   Which one of the following is the BEST way to prevent rumors from becoming a problem?

   A. Refuse to act on rumors, thereby making them less believable
   B. Increase the amount of information passed along by the *grapevine*
   C. Distribute as much factual information as possible
   D. Provide training in report writing

KEY (CORRECT ANSWERS)

1.	C	11.	C
2.	D	12.	A
3.	B	13.	A
4.	B	14.	A
5.	A	15.	C
6.	B	16.	A
7.	B	17.	A
8.	C	18.	B
9.	A	19.	C
10.	B	20.	A

21.	D
22.	A
23.	C
24.	B
25.	C

EXAMINATION SECTION
TEST 1

DIRECTIONS: Each question or incomplete statement is followed by several suggested answers or completions. Select the one that BEST answers the question or completes the statement. *PRINT THE LETTER OF THE CORRECT ANSWER IN THE SPACE AT THE RIGHT.*

1. As a sheriff, you have encountered certain problems in your work and have repeatedly sought help from your immediate superior. This superior has not responded to your appeals for problem-solving. Under the circumstances, it is GENERALLY advisable to

   A. solve your problems as best you can, making certain you cover yourself in the event of failure by keeping a detailed record of the number of times you requested help and were ignored
   B. bypass your immediate superior and seek a relationship with someone above his position after informing your immediate superior of your intention
   C. keep trying to obtain help from your immediate superior, secure in the knowledge that, because of your persistence, you have established a legitimate excuse for making mistakes
   D. ignore difficult problems, concentrating on those matters you can satisfactorily resolve

1.____

2. As a sheriff, you have noticed that your deputy sheriff partner has developed some negative attitudes toward certain aspects of his work. Under the circumstances, it is BEST generally to

   A. show understanding and provide your partner with relevant information
   B. urge your partner to change his point of view immediately or face disciplinary action
   C. inform your superior that you have a trouble-maker on your hands and recommend suitable disciplinary action
   D. leave your partner alone and allow his views to change

2.____

3. As a sheriff, you have told your deputy sheriff partner that he has made an error of judgment in his work. Your partner blames you for the lapse and complains about you to your superior. When you are questioned by your superior, it is MOST advisable to

   A. call attention to your greater experience, and carefully explain how the lapse was really the deputy sheriff's fault
   B. seek to provide data for a rational diagnosis of the matter
   C. deny responsibility, and show how you *go by the book*
   D. present a documented report of the deputy sheriff's incompetence and insubordination

3.____

4. Assume that you are a senior deputy sheriff teamed with an inexperienced deputy sheriff. He is executing a seizure levy and has failed to take a satisfactory inventory. Both of you are still on the defendant's premises. In the circumstances, it is BEST to

4.____

A. redo the inventory with the deputy sheriff, explaining how to avoid similar errors in the future
B. redo the inventory yourself, explaining that the office of the sheriff can't afford errors
C. make certain that the deputy sheriff understands that the error was his fault, then have him redo the inventory to your satisfaction
D. chastise the deputy sheriff privately and inform him that anyone who can't properly inventory shouldn't be a deputy sheriff

5. Anticipating difficulty from a possibly troublesome defendant on an arrest case, you, as a senior deputy sheriff, have instructed your partner, an inexperienced deputy sheriff, to observe your behavior on this assignment and not to participate, except in case of extreme need for assistance. The defendant assaults you as you attempt to make the arrest, and it is only with difficulty that you overcome the assault and make the arrest. Your partner observes all this and does not interfere. In your report on the incident, you state that your partner failed to exercise judgment and initiative in coming to your assistance. When confronted with your statement, your partner claims that he was following explicit instructions and that, in his view, no real need for his assistance existed. The MOST reasonable comment on the above incident is that the 5._____

A. deputy sheriff displayed a lack of initiative and cooperation
B. senior deputy sheriff gave conflicting orders, assuming understanding on the part of the deputy sheriff
C. deputy sheriff showed good judgment in not properly interpreting the senior deputy sheriff's instructions
D. senior deputy sheriff's instructions should have been given in writing, not orally

Questions 6-10.

DIRECTIONS: Questions 6 through 10 are to be answered only on the basis of the information contained in the table on the next page.

DISTRIBUTION OF CITIZENS' RESPONSES TO STATEMENTS CONCERNING SHERIFFS' ARRESTS

(Number of citizens responding = 1171)

		CATEGORIES			
	(A) Strongly Agree	(B) Agree	(C) Disagree	(D) Strongly Disagree	(E) Don't Know
I. Sheriffs act improperly in arresting defendants, even when these persons are rude and ill-mannered	12%	37%	36%	9%	6%
II. Sheriffs frequently use more force than necessary when making arrests	9%	19%	46%	19%	7%
III. Any defendant who insults or physically abuses a sheriff has no complaint if he is sternly handled in return	13%	44%	32%	7%	4%

6. The total percentage of responses to Statement III OTHER THAN *Strongly Agree* and *Disagree* is

   A. 45%   B. 46%   C. 55%   D. 59%

7. The number of *Disagree* responses to Statement II is MOST NEARLY

   A. 71   B. 114   C. 539   D. 820

8. Assume that for Statement II the (B) percentage of responses were doubled and the (A) percentage increased one and a half times. If the (D) and (E) percentages remained the same, the (C) percentage would then be MOST NEARLY

   A. 23%   B. 26%   C. 39%   D. 52%

9. The total number of *Don't Know* responses is MOST NEARLY

   A. 17
   B. 188
   C. 200
   D. a figure which cannot be determined from the table

10. If the percentage of *Disagree* responses to Statement III were 35% less, the resulting percentage would be MOST NEARLY

    A. 11%   B. 14%   C. 15%   D. 21%

Questions 11-15.

DIRECTIONS: Questions 11 through 15 are to be answered SOLELY on the basis of the following reading selection.

In studying the relationships of people to the organizational structure, it is absolutely necessary to identify and recognize the informal organizational structure. These relationships are necessary when coordination of a plan is attempted. They may be with *the boss,* line supervisors, staff personnel, or other representatives of the formal organization's hierarchy, and they may include the *liaison men* who serve as the leaders of the informal organization. An acquaintanceship with the people serving in these roles in the organization, and its formal counterpart, permits a supervisor to recognize sensitive areas in which it is simple to get a conflict reaction. Avoidance of such areas, plus conscious efforts to inform other people of his own objectives for various plans, will usually enlist their aid and support. Planning *without people* can lead to disaster because the individuals who must act together to make any plan a success are more important than the plans themselves.

11. Of the following titles, the one that MOST clearly describes the paragraph is

    A. Coordination of a Function
    B. Avoidance of Conflict
    C. Planning with People
    D. Planning Objectives

12. According to the paragraph, attempts at coordinating plans may fail unless

    A. the plan's objectives are clearly set forth
    B. conflict between groups is resolved

C. the plans themselves are worthwhile
D. informal relationships are recognized

13. According to the paragraph, conflict

    A. may, in some cases, be desirable to secure results
    B. produces more heat than light
    C. should be avoided at all costs
    D. possibilities can be predicted by a sensitive supervisor

14. The paragraph implies that

    A. informal relationships are more important than formal structure
    B. the weakness of a formal structure depends upon informal relationships
    C. liaison men are the key people to consult when taking formal and informal structures into account
    D. individuals in a group are at least as important as the plans for the group

15. The paragraph suggests that

    A. some planning can be disastrous
    B. certain people in sensitive areas should be avoided
    C. the supervisor should discourage acquaintanceships in the organization
    D. organizational relationships should be consciously limited

Questions 16-20.

DIRECTIONS: Questions 16 through 20 are sentences taken from reports on the administration of the office of the sheriff. Some are correct according to ordinary formal usage. Others are incorrect because they contain errors in English usage, spelling, or punctuation. Consider a sentence correct if it contains no errors in English usage, spelling, or punctuation, even if there may be other ways of writing the sentence correctly. Mark your answer:
A. if sentence I only is correct
B. if sentence II only is correct
C. if sentences I and II are correct
D. if neither sentence I nor II is correct.

16. I. A deputy sheriff must ascertain whether the debtor, has any property.
    II. A good deputy sheriff does not cause histerical excitement when he executes a process.

17. I. Having learned that he has been assigned a judgment debtor, the deputy sheriff should call upon him.
    II. The deputy sheriff may seize and remove property without requiring a bond.

18. I. If legal procedures are not observed, the resulting contract is not enforseable.
    II. If the directions from the creditor's attorney are not in writing, the deputy sheriff should request a letter of instructions from the attorney.

19. I. The deputy sheriff may confer with the defendant and may enter this defendants' place of business.
    II. A deputy sheriff must ascertain from the creditor's attorney whether the debtor has any property against which he may proceede.

20. I. The sheriff has a right to do whatever is reasonably necessary for the purpose of executing the order of the court.
    II. The written order of the court gives the sheriff general authority and he is governed in his acts by a very simple principal.

19.____

20.____

KEY (CORRECT ANSWERS)

1.	B	11.	C
2.	A	12.	D
3.	B	13.	D
4.	A	14.	D
5.	B	15.	A
6.	C	16.	D
7.	C	17.	C
8.	A	18.	B
9.	C	19.	D
10.	D	20.	A

TEST 2

DIRECTIONS: Each question or incomplete statement is followed by several suggested answers or completions. Select the one that BEST answers the question or completes the statement. *PRINT THE LETTER OF THE CORRECT ANSWER IN THE SPACE AT THE RIGHT.*

Questions 1-5.

DIRECTIONS: Questions 1 through 5 are to be answered SOLELY on the basis of the following reading selection.

    The dynamics of group behavior may be summed up by saying that the individuals in a group respond to many lines of force arising out of their relationship with every other member of a group, and with the group itself. In addition, each member of a group quite naturally brings with him all the things that have been *bugging* him. Then, the situation or the setting in which the group meets, as well as the circumstances related to the formation of the group, are active working forces exerting some X influence upon each member of the group. Lastly, all of this kinetic energy is at the control of the person seeking to lead the group into some kind of action. If he is to produce something meaningful with the members of a group, he must utilize this energy, contain it, dissipate it in some fashion or be faced with difficulty.

    This dynamic force inherent in any group can be harnessed by a supervisor with leadership qualities, but it must be controlled. It will not be contained by acting without consultation with group members, by refusing to accept suggestions coming from the group, or by refusing to explain or even give notice of contemplated actions. However, it can be controlled by placing the focus upon the members of the group, rather than upon the supervisor, and depending upon the leader-supervisor to provide as many participative experiences for group members as is commensurate with his own decision-making responsibilities. It is true that this is subordinate-centered leadership, but the supervisor can gain strength through permissive leadership without sacrificing basic responsibilities for effective planning and adequate control of operations.

1. Of the following titles, the one that MOST closely describes the reading selection is   1.____

    A. The Supervisor with Dynamic Leadership Potential
    B. Dissipation of Group Energy
    C. Controlling Group Relationships
    D. Sacrificing Basic Responsibilities

2. According to the reading selection, the setting in which the group meets   2.____

    A. can readily be modified either in whole or in part
    B. must be made meaningful in some fashion to foster skills development
    C. can provide the sole source of group dynamics
    D. is one of the forces exerting influence on group members

3. According to the selection, the members of the group   3.____

    A. should control their formation and development
    B. should control the circumstances of their meeting

C. are influenced by the forces creating the group
D. dissipate meaningless energy

4. According to the selection, the effective group leader

    A. controls the focus of the group
    B. focuses his control over the group
    C. controls group forces by focusing upon group members
    D. focuses the group's forces upon himself

5. According to the selection, effective leadership consists in

    A. partially compromising decision-making responsibilities
    B. partially sacrificing some basic responsibilities
    C. sometimes cultivating permissive subordinates
    D. providing participation for members of the group consistent with decision-making imperatives

Questions 6-10.

DIRECTIONS: Questions 6 through 10 consist of one sentence each. Each sentence contains an incorrectly used word. First, decide which is the incorrectly used word. Then, from among the options given, decide which word, when substituted for the incorrectly used word, makes the meaning of the sentence clear.

For Example: The U.S. national income exhibits a pattern of long term deflection.
    A. reflection   B. subjection
    C. rejoicing   D. growth

The word *deflection* in the sentence does not convey the meaning the sentence evidently intended to convey. The word *growth* (answer D) when substituted for the word *deflection* makes the meaning of the sentence clear. Accordingly, the answer to the question is D.

6. The study commissioned by the joint committee fell compassionately short of the mark and would have to be redone.

    A. successfully   B. insignificantly
    C. experimentally   D. woefully

7. He will not idly exploit any violation of the provisions of the order.

    A. tolerate   B. refuse   C. construe   D. guard

8. The defendant refused to be virile and bitterly protested service.

    A. irked   B. feasible   C. docile   D. credible

9. As today's violence has no single cause, so its causes have no single scheme.

    A. deference   B. cure   C. flaw   D. relevance

10. He took the position that the success of the program was insidious on getting additional revenue.

    A. reputed B. contingent
    C. failure D. indeterminate

Questions 11-15.

DIRECTIONS: Each of Questions 11 through 15 consists of a statement containing five words in capital letters. One of these words in capital letters is not in keeping with the meaning which the statement is evidently intended to carry. The five words in capital letters in each statement are reprinted after the statement. Print the letter preceding the one of the five words which does most to spoil the true meaning of the statement in the space at the right.

11. Within each major DIVISION in a properly set up public or private organization, provision is made so that each NECESSARY activity is CARED for and lines of AUTHORITY and responsibility are clear-cut and INFINITE.

    A. division   B. necessary   C. cared
    D. authority   E. infinite

12. In public service, the scale of salaries paid must be INCIDENTAL to the services rendered, with due CONSIDERATION for the attraction of the desired MANPOWER and for the MAINTENANCE of a standard of living COMMENSURATE with the work to be performed.

    A. incidental   B. consideration   C. manpower
    D. maintenance   E. commensurate

13. An understanding of the AIMS of an organization by the staff will AID greatly in increasing the DEMAND of the correspondence work of the office, and will to a large extent DETERMINE the NATURE of the correspondence.

    A. aims   B. aid   C. demand
    D. determine   E. nature

14. BECAUSE the Civil Service Commission strongly feels that the MERIT system is a key factor in the MAINTENANCE of democratic government, it has adopted as one of its major DEFENSES the progressive democratization of its own PROCEDURES in dealing with candidates for positions in the public service.

    A. Because   B. merit   C. maintenance
    D. defenses   E. procedures

15. Retirement and pension systems are ESSENTIAL not only to provide employees with a means of support in the future, but also to prevent longevity and CHARITABLE considerations from UPSETTING the PROMOTIONAL opportunities for RETIRED members of the career service.

    A. essential   B. charitable   C. upsetting
    D. promotional E. retired

Questions 16-20.

DIRECTIONS: Questions 16 through 20 are sentences taken from reports on the administration of the office of the sheriff. Some are correct according to ordinary formal usage. Others are incorrect because they contain errors in English usage, spelling or punctuation. Consider a sentence correct if it contains no errors in English usage, spelling or punctuation even if there may be other ways of writing the sentence correctly. Mark your answer:
A. if sentence I only is correct
B. if sentence II only is correct
C. if sentences I and II are correct
D. if neither sentence I nor II is correct.

16. I. If a deputy sheriff finds that property he has to attach is located on a ship, he should notify his supervisor.
    II. Any contract that tends to interfere with the administration of justice is illegal.

17. I. A mandate or official order of the court to the sheriff or other officer directs it to take into possession property of the judgment debtor.
    II. Tenancies from month-to-month, week-to-week, and sometimes year-to-year are termenable.

18. I. A civil arrest is an arrest pursuant to an order issued by a court in civil litigation.
    II. In a criminal arrest, a defendant is arrested for a crime he is alleged to have committed.

19. I. Having taken a defendant into custody, there is a complete restraint of personal liberty.
    II. Actual force is unnecessary when a deputy sheriff makes an arrest.

20. I. When a husband breaches a separation agreement by failing to supply to the wife the amount of money to be paid to her periodically under the agreement, the same legal steps may be taken to enforce his compliance as in any other breach of contract.
    II. Having obtained the writ of attachment, the plaintiff is then in the advantageous position of selling the very property that has been held for him by the sheriff while he was obtaining a judgment.

KEY (CORRECT ANSWERS)

1.	C	11.	E
2.	D	12.	A
3.	C	13.	C
4.	C	14.	D
5.	D	15.	E
6.	D	16.	C
7.	A	17.	D
8.	C	18.	C
9.	B	19.	B
10.	B	20.	C

EXAMINATION SECTION
TEST 1

DIRECTIONS: Each question or incomplete statement is followed by several suggested answers or completions. Select the one that BEST answers the question or completes the statement. *PRINT THE LETTER OF THE CORRECT ANSWER IN THE SPACE AT THE RIGHT.*

1. Which of the following is MOST advisable in the removal and transportation of objects bearing fingerprints?
   A. Cellophane sheets should never be used for protecting papers.
   B. After removal from the scene, the latent print should be photographed so that the image is the size of the print.
   C. Objects should never be wrapped in a handkerchief or a towel.
   D. Small objects should be placed in a paper bag.

   1.____

2. Which of the following practices concerning attitude and demeanor is LEAST appropriate during the interrogation of a suspect?
   A. The interrogator should occasionally convey a sense of inattentiveness in order to make the suspect feel more relaxed.
   B. The language of the interrogator should be adapted to the suspect's cultural level.
   C. The interrogator should explain the purpose of the investigation to the suspect in general terms.
   D. Slang may be used when it promotes ease of speech or fluency for the suspect.

   2.____

3. In its consideration of the penalties to be imposed for drug offenses, the President's Commission on Law Enforcement and Administration of Justice had recommended that
   A. suspended sentences, probation, and parole be prohibited for all but the first offense of unlawful possession
   B. the policy of mandatory minimum terms of imprisonment be maintained
   C. maximum sentences for possession with intent to sell be made more severe
   D. courts and correctional authorities be given enough discretion to deal flexibly with violators

   3.____

4. In a field study, two police forces were compared in their handling of juvenile delinquents. The first force put particular emphasis on education, training, merit, promotions, and centralized control. The second force relied more on organization by precinct, seniority, and on-the-job experience.

   4.____

In regard to the rates of processing (police contacts short of arrest but requiring an official record) and arrest (formal police action against the juvenile), it was found that
- A. the processing rate for the first force was higher, but the arrest rate was lower
- B. the arrest rate for the first force was higher, but the processing rate was lower
- C. both the processing rate and the arrest rate were significantly higher for the first force
- D. both the processing rate and the arrest rate were significantly lower for the first force

5. The President's Commission on Law Enforcement and Administration of Justice also recommended that undergraduate programs for potential and existing law enforcement personnel emphasize
   - A. vocational subjects
   - B. liberal arts
   - C. management principles
   - D. technical courses

6. In its survey on the capability of selected police departments to control civil disorders, the National Advisory Commission on Civil Disorders found that the MOST critical deficiency of all was inadequacy of
   - A. training programs
   - B. mobilization planning
   - C. logistical support
   - D. intelligence gathering

7. In a report, the National Commission on Marijuana and Drug Abuse has recommended all of the following EXCEPT that
   - A. private possession of marijuana for personal use should no longer be an offense
   - B. an ounce or less of marijuana possessed in public would be contraband subject to summary seizure and forfeiture
   - C. a plea of marijuana intoxication shall be a defense to certain criminal acts committed under the influence
   - D. casual distribution of small amounts of marijuana not involving a profit should no longer be an offense

8. The Governor of the State made all of the following proposals in the area of crime and the courts EXCEPT to
   - A. free judges and courts from much of the burden of thousands of housing violations cases
   - B. reduce from 12 to 6 the number of jurors required in certain civil cases
   - C. authorize presiding judges, rather than attorneys, to initiate questioning of prospective jurors in criminal cases
   - D. require the prosecution to bring to trial all defendants in criminal cases within six months of their arrest

9. In addition, the Governor of the State made all of the following proposals concerning prison reform EXCEPT
   A. establishment of half-way houses close to the homes of inmates nearing parole
   B. intensified recruitment among members of minority groups for correction officer positions
   C. temporary release programs, including occasional furloughs for family visits
   D. creation of citizen observer panels whose members would be appointed jointly by correction officials and inmates

9._____

10. According to Uniform Crime Reports, the number of murders committed in the preceding year increased by the GREATEST percentage in
    A. rural areas   B. large cities
    C. suburban areas   D. metropolitan areas

10._____

11. According to Uniform Crime Reports, which of the following statements concerning arrest trends for juveniles during the preceding year is INCORRECT?
    A. The increase in arrests of females under 18 years of age was more than twice the increase in arrests for males under 18.
    B. A relatively small percentage of the total youth population become involved in criminal acts.
    C. The increase in juvenile arrests for property crimes was significantly higher than the increase in juvenile arrests for violent crimes.
    D. The involvement of young persons in criminal activity as measured by police arrests has greatly exceeded their percentage increase in the national population.

11._____

12. Following are four statements concerning the rights of defendants in criminal proceedings:
    I. Before the police begin to question a suspect, he must be informed of his rights to remain silent and to be represented by a lawyer.
    II. The right to counsel and the guarantee against self-incrimination have been extended to defendants appearing in state criminal courts.
    III. Questioning of a suspect in custody is prohibited unless counsel is present.
    IV. When an investigation shifts to the accusatory stage, a defendant is entitled to counsel, even during interrogation before indictment.
    Which of the following choices lists ALL of the above statements that are TRUE?
    A. I, II, III, IV   B. I, II, IV
    C. II, III, IV   D. II, IV

12._____

13. One method of identifying unknown criminals when eyewitnesses are available is to have an artist draw a composite of the features as described by these eyewitnesses.

13._____

Which of the following steps is LEAST appropriate for the preparation of such a composite drawing?
- A. The witnesses should compare their impressions of the criminal and exchange opinions concerning the dominant characteristics.
- B. After obtaining an oral account, the investigator should have each witness reduce his description to writing.
- C. The artist should make up several preliminary sketches which are variants of the common impression.
- D. The witnesses should separately examine each preliminary sketch, select the closest approximation, and make suggestions for improvement.

14. As a general rule, a witness must testify to facts rather than opinions, inferences, or conclusions. Exceptions to this rule include common experiences that can be described only in the form of conclusions, matters of common knowledge, and opinions based on familiar experiences.
An ordinary witness may testify to all of the following EXCEPT whether
    - A. a hole appeared to be of a certain depth even though exact measurements had not been taken
    - B. the actions of a person whose sanity is in question seemed to be rational or irrational
    - C. a person looked as if he wanted to get away from a certain neighborhood
    - D. a vehicle was moving rapidly or slowly

15. Assume that an officer who is investigating a burglary discovers a tool impression at the door of a building which has been broken into. When a jimmy is found nearby, the officer places the tool against the door to determine whether the blade of the tool fits the impression.
This action by the officer is BASICALLY
    - A. *advisable*, chiefly because the officer can tell immediately whether the jimmy might have been used in the commission of the crime
    - B. *inadvisable*, chiefly because evidence samples should not come into contact with other samples or with contaminating matter
    - C. *advisable*, chiefly because any paint traces on the blade of the tool can then be compared with the material where the door was damaged
    - D. *inadvisable*, chiefly because comparison of samples should not be made until the evidence has been removed to the laboratory

16. Of the following, an officer who has just arrived at the scene of a crime and is ready to begin his investigation should FIRST
    - A. determine which kinds of evidence are most important for solving the particular crime
    - B. stand to one side and make an estimate of the entire situation
    - C. select the method of search that will most efficiently cover all the ground
    - D. form preliminary opinion of what has happened and attempt to verify it by examining various articles

17. In programs designed to treat drug abusers, the one of the following which was found to be MOST important in achieving success is
    A. the desire of the user to stop using drugs
    B. acceptance by the patient of non-drug alternatives
    C. involvement of the patient in group therapy
    D. the employment of ex-abusers as counselors in the treatment program

17._____

18. The one of the following terms which BEST describes the psychological desire to repeat the use of a drug intermittently or continuously because of emotional needs is
    A. addiction   B. euphoria   C. tolerance   D. habituation

18._____

19. It is generally accepted that the effect of repeated use of marijuana in heavy dose is that users will _____ suffer physical withdrawal symptoms if they stop suddenly.
    A. develop a tolerance and will
    B. develop a tolerance but will not
    C. not develop a tolerance but will
    D. not develop a tolerance and will not

19._____

20. In the context of civil disorder, appearances and reality are of almost equal importance in the handling of citizen complaints against the police.
    The one of the following which is MOST consistent with the viewpoint of the foregoing statement is that
    A. the police should not be the only municipal agency subject to outside scrutiny and review
    B. the benefits and liabilities of civilian review boards have both been exaggerated
    C. the police department itself should receive and act on complaints in order to protect police against unfounded charges
    D. in addition to adequate machinery for handling complaints, there must be belief among citizens that the procedures are adequate

20._____

21. In most police departments, the patrol operations of juvenile divisions are supplementary to those of the uniform patrol division.
    When complaints regarding the commission of offenses are received, they should GENERALLY be answered by
    A. beat officers unless it is certain that a juvenile offender is involved
    B. juvenile division officers if it is the type of case in which juveniles are usually involved
    C. beat officers regardless of whether juveniles are involved
    D. juvenile division officers if a juvenile offender is suspected of being involved

21._____

22. Which of the following statements regarding the investigation of arson cases is INCORRECT?
    A. It is essential that a human being actually be present for a building to be considered inhabited.
    B. Direct evidence connecting the offender with the crime is ordinarily lacking.
    C. Every fire is presumed to be of accidental origin until it is proved otherwise.
    D. Qualified experts may testify to the absence of defects and deficiencies which could cause fire.

22.____

23. Funds originally made available to state and local governments as a result of passage of the Safe Streets Act were allocated on the basis of
    A. crime rates
    B. size of population
    C. state planning agency recommendations
    D. requests from local governments

23.____

24. In response to an increase in the amount of crime that is committed in apartment buildings, several local police precincts have started programs to combat indoor crime.
    Under these programs,
    A. bi-weekly meetings are held with tenants to recommend improved security procedures
    B. police in patrol cars park and make periodic vertical patrols of apartment buildings
    C. building superintendents are required to fill out checklists of security deficiencies in their buildings
    D. the number of foot patrolmen is doubled in order to increase police visibility

24.____

25. Suppose that, at a police training lecture, you are told that many of the men in our penal institutions today are second and third offenders.
    Of the following, the MOST valid inference you can make solely on the basis of this statement is that
    A. second offenders are not easily apprehended
    B. patterns of human behavior are not easily changed
    C. modern laws are not sufficiently flexible
    D. laws do not breed crimes

25.____

KEY (CORRECT ANSWERS)

1. C
2. A
3. D
4. C
5. B

6. A
7. C
8. D
9. D
10. A

11. C
12. B
13. A
14. C
15. B

16. B
17. A
18. D
19. D
20. D

21. C
22. A
23. B
24. B
25. B

TEST 2

DIRECTIONS: Each question or incomplete statement is followed by several suggested answers or completions. Select the one that BEST answers the question or completes the statement. *PRINT THE LETTER OF THE CORRECT ANSWER IN THE SPACE AT THE RIGHT.*

Questions 1-3.

DIRECTIONS: Questions 1 through 3 are based on the following example of a police report. The report consists of nine numbered sentences, some of which are not consistent with the principles of good police report writing.

(1) At 10:30 P.M., May 23, I received a radio message from Sergeant William Smith, who directed me to report to the Tremont Motel, 10 Wilson Avenue, to investigate an attempted burglary. (2) When I arrived at the motel at 10:45 P.M., John Jones told me that he had seen a blue sedan park across the street earlier in the evening. (3) A few minutes later, Jones heard a noise at the far end of the motel. (4) Noticing that the door to one of the motel units was open, Jones walked in and saw a man about six feet tall and 25-30 years old. (5) When he saw Jones, the man ran into the next room and escaped through a window. (6) While returning to the motel office, Jones passed several cars parked in front of other units. (7) He then saw the man run across the street and get into the blue sedan, which immediately sped away. (8) No evidence was obtained at the scene of the attempted burglary. (9) Jones could not remember the license number of the car, but he thought it was an out-of-state license plate.

1. A good police report should be arranged in logical order.
   Which of the following sentences from the report does NOT appear in its proper sequence in the report?
   A. 3   B. 5   C. 7   D. 9

   1.____

2. Only material that is relevant to the main thought of a report should be included.
   Which of the following sentences from the report contains material which is LEAST relevant to this report?
   A. 2   B. 3   C. 6   D. 8

   2.____

3. Police reports should include all essential information.
   Which of the following sentences from the report is LEAST complete in terms of providing necessary information?
   A. 2   B. 4   C. 5   D. 9

   3.____

Questions 4-10.

DIRECTIONS: Questions 4 through 10 are to be answered on the basis of the information contained in the following tables and chart.

TABLE 1
Number of Murders by Region, United States: 2015 and 2016

Region	Year	
	2015	2016
Northeastern States	2,521	2,849
North Central States	3,427	3,697
Southern States	6,577	7,055
Western States	2,062	2,211

Number in each case for given year and region represents total number (100%) of murders in that region for that year.

TABLE 2
Murder by Circumstance, U.S. – 2016
(Percent distribution by category)

Region	Total	Spouse Killing Spouses	Parent Killing Child	Other Family Killings	Romantic Triangle & Lovers' Quarrels	Other Arguments	Known Felony Type	Suspected Felony Type
Northeastern States	100.0	9.6	3.7	6.1	7.9	38.4	25.4	8.9
North Central States	100.0	11.3	3.0	8.9	5.0	39.5	22.4	9.9
Southern States	100.0	13.8	2.2	8.8	8.4	46.0	13.9	6.9
Western States	100.0	12.5	4.9	7.0	6.4	32.2	28.0	9.0

CHART 1
Murder by Type of Weapon Used, U.S. – 2016
(Percent Distribution)

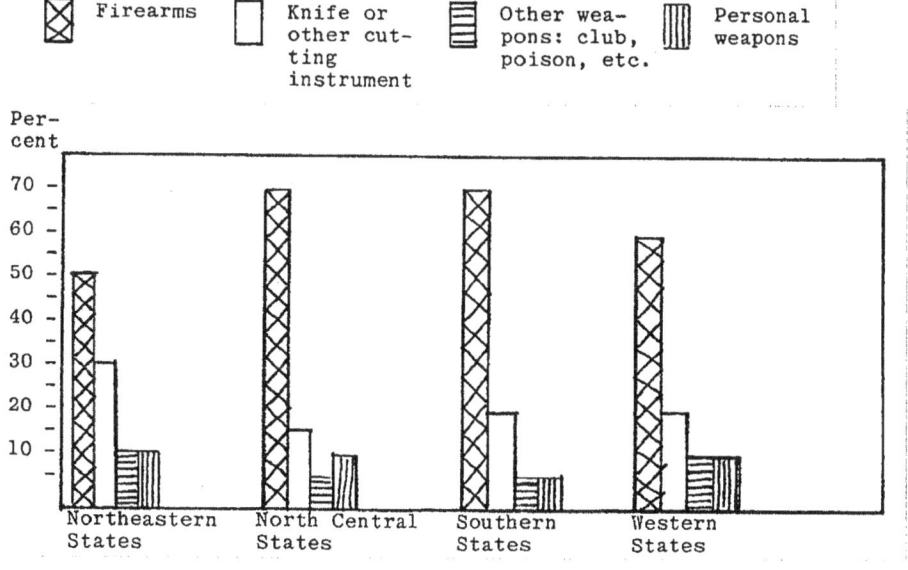

4. The number of persons murdered by firearms in the Western States in 2016 was MOST NEARLY
   A. 220   B. 445   C. 1235   D. 1325

5. In 2016, the number of murders in the category *Parent Killing Child* was GREATEST in the _____ States.
   A. Northeastern
   B. North Central
   C. Southern
   D. Western

6. The difference between the number of persons murdered with firearms and the number of persons murdered with other weapons (club, poison, etc.) in the North Central States in 2016 is MOST NEARLY
   A. 2200   B. 2400   C. 2600   D. 2800

7. In 2016, the ratio of the number of murders in the Western States to the total number of murders in the U.S. was MOST NEARLY
   A. 1 to 4   B. 1 to 5   C. 1 to 7   D. 1 to 9

8. The total number of murders in the U.S. in the category of *Romantic Triangles and Lovers' Quarrels* in 2016 was MOST NEARLY
   A. 850   B. 950   C. 1050   D. 1150

9. Which of the following represents the GREATEST number of murders in 2016? Persons murdered by _____ states.
   A. firearms in the western
   B. knives or other cutting instruments in the southern
   C. knives or other cutting instruments and persons murdered by other weapons (club, poison, etc.) in the northeastern
   D. knives or other cutting instruments, persons murdered by other weapons (club, poison, etc.) and persons murdered by personal weapons in the north central

10. From 2015 to 2016, the total number of murders increased by the GREATEST percentage in the _____ States.
    A. Northeastern   B. North Central   C. Southern   D. Western

Questions 11-13.

DIRECTIONS: Questions 11 through 13 are to be answered SOLELY on the basis of the following passage.

The criminal justice system is generally regarded as having the basic objective of reducing crime. However, one must also consider its larger objective of minimizing the total social costs associated with crime and crime control. Both of these components are complex and difficult to measure completely. The social costs associated with crime come from the long- and short-term physical damage, psychological harm, and property losses to victims as a result of crimes committed. Crime also creates serious indirect effects. It can induce a feeling of insecurity that is only partially reflected in business losses and economic disruption due to anxiety about venturing into high crime rate areas.

Balanced against these costs associated with crime must be the consequences of actions taken to reduce them. Money spent on developing, maintaining, and operating criminal justice agencies is part of the cost of the crime control system. But there are also indirect costs, such as welfare payments to prisoners' families, income lost by offenders who are denied good jobs, legal fees, and wages lost by witnesses. In addition, there are penalties suffered by suspects erroneously arrested or sentenced, the limitation on personal liberty resulting from police surveillance, and the invasion of privacy in maintaining criminal records.

11. Of the following, the MOST appropriate title for this passage would be 11.____
    A. The Effectiveness of Crime Control Efforts
    B. Protecting Citizens' Rights
    C. The Costs of Crime
    D. Improving the Criminal Justice System

12. According to this passage, all of the following are indirect costs of the crime control system EXCEPT 12.____
    A. wages lost by witnesses
    B. money spent for legal services
    C. payments made to the families of prisoners
    D. money spent on operating criminal justice agencies

13. According to this passage, actions taken to reduce crime 13.____
    A. will reduce the indirect costs of the crime control system
    B. may result in a decrease of personal liberty
    C. may cause psychological harm to victims of crime
    D. should immediately start improving the criminal justice system

Questions 14-16.

DIRECTIONS: Questions 14 through 15 are to be answered SOLELY on the basis of the following passage.

Probably the most important single mechanism for bringing the resources of science and technology to bear on the problems of crime would be the establishment of a major prestigious science and technology research program within a research institute. The program would create interdisciplinary teams of mathematicians, computer scientists, electronics engineers, physicists, biologists, and other natural scientists, psychologists, sociologists, economists, and lawyers. The institute and the program must be significant enough to attract the best scientists available, and, to this end, the director of this institute must himself have a background in science and technology and have the respect of scientists. Because it would be difficult to attract such a staff into the Federal Government, the institute should be established by a university, a group of universities, or an independent non-profit organization, and should be within a major metropolitan area. The institute would have to establish close ties with neighboring criminal justice agencies that would receive the benefit of serving as experimental laboratories for such an institute. In fact, the proposal for the institute might be jointly submitted with the criminal justice agencies. The research program would require in order to bring together the necessary *critical mass* of competent staff, an annual budget which might reach 5 million dollars, funded with at least three years of lead time to assure continuity. Such a major scientific and technological research institute should be supported by the Federal Government.

14. Of the following, the MOST appropriate title for the above passage is
    A. Research – An Interdisciplinary Approach to Fighting Crime
    B. A Curriculum For Fighting Crime
    C. The Role of the University in the Fight Against Crime
    D. Governmental Support of Criminal Research Programs

14.____

15. According to the above passage, in order to attract the best scientists available, the research institute should
    A. provide psychologists and sociologists to counsel individual members of interdisciplinary teams
    B. encourage close ties with neighboring criminal justice agencies
    C. be led by a person who is respected in the scientific community
    D. be directly operated and funded by the Federal Government

15.____

16. The term *critical mass*, as used in the above passage, refers MAINLY to
    A. a staff which would remain for three years of continuous service to the institute
    B. staff members necessary to carry out the research program of the institute successfully
    C. the staff necessary to establish relations with criminal justice agencies which will serve as experimental laboratories for the institute
    D. a staff which would be able to assist the institute in raising adequate funds

16.____

Questions 17-19.

DIRECTIONS: Questions 17 through 19 are to be answered SOLELY on the basis of the following passage.

An assassination is an act that consists of a plotted, attempted or actual murder of a prominent political figure by an individual who performs this act in other than a governmental role. This definition draws a distinction between political execution and assassination. An execution may be regarded as a political killing, but it is initiated by the organs of the state, while an assassination can always be characterized as an illegal act. A prominent figure must be the target of the killing, since the killing of lesser members of the political community is included within a wider category of internal political turmoil, namely, terrorism. Assassination is also to be distinguished from homicide. The target of the aggressive act must be a political figure rather than a private person. The killing of a prime minister by a member of an insurrectionist or underground group clearly qualifies as an assassination. So does an act by a deranged individual who tries to kill not just any individual, but the individual in his political role – as President, for example.

17. Of the following, the MOST appropriate title for the above passage would be
    A. Assassination – Legal Aspects   B. Political Causes of Assassination
    C. Assassination – A Definition   D. Categories of Assassination

17.____

18. Assume that a nationally prominent political figure is charged with treason by the state, tried in a court of law, found guilty and hanged by the state. According to the above passage, it would be MOST appropriate to regard his death as a(n)
    A. assassination
    B. execution
    C. aggressive act
    D. homicide

19. According to the above passage, which of the following statements is CORRECT?
    A. The assassination of a political figure is an illegal act.
    B. A private person may be the target of an assassination attempt.
    C. The killing of an obscure member of a political community is considered an assassination event.
    D. An execution may not be regarded as a political killing.

Questions 20-27.

DIRECTIONS: Questions 20 through 27 consist of sentences concerning police operations. Some are correct according to ordinary formal English usage. Others are incorrect because they contain errors in English usage, spelling, or punctuation. Consider a sentence correct if it contains no errors in English usage, spelling, or punctuation, even if there may be other ways of writing the sentence correctly.
Mark your answer:
   A. If only Sentence I is correct;
   B. If only Sentence II is correct;
   C. If Sentences I and II are correct;
   D. If neither Sentence I nor II is correct.

20. I. The influence of recruitment efficiency upon administrative standards is readily apparant.
    II. Rapid and accurate thinking are an essential quality of the police officer.

21. I. The administrator of a police department is constantly confronted by the demands of subordinates for increased personnel in their respective units.
    II. Since a chief executive must work within well-defined fiscal limits, he must weigh the relative importance of various requests.

22. I. The two men whom the police arrested for a parking violation were wanted for robbery in three states.
    II. Strong executive control from the top to the bottom of the enterprise is one of the basic principals of police administration.

23. I. When he gave testimony unfavorable to the defendant loyalty seemed to mean very little.
    II. Having run off the road while passing a car, the patrolman gave the driver a traffic ticket.

24. I. The judge ruled that the defendant's conversation with his doctor was a priviliged communication.
    II. The importance of our training program is widely recognized; however, fiscal difficulties limit the program's effectiveness.

25. I. Despite an increase in patrol coverage, there were less arrests for crimes against property this year.
    II. The investigators could hardly have expected greater cooperation from the public.

26. I. Neither the patrolman nor the witness could identify the defendant as the driver of the car.
    II. Each of the officers in the class received their certificates at the completion of the course.

27. I. The new commander made it clear that those kind of procedures would no longer be permitted.
    II. Giving some weight to performance records is more advisable than making promotions solely on the basis of test scores.

KEY (CORRECT ANSWERS)

1.	D	10.	A	19.	A
2.	C	11.	C	20.	D
3.	A	12.	D	21.	C
4.	D	13.	B	22.	A
5.	C	14.	A	23.	D
6.	B	15.	C	24.	B
7.	C	16.	B	25.	B
8.	D	17.	C	26.	A
9.	B	18.	B	27.	D

EXAMINATION SECTION
TEST 1

DIRECTIONS: Each question or incomplete statement is followed by several suggested answers or completions. Select the one that BEST answers the question or completes the statement. *PRINT THE LETTER OF THE CORRECT ANSWER IN THE SPACE AT THE RIGHT.*

1. Identify the statements that contain clearly defined objectives:
   The objective
   I. in this section is to increase understanding of the principles of management
   II. of the literacy program is to teach prisoners to read
   III. of the work release program is to assist the prisoner in retaining his job and to keep him in the community
   IV. of jail programs is to rehabilitate the offender
   V. of the literacy program is to raise the reading level of the students to the fourth grade reading level

   The CORRECT answer is:

   A. I, III B. II, V C. III, V
   D. III, IV E. II, IV

2. The following are statements about the distinguishing characteristics of *line item* budgets, *performance* budgets, and *program* budgets.
   Indicate by writing the type of budget described in the space at the right.

   A. The focus is on the kinds and level of service performed.
   B. It deals with packages of commonly related activities.
   C. It focuses on specific problems and relevant policy issues.
   D. It is structured around identifiable units of service and their specific costs.
   E. How much is being spent and for what purpose.
   F. It focuses on the results of the performance of the service rather than on dollar costs.
   G. The budget reflects a concern for control.

3. Identify the kind of budget associated with the following questions:

   A. What services are being performed and what cost?
   B. What needs to be done, for whom, and how can it best be done?
   C. How much money did we spend in the past?

4. A significant characteristic of the program budget is that it lends itself to review and analysis.
   Why?

   A. The budget has a built-in accounting system that makes close control possible.
   B. The budget includes measurable objectives.
   C. It is possible to review performance based on units of service.
   D. All of the above

5. The advantages of program budgeting over line item and performance budgeting is:
    I. Tight, administrative control
    II. Forces the administrator to think through his total operation
    III. Measurable objectives
    IV. Simplicity of development
    V. Closer estimates of future costs

    The CORRECT answer is:

    A. I, II
    B. II, III, IV
    C. II, III, V
    D. III, IV, V
    E. II, IV

6. Indicate whether the following statements are true or false:

    A. High pay is more important as a factor in job satisfaction.
    B. When pay is low, increases in salary will increase job satisfaction, but only temporarily.
    C. An excellent method of improving morale of personnel is to assign to the jail, officers who can't make it in the field.
    D. Every officer should learn each post in the jail and can be expected to function equally well on every post.

7. List four methods of determining employee training needs.

    A. _____
    B. _____
    C. _____
    D. _____

8. Employee selection, probation, and training are closely related to each other.
   Select the statement that gives the BEST reason why this is true.
   They are

    A. related because they logically follow each other
    B. all a part of personnel administration
    C. related because each step supports the following step; but any one alone is not the most important
    D. practically the same

9. Sheriff D has hired his wife's third cousin, C, as jail officer. About a year later, he realizes that C is just not shaping up. He lacks interest, is slow to learn, and is forgetful. He cannot fire him, however, because C has passed his probationary period and is on permanent status. The jail staff now includes a marginal officer. Sheriff D feels, however, that the officer's performance can be improved through training.
   What do you think?

    A. Training can improve anyone's performance.
    B. The sheriff had better improve his selection process.
    C. Apparently, C needs motivational training.
    D. The sheriff cannot expect training to correct the mistakes that have been made in selection and orientation.

10. Indicate whether the following statements are true or false:

   A. A large number of security categories is an indication of an effective classification system.
   B. A classification system should have a simple procedure.
   C. The term trusty accurately describes this type of prisoner.
   D. Once classified, a prisoner need not be reviewed again.
   E. The objectives of classification are to evaluate the prisoner and determine the degree of supervision or control he requires.

11. One of the objectives of the jail is to ensure the safety of all prisoners. Identify the statements below that support this objective.
   I. Medical examination for all prisoners
   II. Permitting juveniles to be placed in cells with adult prisoners
   III. A classification system
   IV. Guidelines on admission of prisoners to the jail
   V. Treating all prisoners alike
   VI. Permitting trusties to supervise other prisoners

   The CORRECT answer is:

   A. I, II, III   B. II, V, VI   C. III, IV, V
   D. I, IV, V   E. I, III, IV

12. Correspondence is permitted in order to maintain family and community ties. Identify the statements that support this objective.
   I. One letter a week is permitted.
   II. There is no mail censorship.
   III. The prisoner can write an unlimited number of letters.
   IV. The prisoner can write to his immediate family only.
   V. The prisoner may only write letters of one page.

   The CORRECT answer is:

   A. I, II   B. II, III   C. III, IV
   D. IV, V   E. II, IV

13. Indicate whether the following statements are true or false:

   A. Censoring mail contributes to good security because it prevents prisoners from making escape plans.
   B. Requiring verification of persons to whom the prisoner wishes to write is a good idea because it provides valid identification of the correspondent.
   C. Limitations on mail are in reality a matter of administrative convenience.
   D. Packages keep prisoners happy and as a consequence discourage them from escape attempts.
   E. A prisoner's family should be permitted to send him food parcels in order to supplement his diet.

14. Indicate whether the following statements are true or false:

    A. Both long and short hair can be unsanitary.
    B. Women who have long hair do not have it cut when admitted to the jail.
    C. Length of hair is less important than its cleanliness.
    D. Cutting long hair for sanitary reasons ignores the fact that sanitation can be more easily achieved by washing.
    E. Both long and short hair clogs water drains.
    F. Long hair looks silly on men and, therefore, should not be allowed in the jail.

15. Select the statement that achieves the objective of providing a sanitary jail and protects the health of prisoners.
    All prisoners will bathe

    A. on admission and regularly thereafter
    B. regularly, and all long hair will be cut
    C. regularly; hair will be washed regularly and kept combed. All prisoners with long hair must wear hair nets when assigned to the kitchen, laundry, or any other job near moving machinery.
    D. all of the above

16. Indicate whether the following statements are true or false:

    A. A club carried by the officer in the jail must be considered a weapon.
    B. Weapons should be carried by jail personnel for their own protection.
    C. There is nothing wrong with carrying a derringer well concealed; it may save your life.
    D. Weapons carried in the jail do not provide any protection to the officer.
    E. Visiting law enforcement personnel should be permitted to carry their weapons in the jail since they are responsible persons.
    F. An officer who needs to carry a weapon in the jail should not be working in the jail.
    G. The best place for an armory is outside the jail.

KEY (CORRECT ANSWERS)

1. C
2. A. Performance
   B. Program
   C. Program
   D. Performance
   E. Line item
   F. Program
   G. Line item
3. A. Performance
   B. Program
   C. Line item
4. B
5. C

6. A. False
   B. True
   C. False
   D. False
7. A. Evaluation of employee performance
   B. Review of critical incidents
   C. Introduction of new procedures
   D. Surveying employees
8. C
9. D
10. A. False
    B. True
    C. False
    D. False
    E. True

11. E
12. B
13. A. False
    B. True
    C. False
    D. False
    E. True
14. A. True
    B. True
    C. True
    D. True
    E. True
    F. False
15. C
16. A. True
    B. False
    C. False
    D. True
    E. False
    F. True
    G. True

TEST 2

DIRECTIONS: Each question or incomplete statement is followed by several suggested answers or completions. Select the one that BEST answers the question or completes the statement. *PRINT THE LETTER OF THE CORRECT ANSWER IN THE SPACE AT THE RIGHT.*

1. Which of the following are APPROPRIATE methods of program development? 1.____
   I. Find out what other jails are doing and develop similar programs.
   II. An examination of the annual report will give sufficient information on prisoner needs to develop programs.
   III. A relatively wide range of data about the jail population will be needed.
   IV. There may be a need to develop both statistical
   V. studies and a testing program to get a clear picture of jail population needs.
   The CORRECT answer is:

   A. I, II   B. II, III   C. III, IV
   D. I, IV   E. II, IV

2. You are faced with the following situation: 2.____
   There is increasing pressure from the community to develop jail programs. A survey has been done of the jail population and the findings are as follows:

Education Level		Occupation		Residence	
0-4th Grade	75	General labor	90	Permanent residence	25
5-7 th Grade	40	Construction labor	22	No permanent residence	114
8-12th Grade	20				
Over 12th	4	Skilled operators	6		139
	139	Clerical	21		
			139		

   Given the above figures, what would you do about program development?
   I. Start an illiteracy program, since a large number have a 4th grade education or less.
   II. Begin a work release program because there are 25 persons who have permanent residence.
   III. Test the 0-4th grade group to find out the level of literacy.
   IV. Develop a vocational training program for the general laborers.
   V. Although I might be interested in developing a work release program, I would want to know more about the group who claim permanent residence: such as marital status, job skills, and any kinds of problems they might have.
   VI. Set up a literacy program with volunteers from the community. Prisoners who need it will volunteer, and the participation from the community will solve the problems of criticism about a lack of programs in the jail.
   The CORRECT answer is:

   A. I, II, III   B. III, IV, V   C. II, III, V
   D. III, V   E. III, VI

3. Select the statements that are TRUE program objectives. 3.____
   I. It is the objective of the AA program to give the prisoner an understanding of his drinking problem.
   II. The objective of a work release program is to prevent job loss due to confinement.

III. The purpose of the AA program is to make help available to the problem drinker.
IV. The objective of a literacy program is to raise the reading level of illiterate prisoners to the 5th grade reading level.
V. The objective of the AA program is to have the prisoner recognize and admit his drinking problem.
VI. The objective of jail programs is to rehabilitate prisoners.
VII. The objective of a work release program is to restore the prisoner to the community.
VIII. The objective of a literacy program is to teach prisoners to read.

The CORRECT answer is:

A. I, IV, V
B. I, II, III
C. VI, VII
D. IV, V
E. V, VI

4. Which of the following represents the PROPER sequence in program development? 4.____

A. Funds, prisoner needs, program objectives, program selection, personnel
B. Program selection, prisoner needs, program objectives, funds, personnel
C. Prisoner needs, objectives, program selection, funds, personnel
D. Objectives, prisoner needs, funds, program selection, personnel

5. Select the statements that MOST clearly express the characteristics of work release. 5.____
   I. It exposes the prisoner to many temptations - especially the alcoholic.
   II. It gives the prisoner an opportunity to contribute to the support of his family.
   III. It provides the prisoner with an opportunity to serve his sentence much more easily than if he were confined.
   IV. It provides cheap labor to local employers.
   V. The prisoner is faced with the problem of making decisions that he would not normally make if he were confined.
   VI. It gives the prisoner the opportunity to see his family more often.
   VII. It provides an opportunity for the prisoner to retain his ties in the community.

The CORRECT answer is:

A. I, II, III
B. II, III, IV
C. III, IV, V
D. V, VI, VII
E. II, V, VII

6. Which of the following kinds of prisoners should NOT be selected for work release? 6.____
   I. All alcoholics
   II. Persons with poor work records
   III. Persons with jobs in the community
   IV. Sex offenders
   V. Drunk drivers
   VI. Prisoners who do not have permanent residence in the
   VII. community
   VIII. The prisoner charged with assault and battery against his wife

The CORRECT answer is:

A. I, III
B. II, IV
C. III, V
D. IV, VI
E. V, VII

KEY (CORRECT ANSWERS)

1. C
2. D
3. D, E
4. C
5. E
6. D

TEST 3

DIRECTIONS: Each question or incomplete statement is followed by several suggested answers or completions. Select the one that BEST answers the question or completes the statement. *PRINT THE LETTER OF THE CORRECT ANSWER IN THE SPACE AT THE RIGHT.*

1. Select the statement that BEST defines the role of the jail administrator.   1._____

    A. The jail administrator is the person most knowledgeable about jails and is, therefore, one of the most important members of the planning committee.
    B. Although it is not necessary that the jail administrator be a member of the planning committee, he should appoint its members and approve the final report.
    C. The jail administrator is the initiator, coordinator, and consultant to the planning committee.
    D. All of the above

2. List the various kinds of data that are needed for a jail study. The main headings are given.   2._____
Fill in the kinds of data which are included within those categories.

    A. Jail population studies (list six):
    1. _____   2. _____
    3. _____   4. _____
    5. _____   6. _____
    B. Population forecasting (list three):
        1. _____
        2. _____
        3. _____

3. The jail is not an independent agency, and the activities of other branches of government influence jail population. List the two agencies that have the MOST immediate influence on the jail.   3._____

    A. _____
    B. _____

4. Sheriff D has been concerned about the conditions of his jail for some time. There has been an increase in the jail population which indicates to him the need for some expansion. A week ago, he was visited by a consultant from a steel company who helpfully surveyed the jail and recommended that the county needed a new jail.   4._____
Do you feel this is the PROPER approach to jail planning?

    A. *No;* the opinion of one man is not enough. The sheriff should consult with other experts.
    B. *Yes;* the consultant obviously knows his business. The sheriff should take his recommendations to the county governing board.
    C. *No;* having defined his problem as lack of space, the sheriff should propose an evaluation of the jail by a group of experts who can supply information that would support the sheriff's recommendation for a formal planning study.
    D. *Yes;* the sheriff is an expert on jails and can determine if the consultant's report is accurate.

5. A number of problems will arise after a jail is built. What are the two MAIN problems, usually? 5._____

   A. _____
   B. _____

6. The planning group has submitted a report and specifications for a new jail to the county council. An architect has been selected and the specifications have been turned over to him to translate into building plans. The architect has designed three jails in the past five years and will not require any additional information than that contained in the report and specifications. 6._____
   Select the APPROPRIATE response to this situation.

   A. The architect's past experience will be very helpful in designing the new jail. He should not need any further information if the planning was done well.
   B. Although the architect is experienced in jail design, he will need assistance in translating specifications into operational realities. All jails are not the same and cannot be built as though they have similar functions and similar problems.
   C. Since the most important function of a jail is to hold prisoners, there is little reason for great variations in interior jail design.
   D. This architect is well suited for the job. He may be left to his own devices and predilections.

KEY (CORRECT ANSWERS)

1. C
2. A. (1) Daily average count
      (2) High and low admission rates
      (3) Seasonal population highs and lows
      (4) Age
      (5) Sex
      (6) Kinds of offenses
   B. (1) Projections of the community population
      (2) Present and projected arrest rates
      (3) Present and projected crime rates

3. A. Courts
   B. Police
4. C
5. A. Location - too far from the courts Police
   B. Not enough single cells
6. B

TEST 4

DIRECTIONS: Each question or incomplete statement is followed by several suggested answers or completions. Select the one that BEST answers the question or completes the statement. *PRINT THE LETTER OF THE CORRECT ANSWER IN THE SPACE AT THE RIGHT.*

1. Prisoner L was attacked and beaten by the prisoner who shared his two-man cell. He was hospitalized for internal injuries and a broken leg. Investigation revealed that his attacker, prisoner E, was mentally ill and had a long history of mental illness and assaultive behavior. The county and the sheriff were co-defendants in the suit that resulted from the investigation.
   What step could have been taken to avoid this situation?

   A. Keep all prisoners in separate cells.
   B. Very little could be done. It is not possible to supervise prisoners all the time.
   C. A classification and evaluation procedure would have prevented this occurrence.
   D. The jail needed an evaluation and classification procedure, a trained admissions officer who could evaluate prisoners, and separate housing for dangerous prisoners.

1._____

2. Prisoner J reported to sick call with a black eye, three loose teeth, and bruises on his back. He claims that he was fined by a kangaroo court and beaten and robbed when he refused to pay. He threatens to sue the county and the sheriff for not providing him with protection from other prisoners.
   How could this incident have been prevented?
   I. Establish a rule against kangaroo courts
   II. Prisoner J was in a fight, but there is no evidence of a kangaroo court
   III. Improve supervisory procedures
   IV. Establish an evaluation program that will identify troublemakers
   V. Very little can be done. It is impossible to prevent the formation of kangaroo courts.
   VI. Not permit money in the jail.
   The CORRECT answer is:

   A. I, II   B. II, III   C. III, VI
   D. VI, VII   E. III, V

2._____

3. The jail in an urban county is large and holds persons charged with a variety of crimes. There has been a history of sexual assaults, beatings, kangaroo courts, and escapes for a number of years. The last administrator was indicted for mismanagement and both he and the county have been successfully sued by prisoners who had suffered injuries while confined. The new administrator has been in office one year, but there has been no change in procedures. He and the county are being sued by a prisoner who was severely beaten and robbed by a kangaroo court.
   According to past court decisions, which one of the following statements may be the APPROPRIATE finding of the court?

   A. Although these problems are of long standing, the sheriff has not had sufficient time to put into effect the appropriate procedures that would remedy the situation and prevent assaults such as this one from occurring

3._____

55

B. The sheriff has been well aware of the history of the jail and its problems. In fact, the assaults were a major feature of his campaign. Knowing the problems and aware of his responsibility for the safety of prisoners, he was in a position to anticipate danger but has taken no steps to prevent injury to prisoners
C. Both of the above
D. None of the above

4. Prisoner B suffered what apparently was a heart attack in his cell during the evening. It required a locksmith to get the door open. The key was worn and would not turn the lock. By the time the cell door was opened, Prisoner B was dead.
What step should have been taken to prevent this incident?

 A. Medical exam at admission would have discovered this condition.
 B. A key control system would have revealed the defective key.
 C. A procedure for responding to medical emergencies is needed.
 D. A duplicate key system with a key and lock inspection and reporting system

5. How do you feel the courts will rule in a case where a prisoner suffers injury or death because the cell door cannot be opened due to defective equipment?

 A. Probably find the sheriff not liable, because he has not shown malice or irresponsibility
 B. Probably find the sheriff liable because he should be aware of the condition of his jail and take the appropriate steps to protect his prisoners
 C. Both of the above
 D. None of the above

6. Prisoner W was found dead in his cell in the morning. Apparently, the head wound he had received prior to his arrest was much more serious than the jail staff had realized. The sheriff claims that he cannot be held liable for the death since he is required by law to accept all persons who are lawfully arrested.
How have courts ruled in cases similar to this?

 A. The courts have ruled that since the sheriff is required by law to accept lawfully arrested persons, he is powerless to reject those who may be in need of medical care. He, therefore, has no liability.
 B. The courts have ruled that the sheriff is bound to exercise ordinary and reasonable care for the preservation of a prisoner's life and health. He would, therefore, be liable, even though he was required by law to accept injured prisoners.
 C. Both of the above
 D. None of the above

7. The county jail has a new sheriff and a number of new deputies. There is no training program, and supervision of personnel is non-existent. The sheriff claims to know his deputies well since they are his friends. A prisoner is now suing the sheriff and the county claiming injuries received from a beating by one of the deputies. The prisoner claims that the deputy has a reputation in the community for a violent temper and has a history of numerous fights. He further claims that the sheriff is a close friend of the deputy and knows his reputation. If the prisoner's statements are accepted by the court as fact, how do you think the court will rule?

A. The court will not find the sheriff liable, because he cannot be held responsible for the official acts of his employees.
B. The court will find the sheriff liable. He has failed to exercise care in the selection of his employees and knew about the deputy's incompetence.
C. The court will not find the sheriff liable. Although he knew about his deputy's violent temper and history of fighting, he had no way of knowing that the deputy would assault prisoners. If he had known of his deputy's unfitness, and had not discharged him, he would be liable.
D. None of the above

8. Sheriff O consistently refuses to make any exceptions for attorney visits and insists that they conform to the regular visiting hours. Some attorneys have complained to him that this policy is causing undue hardship to both then and their clients. Today an attorney appeared at the jail at 6:00 P.M. and requested to visit with prisoner T. At this time of the evening, the prisoners have been fed and counted. The jail does not have any evening activities; it is not understaffed, and the prisoner is not an escape risk. Do you feel a visit should be permitted?

   A. *No.* The attorney can return the next day at a reasonable hour.
   B. *Yes.* There are no activities that might cause a scheduling conflict.
   C. *No.* Permitting a prisoner out of his cell at this time of night could be dangerous.
   D. *Yes.* This is an area of administrative discretion. In order to deny such visits, the sheriff must show good reason such as danger to the jail or interference with vital activities. The plea of inconvenience is not adequate as a reason for denying a visit.

9. Attorney B has written a strong letter to Sheriff F protesting the inspection of mail between him and his clients. He has stated in no uncertain terms that if this *censorship,* as he calls it, continues, he will take the sheriff to court for interfering with the attorney-client relationship.
   What should the sheriff do?

   A. Change his policy and permit unrestricted and uninspected mail from this attorney to enter the jail
   B. Inform the attorney that there will be no change in mail inspection policy and the reasons why
   C. Avoid a court fight and change mail policy to permit mail between attorneys and their clients to enter the jail uninspected
   D. Ignore the letter; the attorney knows the law on these matters and is bluffing

10. Prisoner A has requested permission to purchase a law book from the publisher. Which of the following statements contains the PROPER decision?

    A. Deny. He has no appeal pending.
    B. Review his request and, if the book will be useful to him in preparing his case, approve the purchase.
    C. Deny. Rumor has it that the prisoner is doing legal work for other prisoners.
    D. Suggest that he consider hiring an attorney.
    E. Approve the request.

11. Prisoner K has been in the process of appealing his conviction. Unfortunately, he is illiterate and without funds. Furthermore, his *attorney,* Prisoner G, is now in segregation for writing documents for prisoners - he had been working on K's paper when he was caught in a cell inspection. You have an interview with K at his request. He insists that he has a reasonable chance of success in his appeal and complains that you have no right to block his legal activities by locking up the *jail house lawyer,* Prisoner G. He also threatens to write a letter of complaint to the court.
What should you do?

     A. Release G from segregation and avoid any censure from the court
     B. Give K a list of lawyers and let him select one
     C. Refer K to legal aid, even though you know this agency has no funds to handle appeals
     D. Since you cannot provide any reasonable alternative, it will be necessary to release G from segregation to help K with his appeal

11._____

12. Identify those conditions that would probably create an opportunity for court intervention in disciplinary matters.
     I. A policy that permits lower rank personnel to place prisoners in isolation or segregation without the administrator's approval
     II. Weekly review of all prisoners in isolation
     III. Reduction of food to two meals a day
     IV. Sleeping pad and blanket placed in cell every evening
     V. No lights
     VI. Regular use of washing and bathing facilities outside of cell
    The CORRECT answer is:

     A. I, II, III   B. II, III, IV   C. I, III, V
     D. III, V, VI   E. II, IV, VI

12._____

13. Prisoner V has been confined in isolation for 20 days. He is uncertain about when he will be returned to the population since he has not been interviewed since he was placed on punishment status. The cell is well lit, ventilated, and has a cot, mattress, and blanket. V is permitted to write and may have visits as long as he bathes and shaves regularly. While in isolation, he is not permitted any reading material; since he has very little opportunity for exercise, he is fed two meals a day.
Which one of the statements below CORRECTLY describes the conditions above?

     A. The conditions of isolation are above average and are within guidelines that will prevent court intervention.
     B. The conditions of segregation may be above average when compared to other jails. However, the standards of his confinement are lower than that of other prisoners because he is receiving two meals per day.
     C. Both of the above
     D. None of the above

13._____

14. Prisoner O claims to belong to some obscure and unusual religion. He claims that in order to practice his faith, he requires another person of similar faith to join him in prayer at least once a week for a two-hour period. He insists that he can eat only green vegetables and lamb. The sheriff has refused permission for a two-hour visit because he does not have staff to supervise, or the facilities, and will not authorize any special foods. O threatens to go to court because he claims the right to practice his religion. What should the sheriff do?

14.____

   A. O has the right under the Constitution to practice his religion. The sheriff should permit the two-hour visit. The diet request should be denied, however, because it would cause a hardship to the jail.
   B. O has the right to believe anything he wishes. However, he does not have an absolute right to practice his religion if it presents a danger to the community. In this instance, refusal of the two-hour visit is based on security and supervisory problems. Denial of food is proper since such a diet for one person would be extremely burdensome to the jail.
   C. Both of the above
   D. None of the above

15. Three youthful prisoners have been sentenced to the jail for 30 days each for disorderly conduct. They have made a request to have the local underground newspaper mailed to them. The sheriff has reviewed a copy of the paper and feels it is *dirty, revolutionary,* and *communist* and should not be permitted in the jail.
    Which statement below is a PROPER response to the sheriff's position?

15.____

   A. Underground papers fall into the same category as pornography and should be prohibited from entering the jail.
   B. The courts have upheld this kind of censorship. The sheriff is on safe ground in denying these prisoners the paper.
   C. The sheriff is voicing personal opinions. He has not shown that the paper will threaten the security or good order of the jail. A court may have to decide on this if the prisoners decide to press their case. It would be wise for the sheriff to re-examine the paper to determine if his objections are objective or personal.
   D. None of the above

KEY (CORRECT ANSWERS)

1. D	6. B	11. D
2. C	7. B	12. C
3. B	8. D	13. B
4. D	9. B	14. B
5. B	10. E	15. C

TEST 5

DIRECTIONS: Each question or incomplete statement is followed by several suggested answers or completions. Select the one that BEST answers the question or completes the statement. *PRINT THE LETTER OF THE CORRECT ANSWER IN THE SPACE AT THE RIGHT.*

1. Sheriff P has only recently been elected. As administrator of the jail, he feels a responsibility to the community for running an efficient operation. He is also interested in running for re-election in another two years. Today, two prisoners escaped from the jail.
How should he handle this situation so that he develops public confidence in his administration?

    A. Sheriff P should come up with an explanation for the escape that will not make him look incompetent. It is most important that he begin his term in office with as good an image as possible.
    B. Since he is newly elected, he can blame the escape on the old administration.
    C. He should give the facts about the escape, indicate how he intends to clear up the deficiencies that were the underlying cause and, if necessary, point out some of the problems that may contribute to further incidents. Blaming the past administration is hardly a positive approach.
    D. None of the above

1.____

2. Sheriff N is sincerely interested in operating a clean, efficient operation. He feels that it is important to let the community know about the jail. He, therefore, accepts numerous speaking engagements from businessmen, organizations, and fraternal orders. He is an excellent storyteller and entertains his audiences with descriptions of prisoners and the kinds of crimes they commit. He feels very strongly that his audiences are interested in prisoners and their crimes and that since he satisfies their interest, he is developing a good community relations program.
Do you agree?

    A. *No.* Stories about prisoners and their crimes have nothing to do with community relations.
    B. *Yes.* You can't have much of a call for speaking engagements if you aren't an interesting speaker.
    C. *Yes.* If he can keep the public interested in prisoners, they will remain interested in the jail.
    D. *No.* Telling interesting stories does not inform the public about the jail, nor is speechmaking the only component of a community relations program.

2.____

3. You are in the process of reviewing your jail operation as a step in improving your community relations program. There are a number of changes you can make that will make a good impression on the community without jeopardizing jail safety or security. At this time you are considering liberalizing correspondence and visiting.
Will this or will this not contribute to a community relations program?

    A. *No.* Only a small part of the community is represented by prisoners and their families.
    B. *No.* If you are going to liberalize correspondence and visiting, do it for a sensible reason.

3.____

C. *Yes.* You have determined that liberalizing this procedure will not endanger the security of the jail. You have also identified a significant public and are meeting their needs.
D. None of the above

4. Sheriff A has developed an excellent relationship with reporter B. Yesterday he took B through the jail for an inside story about an escape that had occurred that morning. Other news media were not notified until noon. As usual, B wrote an excellent story, much of it favorable to Sheriff A.
What do you think of Sheriff A's behavior?

    4.____

A. Poor press relations. He should not give any reporter an opportunity for a scoop.
B. Poor policy. It is not good practice to become too friendly with reporters.
C. Good press relations. Because he had a sympathetic reporter, he was given favorable publicity.
D. None of the above

5. A jail is planning a formal graduation ceremony for those prisoners who have completed a literacy program. Sheriff A is debating on whether or not to invite prisoners' families and notify the news media.
What should he do?

    5.____

A. Notify the news media - it will be good publicity.
B. Don't invite anyone. This is too small an event to be of interest to anyone.
C. Invite only selected news media - too many would endanger the jail's security.
D. Invite the news media but not the prisoners' families; they may create security and contraband problems.
E. Invite both news media and immediate family members. The event is an excellent means of informing the community of a jail program. Family members and prisoners will realize the importance of the program by participating in a ceremony.

6. A newspaper sent a young reporter to cover the story about the escape of three prisoners. Although the story was essentially correct, the reporter made a few minor errors.
What action should the sheriff take?

    6.____

A. Call the editor and complain about the reporter's inaccuracies.
B. Call the reporter and let him know that his story contained errors.
C. Call the editor and advise him that any inaccuracies in the future and the reporter will not be allowed in the jail.
D. Ignore the errors since they were minor.

7. The jail has admitted a prisoner who is accused of a double murder. Community interest is high, and the news media are all insisting on interviews with the jail administrator and with the accused. The jail is small and does not have facilities for many reporters.
What should the jail administrator do?

    7.____

A. Permit only a few reporters in at one time, until all have had an opportunity to conduct interviews.
B. Meet with the reporters outside the jail and give them an interview. Refuse to allow interviews with the prisoner.

C. Have the reporters select representatives to conduct interviews in the jail.
D. Have the reporters select a representative to conduct interviews with the administrator. Do not permit any interviews with the prisoner unless he agrees and is accompanied by his attorney.

8. The jail has had a serious escape that was effected by sawing bars and picking locks. The chief jailer has been interviewed by the news media and maintains that the escape was caused by the incompetence of the officers on duty that night. The sheriff has also been interviewed and stated that the jail is old and needs to be replaced. Which statement below BEST describes this situation?

    A. The chief jailer is probably right. After all, he spent more time in the jail than the sheriff.
    B. The sheriff as the administrator has the responsibility for news releases.
    C. It is obvious that the sheriff has not given much thought to developing a procedure for giving news releases. If he had, responsibility for releasing information about the jail would be clearly assigned and there would not be an opportunity for conflicting statements.
    D. The chief jailer and the sheriff are probably both right about the causes of the escape.

KEY (CORRECT ANSWERS)

1. C
2. D
3. C
4. A
5. E
6. D
7. D
8. C

EXAMINATION SECTION
TEST 1

DIRECTIONS: Each question or incomplete statement is followed by several suggested answers or completions. Select the one that BEST answers the question or completes the statement. *PRINT THE LETTER OF THE CORRECT ANSWER IN THE SPACE AT THE RIGHT.*

Questions 1-3.

DIRECTIONS: Questions 1 to 3 measure your ability to fill out forms correctly and to remember information and ideas. Below and on the following two pages are directions for completing two kinds of forms, a correctly completed sample of each form, and a section from a procedures manual. You should memorize the sets of directions and the section from the procedures manual.

In the test, you will be (1) asked questions about the information and ideas in the manual and (2) presented with completed forms and asked to identify entries that are INCORRECT (contain wrong information, incomplete information, information in wrong order, etc.).

DIRECTIONS FOR COMPLETING CASE REPORT FORM

A case report form (see completed sample) is to be filled out by each officer at the time of the preliminary investigation. The entry for each numbered box is as follows:

Box 1 - The time the assignment was received.

Box 2 - The day, date, and time of the occurrence, in that order. Names of months and days may be abbreviated.

Box 3 - The manner in which the report was received. Use P = person, TOC = Through Official Channels (911 or other emergency numbers), M = mail, or T = telephone.

Box 4 - Name of the person notifying the department.

Box 5 - The address of the occurrence. include number, street, and village, and name of establishment, if appropriate. Do NOT abbreviate the name of a street, village, or establishment. If no street address is available, supply directions.

Box 6 - Victim's name, last name first.

Box 7 - Victim's birthdate - month, day, and year. Use the style shown in the completed sample.

Box 8 - Victim's sex and race: F = female, M = male, B = black, W = white, Y = yellow, O = other.

Box 9 - Relationship of victim to the offender (be as specific as possible):
HU = husband, WI = wife, MO = mother, FA = father,

SO = son, DA = daughter, BR = brother, SI = sister,
AQ = acquaintance, ST = stranger, UN = unknown.

SAMPLE OF COMPLETED CASE REPORT FORM

1. Time Received 5:57 PM		2. Date and Time of Occurrence Wed., Oct. 17, 2017, 1:00 PM	
3. Original Complaint Received TOC		4. Reported by Jeffrey Greene	
5. Place of Occurrence Sam's Stationery Shop, 130 Main St., Brooketown			
6. Victim's Name Silver, Sam	7. Date of Birth 3/17/72		8. Sex and Race M - W
7. Relationship to the Offender ST			

DIRECTIONS FOR COMPLETING
AUTOMOBILE FIELD INTERVIEW FORM

An automobile field interview form (see completed sample on the following page) is to be filled out when a car is stopped under suspicious circumstances, but no arrests are made. The entry for each numbered box is as follows:

Box 1 - Driver's name, last name first.

Box 2 - Village of residence, if within the county

Box 3 - Type of vehicle: S = sedan, C = convertible, SW = station wagon, V = van, T = truck.

Box 4 - Vehicle registration number.

Box 5 - Time and place of interview: location (street address only), time (per 24-hour clock), date, in that order.

Box 6 - Type of area: C = commercial, H = highway, R = residential, I = industrial, S = school

Box 7 - Patrol post number: precinct number is first digit; sector number is last two digits.

Box 8 - Officer's name and shield number, in that order.

SAMPLE OF COMPLETED AUTOMOBILE FIELD INTERVIEW FORM

1. Operator Robbins, Susan		2. Village Shady Brook	
3. Type of Vehicle C		4. Registration C 7237	
5. Time and Place of Interview Merry Road at Elm Street, 1428, 2/7/17			
6. Type of Area R	7. Post No. 221		8. Officer Sally Dodd, 2212

EXAMINATION SECTION
TEST 1

DIRECTIONS: Each question or incomplete statement is followed by several suggested answers or completions. Select the one that BEST answers the question or completes the statement. *PRINT THE LETTER OF THE CORRECT ANSWER IN THE SPACE AT THE RIGHT.*

Questions 1-3.

DIRECTIONS: Questions 1 to 3 measure your ability to fill out forms correctly and to remember information and ideas. Below and on the following two pages are directions for completing two kinds of forms, a correctly completed sample of each form, and a section from a procedures manual. You should memorize the sets of directions and the section from the procedures manual.

In the test, you will be (1) asked questions about the information and ideas in the manual and (2) presented with completed forms and asked to identify entries that are INCORRECT (contain wrong information, incomplete information, information in wrong order, etc.).

DIRECTIONS FOR COMPLETING CASE REPORT FORM

A case report form (see completed sample) is to be filled out by each officer at the time of the preliminary investigation. The entry for each numbered box is as follows:

Box 1 - The time the assignment was received.

Box 2 - The day, date, and time of the occurrence, in that order. Names of months and days may be abbreviated.

Box 3 - The manner in which the report was received. Use P = person, TOC = Through Official Channels (911 or other emergency numbers), M = mail, or T = telephone.

Box 4 - Name of the person notifying the department.

Box 5 - The address of the occurrence. include number, street, and village, and name of establishment, if appropriate. Do NOT abbreviate the name of a street, village, or establishment. If no street address is available, supply directions.

Box 6 - Victim's name, last name first.

Box 7 - Victim's birthdate - month, day, and year. Use the style shown in the completed sample.

Box 8 - Victim's sex and race: F = female, M = male, B = black, W = white, Y = yellow, O = other.

Box 9 - Relationship of victim to the offender (be as specific as possible):
HU = husband, WI = wife, MO = mother, FA = father,

SO = son, DA = daughter, BR = brother, SI = sister,
AQ = acquaintance, ST = stranger, UN = unknown.

SAMPLE OF COMPLETED CASE REPORT FORM

1. Time Received 5:57 PM		2. Date and Time of Occurrence Wed., Oct. 17, 2017, 1:00 PM	
3. Original Complaint Received TOC		4. Reported by Jeffrey Greene	
5. Place of Occurrence Sam's Stationery Shop, 130 Main St., Brooketown			
6. Victim's Name Silver, Sam	7. Date of Birth 3/17/72		8. Sex and Race M - W
7. Relationship to the Offender ST			

DIRECTIONS FOR COMPLETING
AUTOMOBILE FIELD INTERVIEW FORM

An automobile field interview form (see completed sample on the following page) is to be filled out when a car is stopped under suspicious circumstances, but no arrests are made. The entry for each numbered box is as follows:

Box 1 - Driver's name, last name first.

Box 2 - Village of residence, if within the county

Box 3 - Type of vehicle: S = sedan, C = convertible, SW = station wagon, V = van, T = truck.

Box 4 - Vehicle registration number.

Box 5 - Time and place of interview: location (street address only), time (per 24-hour clock), date, in that order.

Box 6 - Type of area: C = commercial, H = highway, R = residential, I = industrial, S = school

Box 7 - Patrol post number: precinct number is first digit; sector number is last two digits.

Box 8 - Officer's name and shield number, in that order.

SAMPLE OF COMPLETED AUTOMOBILE FIELD INTERVIEW FORM

1. Operator Robbins, Susan		2. Village Shady Brook	
3. Type of Vehicle C		4. Registration C 7237	
5. Time and Place of Interview Merry Road at Elm Street, 1428, 2/7/17			
6. Type of Area R	7. Post No. 221		8. Officer Sally Dodd, 2212

3 (#1)

CASE REPORT MANUAL
Section 1 - Solvability Factors

A solvability factor can be defined as any information about a crime that can provide a means to determine who committed it. In other words, a solvability factor is a useful clue to the identity of the perpetrator.

Based on national-level research, the following twelve universal factors have been identified:

1. Existence of witnesses to the crime
2. Knowledge of a perpetrator's name
3. Knowledge of a perpetrator's whereabouts
4. Description of a perpetrator
5. Identification of a perpetrator
6. Property that has traceable characteristics such as a registration number
7. Existence of a distinctive MO
8. Presence of significant physical evidence such as a set of burglar's tools
9. Description of a perpetrator's automobile
10. Positive results from a crime scene evidence search, such as fingerprints or footprints
11. Belief that a crime may be solved with publicity and/or reasonable investigative effort
12. Opportunity for only one person to have committed the crime

The presence of at least one of these solvability factors is necessary for there to be a reasonable chance for a solution to the crime. When there is no solvability factor, the chance of crime solution is limited. Therefore, the police officer who arrives at the scene of a crime first must make the greatest possible effort to identify solvability factors. This effort should include identification of witnesses and a thorough search of the crime scene.

DIRECTIONS: After you have memorized the directions and manual section, try to answer the following questions without referring to the study materials.

1. Which of the following crimes is *most likely* to have a solvability factor? 1.____

   A. A pickpocket takes several wallets on a crowded bus.
   B. Two muggers take money from a blind man in an alley.
   C. A hospital drug cabinet is broken into during a major emergency.
   D. A kidnapper escapes in a van decorated with pink, yellow, and avocado-green paint.

2. At 7:30 AM on Wednesday, February 6, 2017, Patrol Officer Alex White was assigned to investigate a suspected child-beating. The boy had been brought to the hospital, and Dr. Paul Cohen called the local station house at 7:20 AM. David Pepson, a White boy born on June 27, 2015, was brought from his home by his mother, who claims that her husband had punished David an hour earlier for making loud noises. David resides with his parents at 86 Whitewood Lane in Middletown. 2.____

	CASE REPORT FORM			
1.	Time Received 7:30 AM	2.	Date and Time of Occurrence Wed., February 6, 2017, 5:00 AM	
3.	Original Complaint Received T	4.	Reported by Dr. Paul Cohen	
5.	Place of Occurrence 86 Whitewood Lane, Middletown			
6.	Victim's Name David Pepson	7.	Date of Birth 6/27/15	8. Sex and Race M - W
9.	Relationship to the Offender FA			

Of the following, the box in the form above which is filled out INCORRECTLY is Box
    A. 3   B. 4   C. 8   D. 9

3. Officer Steven Brown, 7234, stopped a station wagon in the business section of Westville. He talked to the driver, John Caseman, on Rocky Road near South Bend and the western boundary of section 16 of precinct 2 at 8:20 PM on 3/8/17. The vehicle, registration number 2729H belongs to Mr. Caseman, who resides in Silverton.

AUTOMOBILE FIELD INTERVIEW FORM

1.	Operator Caseman, John	2.	Village Westville
3.	Type of Vehicle V	4.	Registration 2729H
5.	Time and Place of Interview Rocky Road near South Bend, 2020, 3/8/17		
6.	Type of Area C	7. Post No. 216	8. Officer Steven Brown, 7234

Of the following, the box in the form above which is filled out INCORRECTLY is Box
    A. 1   B. 3   C. 5   D. 7

Questions 4-6.

DIRECTIONS: Questions 4 to 6 measure your ability to recall information in a set of bulletins. To do well in the test, you must memorize both the pictorial and the written portions of each of the following eight bulletins.

Date of Issuance 5/13/17

INFORMATION WANTED

by

Police Department. County of Allamin
Hooblertown, Indiana 43102

The Allamin County Police Department homicide squad requests all auto repair shops, dealers and General Motors parts dealers in the precinct be contacted and questioned relative to the below described vehicle which is wanted for a felony - leaving the scene of a fatality. If vehicle is located, contact the homicide squad, (731) 624-1372. Refer to Homicide Case 130.

Place of Occurrence:	Midway State Road, South Strata, Indiana
Time of Occurrence:	0240 hours on March 3, 2017
Vehicle Wanted:	1980 Oldsmobile Cutlass Supreme, color green
Damage:	The Vehicle will have damage to the plastic grill located in the vicinity of the right front headlights. The chrome strip which is affixed to the center of the hood was recovered at the scene.
Parts:	The following parts will be needed to repair the vehicle: 1. Hood - GM Part No. 557547 or 557557 2. Plastic Grill - GM Part No. 22503156

6 (#1)

WANTED
by

Police Department. County of Paradise
Cobbs Cove, Louisiana 41723
for
MURDER

BULLETIN NO. 9-17

No. FJ110M

Note
Seiko watch with Gold Face and three section band is not a standard import into this area.

Occurrence:	Blue Jay Way and Nickel Drive, Yellowbird, 0530 hours on April 12, 2017.
Modus Operandi:	The deceased returned to his home at 2 Blue Jay Way, Yellowbird, at about 0530 hours, April 12, 2017. Four male whites were waiting in the vicinity of his garage and robbed him of U.S. currency and the above watch. They ran to the intersection of Blue Jay Way and Nickel Drive and got into a late model, shiny dark color, four door sedan with large tail-lights. The deceased chased them to the corner. One shot was fired causing his death.
Subjects:	Four Male Whites, dark hair.
Property:	One Seiko Quartz - Sports 100 - wrist watch, yellow metal face and crystal retainer. The band is an expandable three-section, white, yellow, white metal.
Note:	Anyone with information is requested to contact the Paradise County Homicide Squad.

W A N T E D
by
Police Department. County of Whitewall
Short Hills, Kentucky 27135

for
MURDER

BULLETIN NO. 15-17

RC-550JW/C

Occurrence:	Public street, Brown Avenue, 60 ft. north of Camino Street, South Hill, KY, at 2340 hours, 6/25/17.
Modus Operandi:	The victim of the murder was walking south on Brown Avenue when he was accosted by the suspect and shot in the head by the suspect.
Subject:	Male, Black, 25-28 years, 5'9"-6' tall, thin build, short dark hair, medium dark skin, wearing a dark waist-length jacket, sneakers - armed with a gun.
Property:	The above property, a JVC AM-FM cassette radio, Model RC 550JW/C made of black plastic with chrome trim was stolen during the commission of a murder on Brown Avenue in South Hill. The battery compartment door is missing from the radio.
Note:	Anyone with information concerning the murder or the radio is asked to call the Whitewall Homicide Squad.

8 (#1)

<u>W A N T E D</u>
by
<u>Police Department, County of Larinda</u>
<u>Blue Ridge, CA 97235</u>

BULLETIN NO. 6-17

for
<u>BURGLARY</u>

#1

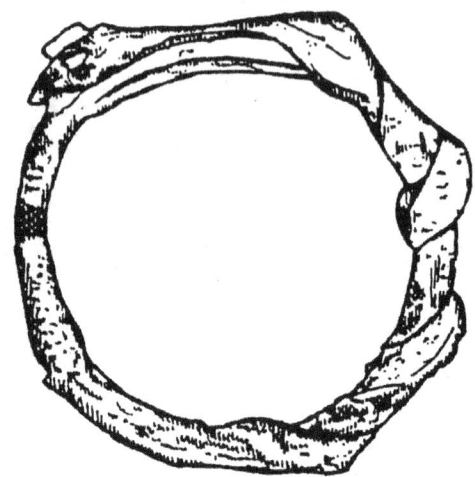
#2

Date of Occurrence:	August 17, 2017 - 1930 to 2230 hours.
Place of Occurrence:	Private home, 37 Cliffmount Dr., Palasino, CA
Property:	Two distinctive, original designer rings taken.
	1. Ladies, yellow gold, 18K ring, size 8, an alligator with green emerald eye.
	2. Mans, yellow gold ring, a snake with 1/4 carat white diamond head and white diamond chips for eyes.
Value:	1. $5,000 2. $7,500
Note:	Any information - contact Burglary Squad, Refer to DD 4-25.

WANTED
by

BULLETIN NO. 12-17

Police Department, County of Canton
Midship, Texas 84290

for
BURGLARY

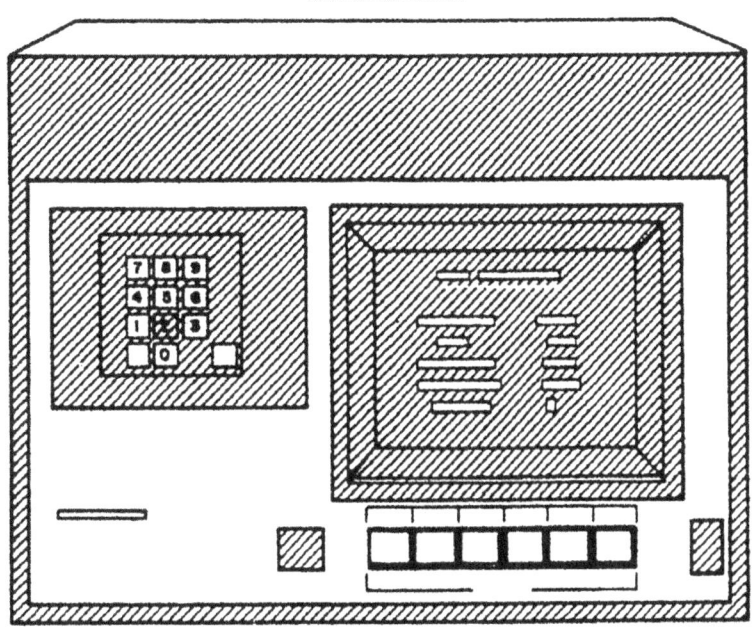

Date of Occurrence: July 31, 2017 - 1640 hours to August 1 - 0720 hours.
Place of Occurrence: 606 Hillmont Drive, Alston, TX Freemont Testing Systems
Property: Three engine analysers, color red, measuring 14" x 20" x 19"
Serial Numbers: 1. AN-0059 2. BP-0079 3. CR-0099
Value: $6,666.00 each.
Note: Request officers on patrol check service stations on post for the above items. Any information contact Detective Bryant, Third Squad, and refer to DD 3-52.

10 (#1)

WANTED
by

BULLETIN NO. 5-17

Police Department, County of Marina
Waterford, CT 03612

for
ROBBERY

2014 PHOTO

Occurrences:	Robberies of gas stations and boutiques in North End precincts of Marina County.
Modus Operandi:	Subject enters store and uses telephone or shops. He then produces sawed-off shotgun or revolver from under his coat and announces robbery.
Subject:	Harry Hamilton, Male, White, DOB 6/22/73, 5'10", 180 lbs., medium complexion, severely pockmarked face.
Further Details:	Contact Robbery Squad at (203) 832-7663. Refer to Robbery Case 782. Robbery Squad has warrant for subject. IF THIS PERSON ENTERS YOUR STORE DIAL 911 OR THE ABOVE NUMBER

WANTED by

BULLETIN NO. 30-17

Police Department, County of Panfield
Lanser, South Carolina 30012

for
ROBBERY

#1

2014 PHOTO
#2

Occurrence:	3 North Avenue, Anita, South Carolina, on 11/26/17 at 2310 hours.
Modus Operandi:	The above subjects forced their way into the private residence of a rug dealer, accosted the dealer, his wife, and brother, demanding jewelry, currency, escaped on foot after binding victims.
Subjects:	No. 1 - Male, White, 40-45 years, 200 lbs., heavy build, bald shaved head, fair complexion, mustache, goatee, large hooked nose, black leather jacket, armed with a knife. No. 2 - Male, White, 6'1" tall, medium build, brown hair, subject identified as Mark Nine, DOB 4/16/78, last known address 1275 East 61st Street, Brooklyn, NY in 2011, hard drug user, armed with a hand gun, subject has been indicted for residence robbery. See Wanted Bulletin 21-12.
Possible 3rd Suspect:	Male, Hispanic, 30-35 years, 5'6", thin build, collar-length black wavy hair, eyes close together, with a large Doberman. Subject observed in the area before robbery talking to bald, stocky male. Also seen entering a vehicle containing 3 or 4 males after the robbery.
Loss:	U.S. currency and jewelry valued at $3,000 to $4,000.

Further Details: Contact Robbery Squad.

12 (#1)

WANTED
by
Police Department, County of Fantail
Sweet Waters, Vermont 04610

BULLETIN NO.
1-17

for
HI-JACKING

Occurrence: Vicinity of Nikon Plaza, off Jewel Avenue & Brook Bubble Road, Sweet Waters, VT at 1820 hours, 2/6/17.

Modus Operandi: Subjects accosted the driver of a United Parcel tractor/trailer, forcing him into a pale yellow van-type vehicle, make and year unknown. Vehicle contained a black and yellow leopard rug. Driver released after two (2) hours, in the vicinity of West Lake, VT. Tractor/trailer recovered in White River, New Hampshire.

Subjects: Four (4) male Whites, one possibly named Joe, armed with hand guns. No further description.

Loss: Photo of above item: one (1) of four (4) broadcasting TV zoom lenses made by Nikon, valued at $7,000. Also included in the Nikon loss were current models of cameras, lenses, calculators, valued at $196,000. Medical supplies, mfg. by True Tell Inc., value $49,000. High quality medical examination scopes, industrial fiberscopes, cassette recorders and cameras, all mgf. by Canon Inc. valued at over $250,000. Sweaters, young mens, vee-neck design, mfg. Milford, Inc., labeled Dimension, Robt. Klein, J.C. Penney. Valued at over $20,450. Above items bearing serial numbers have been entered in NCIC.

Further Details: Contact Robbery Squad.

DIRECTIONS: After you have memorized both the pictorial and written portions of the bulletins, try to answer the following questions WITHOUT referring to the study materials.

4. Which of the following statements about the contents of the *Information Wanted* bulletin is or are true?

    I. The subject vehicle is involved in a felony.
    II. The subject vehicle is green-colored.

    The CORRECT answer is:

    A. I *only*
    B. II *only*
    C. Both I and II
    D. Neither I nor II

5.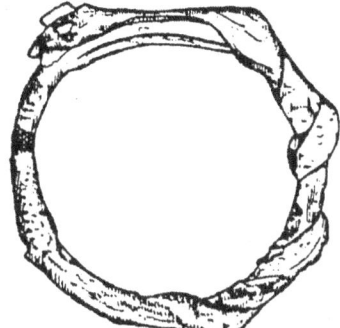

    Which of the following statements about the object above is or are true?

    I. It was taken in the robbery of a residence.
    II. Its value is between $1,000 and $2,000.

    The CORRECT answer is:

    A. I *only*
    B. II *only*
    C. Both I and II
    D. Neither I nor II

6. Which of the following, if any, fits the description of the individual who is wanted for the robbery of several gas stations?

    A.
    B.

C.   D.   None of these

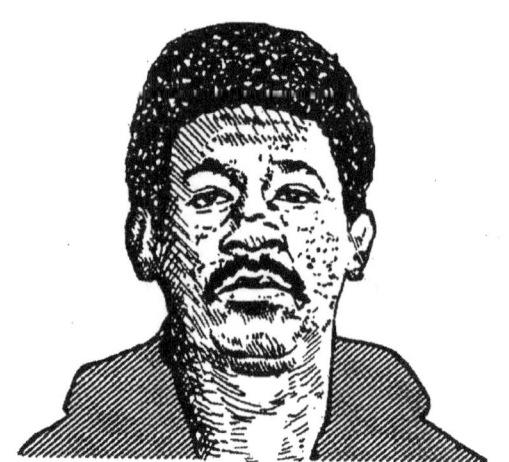

Questions 7-10.

DIRECTIONS: Questions 7 to 10 measure your ability to memorize and recall addresses, identification numbers and codes, and similar data.
In the test, you will be asked questions about the following body of information. You will NOT have the information in front of you when you take the test.

RADIO SIGNALS
01 - Back in Service
02 - Acknowledgement(OK)
06 - On Coffee
08 - Off Meal, Coffee, Personal
27 - Valid License
33 - Clear Channel (Any Emergency Request)
41 - One-Car Assistance Request
63 - Responding to Command
78 - Police Officer in Danger
99 - Possible Emergency Situation, Respond Quietly

TRUCK-TRACTOR IDENTIFICATION NUMBERS
VIN* Plate

Make	Location
Autocar	8
Brockway	2
Diamond Reo	9
Ford	10
GMC	4
Kenworth	1
Peterbuilt	7
White	5

*Vehicle Identification Number

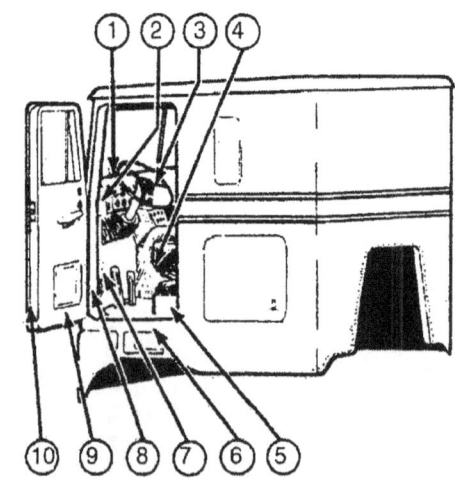

Location of County Precinct Houses

First -   In H,* on S side of Merrick Rd., just E of Grand Avenue.
Second -   In OB,* 1/8 mi. E of Seaford-Oyster Bay Expressway, 1/8 mi. S. of Jericho Trnpk.
Third -   In NH,* 1/8 mi. N of Hillside Ave., 1/8 mi. W of Willis Avenue
Fourth -   In H, on E side of Broadway, just N of Rockaway Avenue
Fifth -   In H, on S side of Dutch Broadway, 1/4 mi. N of Exit 14 of Southern State Parkway
Six -   In NH, just E of Community Drive, and just S of Whitney Pond Park. Seventh - In H, on side of Merrick Rd., just W of Seaford-Oyster Bay Expressway
Eighth -   In H, on E side of Wantagh Ave., just N of Hempstead Farmingdale Trnpk.

Location of Universities, Colleges, and Institutes
Adelphi U. -   In H,* 1/4 mi. E of Nassau Blvd., 1/4 mi. S of Stewart Ave.
Hofstra U. -   In H, at Oak and Fulton Streets.
Molloy College -   In H, on Hempstead Ave., just S of Southern State Pkway., and midway between Exits 19 and 20.
C. W. Post College - In OB,* on Northern Blvd., 1 1/2 mi. W of Massapequa-Glen Cove Rd.
Nassau Community College - In H, on Stewart Ave., 1/2 mi. E of Clinton Rd.
Long Island Agri. & Tech. Institute - In OB, 1/2 mi. E of Round Swamp Rd., between Bethpage State Park and Old Bethpage Village Restoration.
N.Y. Inst. of Technology - In OB, on Northern Blvd., just E of line dividing OB and NH.
U.S. Merchant Marine Acad. - In NH,* at NW end of Elm Point Rd.

---
*H - Town of Hempstead; NH - Town of North Hempstead; OB - Town of Oyster Bay.

DIRECTIONS: After you have memorized the listed data, try to answer the following questions WITHOUT referring to the list.

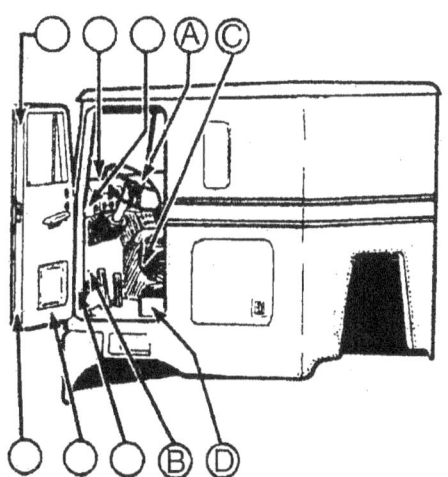

7. On a GMC truck-tractor, above, the VIN is located at   7._____

    A. A   B. B   C. C   D. D

8. The radio signal for *back in service* is   8._____

    A. 01   B. 04   C. 08   D. none of these

9. The Third Precinct House is located in 9.____
    A. NH, 1/8 mi. N of Hillside Ave., 1/8 mi. W of Willis Ave.
    B. NH, 1/4 mi. S of I.U. Willets Rd., 1/4 mi. E of Herricks Rd.
    C. Williston Park, on Willis Ave., 1/4 mi. S of Northern State Parkway
    D. Mineola, on Mineola Blvd., 1/2 mi. N of Jericho Trnpk.

10. The U.S. Merchant Marine Academy is at the NW end of _____ Rd. 10.____
    A. Sands Point   B. Mill Neck
    C. Kings Point   D. Elm Point

KEY (CORRECT ANSWERS)

1. D
2. D
3. B
4. C
5. A

6. D
7. C
8. A
9. A
10. D

EVALUATING INFORMATION AND EVIDENCE
EXAMINATION SECTION
TEST 1

DIRECTIONS: Each question or incomplete statement is followed by several suggested answers or completions. Select the one that BEST answers the question or completes the statement. *PRINT THE LETTER OF THE CORRECT ANSWER IN THE SPACE AT THE RIGHT.*

Questions 1-9.

DIRECTIONS: Questions 1 through 9 measure your ability to (1) determine whether statements from witnesses say essentially the same thing and (2) determine the evidence needed to make it reasonably certain that a particular conclusion is true.

1. Which of the following pairs of statements say essentially the same thing in two different ways?
   I. Some employees at the water department have fully vested pensions.
      At least one employee at the water department has a pension that is not fully vested.
   II. All swans are white birds.
      A bird that is not white is not a swan.
   The CORRECT answer is:
   A. I only	B. I and II	C. II only	D. Neither I nor II

1.____

2. Which of the following pairs of statements say essentially the same thing in two different ways?
   I. If you live in Humboldt County, your property taxes are high.
      If your property taxes are high, you live in Humboldt County.
   II. All the Hutchinsons live in Lindsborg.
      At least some Hutchinsons do not live in Lindsborg.
   The CORRECT answer is;
   A. I only	B. I and II	C. II only	D. Neither I nor II

2.____

3. Which of the following pairs of statements say essentially the same thing in two different ways?
   I. Although Spike is a friendly dog, he is also one of the most unpopular dogs on the block.
      Although Spike is one of the most unpopular dogs on the block, he is a friendly dog.
   II. Everyone in Precinct 19 is taller than Officer Banks.
      Nobody in Precinct 19 is shorter than Officer Banks.
   The CORRECT answer is:
   A. I only	B. I and II	C. II only	D. Neither I nor II

3.____

2 (#1)

4. Which of the following pairs of statements say essentially the same thing in two different ways?
   I. On Friday, every officer in Precinct 1 is assigned parking duty or crowd control, or both.
      If a Precinct 1 officer has been assigned neither parking duty nor crowd control, it is not Friday.
   II. Because the farmer mowed the hay fields today, his house will have mice tomorrow.
      Whenever the farmer mows his hay fields, his house has mice the next day.
   The CORRECT answer is:
   A. I only   B. I and II   C. II only   D. Neither I nor II

   4.____

5. Summary of Evidence Collected to Date:
   I. Fishing in the Little Pony River is against the law.
      Captain Rick caught an 8-inch trout and ate it for dinner.
   Prematurely Drawn Conclusion: Captain Rick broke the law.
   Which of the following pieces of evidence, if any, would make it reasonably certain that the conclusion drawn is true?
   A. Captain Rick caught his trout in the Little Pony River.
   B. There is no size limit on trout mentioned in the law.
   C. A trout is a species of fish.
   D. None of the above

   5.____

6. Summary of Evidence Collected to Date:
   I. Some of the doctors in the ICU have been sued for malpractice.
   II. Some of the doctors in the ICU are pediatricians.
   Prematurely Drawn Conclusion: Some of the pediatricians in the ICU have never been sued for malpractice.
   Which of the following pieces of evidence, if any, would make it reasonably certain that the conclusion drawn is true?
   A. The number of pediatricians in the ICU is the same as the number of doctors who have been sued for malpractice.
   B. The number of pediatricians in the ICU is smaller than the number of doctors who have been sued for malpractice.
   C. The number of ICU doctors who have been sued for malpractice is smaller than the number who are pediatricians.
   D. None of the above

   6.____

7. Summary of Evidence Collected to Date:
   I. Along Paseo Boulevard, there are five convenience stores.
   II. EZ-GO is east of Pop-a-Shop.
   III. Kwik-E-Mart is west of Bob's Market.
   IV. The Nightwatch is between EZ-GO and Kwik-E-Mart.
   Prematurely Drawn Conclusion: Pop-a-Shop is the westernmost convenience store on Paseo Boulevard.

   7.____

Which of the following pieces of evidence, if any, would make it reasonably certain that the conclusion drawn is true?
   A. Bob's Market is the easternmost convenience store on Paseo.
   B. Kwik-E-Mart is the second store from the west.
   C. The Nightwatch is west of the EZ-GO.
   D. None of the above

8. <u>Summary of Evidence Collected to Date:</u> 8._____
   Stark drove home from work at 70 miles an hour and wasn't breaking the law.
   <u>Prematurely Drawn Conclusion</u>: Stark was either on an interstate highway or in the state of Montana.
   Which of the following pieces of evidence, if any, would make it reasonably certain that the conclusion drawn is true?
   A. There are no interstate highways in Montana.
   B. Montana is the only state that allows a speed of 70 miles an hour on roads other than interstate highways.
   C. Most states don't allow speed of 70 miles an hour on state highways.
   D. None of the above

9. <u>Summary of Evidence Collected to Date:</u> 9._____
   I. Margaret, owner of MetroWoman magazine, signed a contract with each of her salespeople promising an automatic $200 bonus to any employee who sells more than 60 subscriptions in a calendar month.
   II. Lynn sold 82 subscriptions to MetroWoman in the month of December.
   <u>Prematurely Drawn Conclusion</u>: Lynn received a $20 bonus.
   Which of the following pieces of evidence, if any, would make it reasonably certain that the conclusion is true?
   A. Lynn is a salesperson.
   B. Lynn works for Margaret.
   C. Margaret offered only $200 regardless of the number of subscriptions sold.
   D. None of the above

Questions 10-14.

DIRECTIONS: Questions 10 through 14 refer to Map #3 and measure your ability to orient yourself within a given section of town, neighborhood or particular area. Each of the questions describes a starting point and a destination. Assume that you are driving a car in the area shown on the map accompanying the questions. Use the map as a basis for the shortest way to get from one point to another without breaking the law.
On the map, a street marked by arrows, or by arrows and the words "One Way," indicates one-way travel and should be assumed to be one-way for the entire length, even when there are breaks or jogs in the street. EXCEPTION: A street that does not have the same name over the full length.

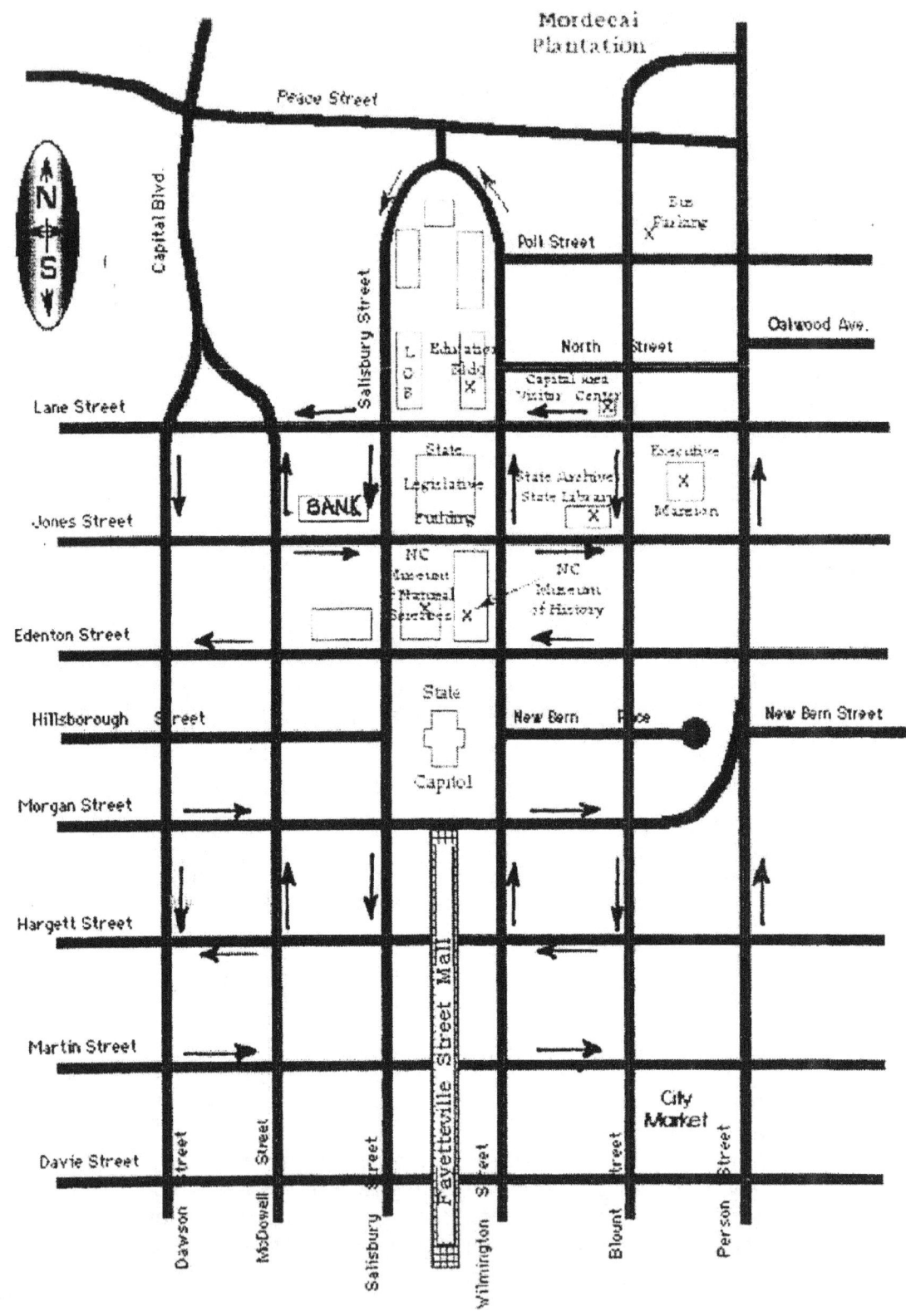

5 (#1)

10. The SHORTEST legal way from the south end of the Fayetteville Street Mall, at Davie Street, to the city of Raleigh Municipal Building is
    A. west on Davie, north on McDowell
    B. west on Davie, north on Dawson
    C. east on Davie, north on Wilmington, west on Morgan
    D. east on Davie, north on Wilmington, west on Hargett

10.____

11. The SHORTEST legal way from the City Market to the Education Building is
    A. north on Blount, west on North
    B. north on Person, west on Lane
    C. north on Blount, west on Lane
    D. west on Martin, north on Wilmington

11.____

12. The SHORTEST legal way from the Education Building to the State Capitol is
    A. south on Wilmington
    B. north on Wilmington, west on Peace, south on Capitol, bear west to go south on Dawson, and east on Morgan
    C. west on Lane, south on Salisbury
    D. each on North, south on Blount, west on Edenton

12.____

13. The SHORTEST legal way from the State Capitol to Peace College is
    A. north on Wilmington, jog north, east on Peace
    B. east on Morgan, north on Person, west on Peace
    C. west on Edenton, north on McDowell, north on Capitol Blvd., east on Peace
    D. east on Morgan, north on Blount, west on Peace

13.____

14. The SHORTEST legal way from the State Legislative Building to the City Market is
    A. south on Wilmington, east on Martin
    B. east on Jones, south on Blount
    C. south on Salisbury, east on Davie
    D. east on Lane, south on Blount

14.____

Questions 15-19.

DIRECTIONS: Questions 15 through 19 refer to Figure #3, on the following page, and measure your ability to understand written descriptions of events. Each question presents a description of an accident or event and asks you which of the following five drawings in Figure #3 BEST represents it.
In the drawings, the following symbols are used:
Moving vehicle ⌂   Non-moving vehicle ▲
Pedestrian or bicyclist •
The path and direction of travel of a vehicle or pedestrian is indicated by a solid line.
The path and direction of travel of each vehicle or pedestrian directly involved in a collision from the point of impact is indicated by a dotted line.

6 (#1)

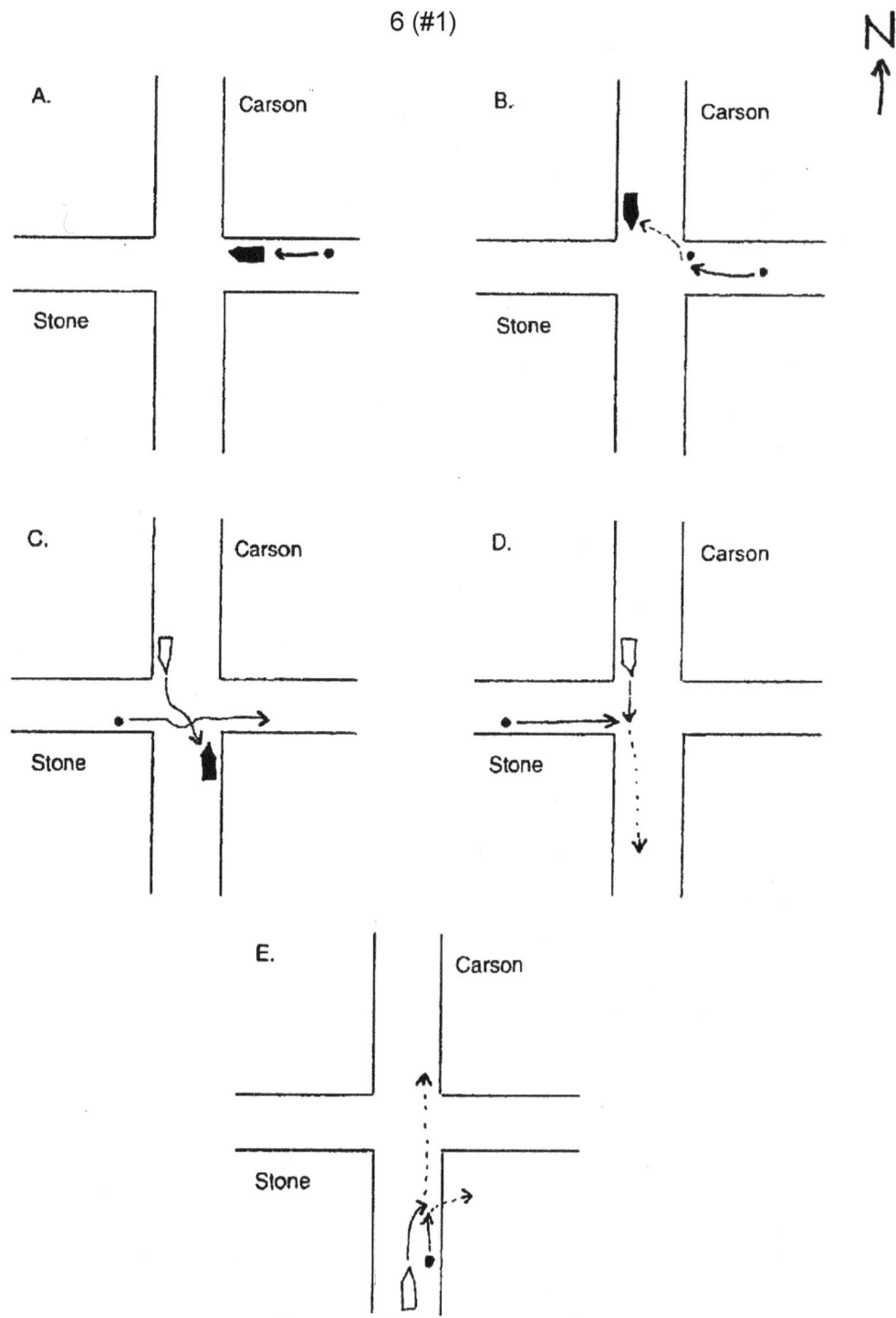

In the space at the right, print the letter of the drawing that BEST fit the descriptions written below.

15. A driver headed north on Carson veers to the right and strikes a bicyclist who is also headed north. The bicyclist is thrown from the road. The driver flees north on Carson.

15._____

16. A driver heading south on Carson runs the stop sign and barely misses colliding with an eastbound cyclist. The cyclist swerves to avoid the collision and continues traveling east. The driver swerves to avoid the collision and strikes a car parked in the northbound lane on Carson.

16._____

17. A bicyclist heading west on Stone collides with a pedestrian in the crosswalk, then veers through the intersection and collides with the front of a car parked in the southbound lane on Carson.

17._____

18. A driver traveling south on Carson runs over a bicyclist who has run the stop sign, and then flees south on Carson.

18._____

19. A bicyclist heading west on Stone collides with the rear of a car parked in the westbound lane.

19._____

Questions 20-22.

DIRECTIONS: In Questions 20 through 22, choose the word or phrase CLOSEST in meaning to the word or phrase printed in capital letters.

20. INSOLVENT
    A. bankrupt   B. vagrant   C. hazardous   D. illegal

20._____

21. TENANT
    A. laborer   B. occupant   C. owner   D. creditor

21._____

22. INFRACTION
    A. portion   B. violation   C. remark   D. detour

22._____

Questions 23-25.

DIRECTIONS: Questions 23 through 25 measure your ability to do fieldwork-related arithmetic. Each question presents a separate arithmetic problem for you to solve.

23. Officer Jones has served on the police force longer than Smith. Smith has served longer than Moore. Moore has served less time than Jones, and Park has served longer than Jones.
Which officer has served the LONGEST on the police force?
    A. Jones   B. Smith   C. Moore   D. Park

23._____

24. A car wash has raised the price of an outside-only wash from $4 to $5. The car wash applies the same percentage increase to its inside-and-out wash, which was $10.
What is the new cost of the inside-and-out wash?
    A. $8   B. $11   C. $12.50   D. $15

24._____

25. Ron and James, college students, make $10 an hour working at the restaurant. Ron works 13 hours a week and James works 20 hours a week.
To make the same amount that Ron earns in a year, James would work about _____ weeks.

   A. 18   B. 27   C. 34   D. 45

25.____

KEY (CORRECT ANSWERS)

1. C
2. D
3. B
4. B
5. A

6. D
7. B
8. B
9. B
10. A

11. B
12. C
13. A
14. B
15. E

16. C
17. B
18. D
19. A
20. A

21. B
22. B
23. D
24. C
25. C

SOLUTIONS TO QUESTIONS 1-9

P implies Q = original statement

Not Q implies not P = contrapositive of the original statement. A statement and its contrapositive are logically equivalent.

Q implies P = converse of the original statement

Not P implies not Q = inverse of the original statement. The converse and inverse of an original statement are logically equivalent.

P implies Q = Not P or Q.

1. The CORRECT answer is C.
   Item I is wrong because "some employees" means "at least one employee" and possibly "all employees." If it is true that all employees have fully vested pensions, then the second statement is false. Item II is correct because the second statement is the contrapositive of the first statement.

2. The CORRECT answer is D.
   Item I is wrong because the converse of a statement does not necessarily follow from the original statement. Item II is wrong because statement I implies that there are no Hutchinson family members who live outside Lindsborg.

3. The CORRECT answer is B. Item I is correct because it is composed of the same two compound statements that are simply mentioned in a different order. Item II is correct because if each person is taller than Officer Banks, then there is no person in that precinct who can possibly be shorter than Officer Banks.

4. The CORRECT answer is B.
   Item I is correct because the second statement is the contrapositive of the first statement. Item II is correct because each statement indicates that mowing the hay fields on a particular day leads to the presence of mice the next day.

5. The CORRECT answer is A.
   If Captain Rick caught his trout in the Little Pony River, then we can conclude that he was fishing there. Since statement I says that fishing in the Little Pony Rive is against the law, we conclude that Captain Rick broke the law.

6. The CORRECT answer is D.
   The number of doctors in each group, whether the same or not, has no bearing on the conclusion. There is nothing in evidence to suggest that the group of doctors sued for malpractice overlaps with the group of doctors that are pediatricians.

7. The CORRECT answer is B.
   If we are given that Kwik-E-Mart is the second store from the west, then the order of stores from west to east, is Pop-a-Shop, Kwik-E-Mart, Nightwatch, EZ-GO, and Bob's Market.

8. The CORRECT answer is B.
We are given that Stark drove at 70 miles per hour and didn't break the law. If we also know that Montana is the only state that allows a speed of 70 miles per hour, then we can conclude that Stark must have been driving in Montana or else was driving on some interstate.

9. The CORRECT answer is B.
The only additional piece of information needed is that Lynn works for Margaret. This will guarantee that Lynn receives the promised $200 bonus.

TEST 2

DIRECTIONS: Each question or incomplete statement is followed by several suggested answers or completions. Select the one that BEST answers the question or completes the statement. *PRINT THE LETTER OF THE CORRECT ANSWER IN THE SPACE AT THE RIGHT.*

Questions 1-9.

DIRECTIONS: Questions 1 through 9 measure your ability to (1) determine whether statements from witnesses say essentially the same thing and (2) determine the evidence needed to make it reasonably certain that a particular conclusion is true.
To do well on this part of the test, you do NOT have to have a working knowledge of police procedures and techniques. Nor do you have to have any more familiarity with criminals and criminal behavior than that acquired from reading newspapers, listening to radio or watching TV. To do well in this part, you must read and reason carefully.

1. Which of the following pairs of statements say essentially the same thing in two different ways?
   I. All of the teachers at Slater Middle School are intelligent, but some are irrational thinkers.
      Although some teachers at Slater Middle School are irrational thinkers, all of them are intelligent.
   II. Nobody has no friends.
       Everybody has at least one friend.
   The CORRECT answer is:
   A. I only   B. I and II   C. II only   D. Neither I nor II

2. Which of the following pairs of statements say essentially the same thing in two different ways?
   I. Although bananas taste good to most people, they are also a healthy food.
      Bananas are a healthy food, but most people eat them because they taste good.
   II. If Dr. Jones is in, we should call at the office.
       Either Dr. Jones is in, or we should not call at the office.
   The CORRECT answer is:
   A. I only   B. I and II   C. II only   D. Neither I nor II

3. Which of the following pairs of statements say essentially the same thing in two different ways?
   I. Some millworker work two shifts.
      If someone works only one shift, he is probably not a millworker.
   II. If a letter carrier clocks in at nine, he can finish his route by the end of the day.
       If a letter carrier does not clock in at nine, he cannot finish his route by the end of the day.
   The CORRECT answer is:
   A. I only   B. I and II   C. II only   D. Neither I nor II

91

2 (#2)

4. Which of the following pairs of statements say essentially the same thing in two different ways?
   I. If a member of the swim team attends every practice, he will compete in the next meet.
      Either a swim team member will compete in the next meet, or he did not attend every practice.
   II. All the engineers in the drafting department who wear glasses know how to use AutoCAD.
      If an engineer wears glasses, he will know how to use AutoCAD.
   The CORRECT answer is:
   A. I only   B. I and II   C. II only   D. Neither I nor II

5. Summary of Evidence Collected to Date:
   All of the parents who attend the weekly parenting seminars are high school graduates.
   Prematurely Drawn Conclusion: Some parents who attend the weekly parenting seminars have been convicted of child abuse.
   Which of the following pieces of evidence, if any, would make it reasonably certain that the conclusion drawn is true?
   A. Those convicted of child abuse are often high school graduates.
   B. Some high school graduates have been convicted of child abuse.
   C. There is no correlation between education level and the incidence of child abuse.
   D. None of the above

6. Summary of Evidence Collected to Date:
   I. Mr. Cantwell promised to vote for new school buses if he was reelected to the board.
   II. If the new school buses are approved by the school board, then Mr. Cantwell was not reelected to the board.
   Prematurely Drawn Conclusion: Approval of the new school buses was defeated in spite of Mr. Cantwell's vote.
   Which of the following pieces of evidence, if any, would make it reasonably certain that the conclusion drawn is true?
   A. Mr. Cantwell decided not to run for reelection.
   B. Mr. Cantwell was reelected to the board.
   C. Mr. Cantwell changed his mind and voted against the new buses.
   D. None of the above

7. Summary of Evidence Collected to Date:
   I. The station employs three detectives: Francis, Jackson, and Stern. One of the detectives is a lieutenant, one is a sergeant, and one is a major.
   II. Francis is not a lieutenant.
   Prematurely Drawn Conclusion: Jackson is a lieutenant.
   Which of the following pieces of evidence, if any, would make it reasonably certain that the conclusion drawn is true?
   A. Stern is not a sergeant.   B. Stern is a major.
   C. Francis is a major.   E. None of the above

8. Summary of Evidence Collected to Date:
   I. In the office building, every survival kit that contains a gas mask also contains anthrax vaccine.
   II. Some of the kits containing water purification tablets also contain anthrax vaccine.

   Prematurely Drawn Conclusion: If the survival kit near the typists' pool contains a gas mask, it does not contain water purification tablets.
   Which of the following pieces of evidence, if any, would make it reasonably certain that the conclusion drawn is true?

   A. Some survival kits contain all three items.
   B. The survival kit near the typists' pool contains anthrax vaccine.
   C. The survival kit near the typists' pool contains only two of these items.
   D. None of the above

8._____

9. Summary of Evidence Collected to Date:
   The shrink-wrap mechanism is designed to shut itself off if the heating coil temperature drops below 400 during the twin cycle.
   Prematurely Drawn Conclusion: If the machine was operating the twin cycle on Monday, it was not operating properly.
   Which of the following pieces of evidence, if any, would make it reasonably certain that the conclusion drawn is true?

   A. On Monday, the heating coil temperature reached 450.
   B. When the machine performs functions other than the twin cycle, the heating coil temperature sometimes drops below 400.
   C. The shrink-wrap mechanism did not shut itself off on Monday.
   D. None of the above

9._____

Questions 10-14.

DIRECTIONS: Questions 10 through 14 refer to Map #3 and measure your ability to orient yourself within a given section of town, neighborhood or particular area. Each of the questions describes a starting point and a destination. Assume that you are driving a car in the area shown on the map accompanying the questions. Use the map as a basis for the shortest way to get from one point to another without breaking the law.

On the map, a street marked by arrows, or by arrows and the words "One Way," indicates one-way travel and should be assumed to be one-way for the entire length, even when there are breaks or jogs in the street. EXCEPTION: A street that does not have the same name over the full length.

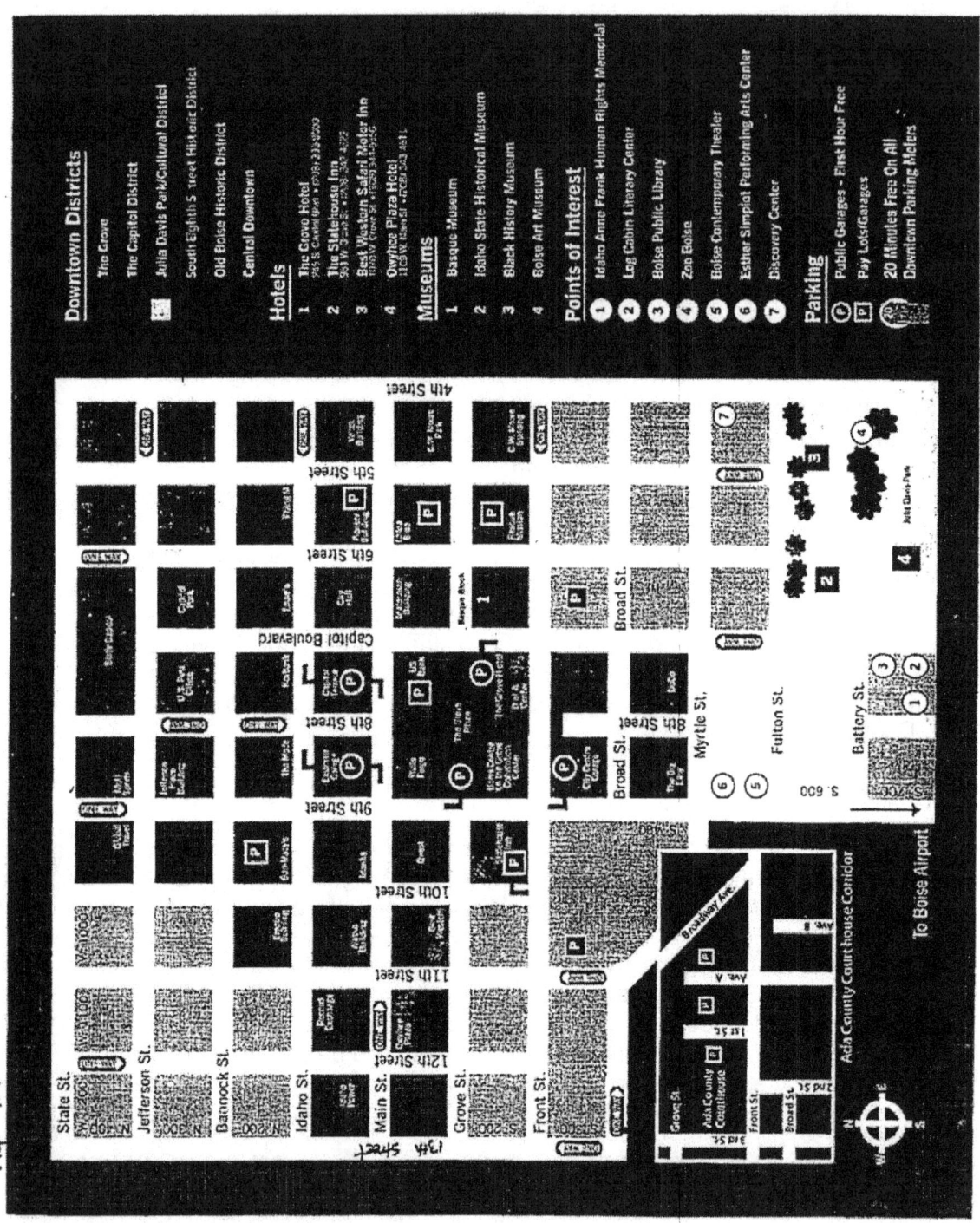

10. The SHORTEST legal way from the State Capitol to Idaho Power is 10._____
    A. south on Capitol Blvd., west on Main, north on 12th
    B. south on 8th, west on Main
    C. west on Jefferson, south on 12th
    D. south on Capitol Blvd., west on Front, north on 12th

5 (#2)

11. The SHORTEST legal way from the Jefferson Place Building to the Statesman Building is
    A. east on Jefferson, south on Capitol Blvd.
    B. south on 8th, east on Main
    C. east on Jefferson, south on 4th, west on Main
    D. south on 9th, east on Main

11.____

12. The SHORTEST legal way from Julia Davis Park to Owyhee Plaza Hotel is
    A. north on 5th, west on Front, north on 11th
    B. north on 6th, west on Main
    C. west on Battery, north on 9th, west on Front, north on Main
    D. north on 5th, west on Front, north on 13th, east on Main

12.____

13. The SHORTEST legal way from the Big Easy to City Hall is
    A. north on 9th, east on Main
    B. east on Myrtle, north on Capitol Blvd.
    C. north on 9th, east on Idaho
    D. east on Myrtle, north on 6th

13.____

14. The SHORTEST legal way from the Boise Contemporary Theater to the Pioneer Building is
    A. north on 9th, east on Main
    B. north on 9th, east on Myrtle, north on 6th
    C. east on Fulton, north on Capitol Blvd., east on Main
    D. east on Fulton, north on 6th

14.____

Questions 15-19.

DIRECTIONS: Questions 15 through 19 refer to Figure #3, on the following page, and measure your ability to understand written descriptions of events. Each question presents a description of an accident or event and asks you which of the following five drawings in Figure #3 BEST represents it.
In the drawings, the following symbols are used:
Moving vehicle ◊   Non-moving vehicle ♦
Pedestrian or bicyclist •
The path and direction of travel of a vehicle or pedestrian is indicated by a solid line.
The path and direction of travel of each vehicle or pedestrian directly involved in a collision from the point of impact is indicated by a dotted line.

In the space at the right, print the letter of the drawing that BEST fit the descriptions written below.

6 (#2)

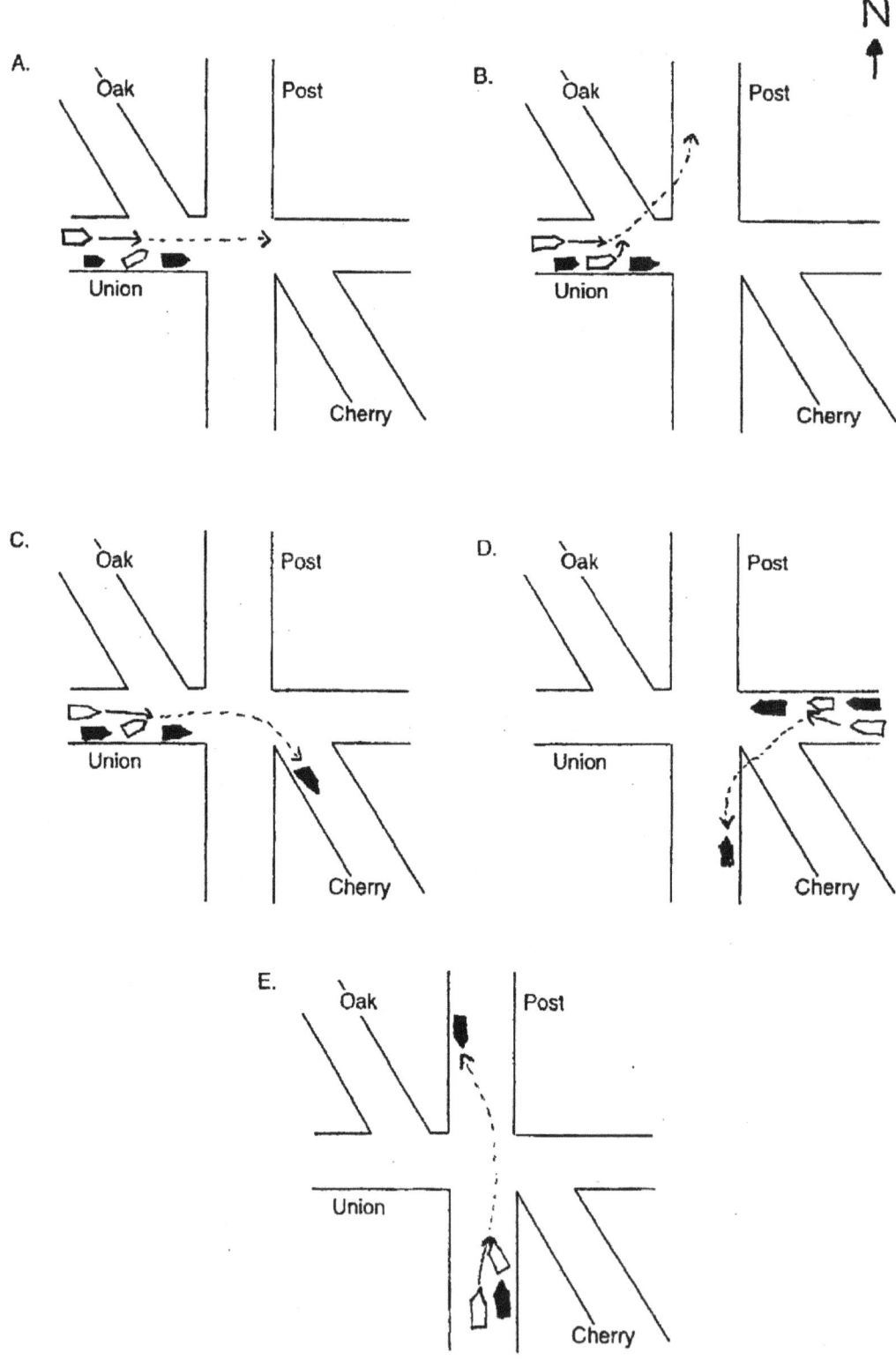

SOLUTIONS TO QUESTIONS 1-9

P implies Q = original statement

Not Q implies not P = contrapositive of the original statement. A statement and its contrapositive are logically equivalent.

Q implies P = converse of the original statement

Not P implies not Q = inverse of the original statement. The converse and inverse of an original statement are logically equivalent.

P implies Q = Not P or Q.

1. The CORRECT answer is B.
   For Item I, the irrational thinking teachers at the Middle School belong the group of all Middle School teachers. Since all teachers at the Middle School are intelligent, this includes the subset of irrational thinkers. For item II, if no one person has no friends, this implies that each person must have at least one friend.

2. The CORRECT answer is A.
   In item I, both statements state that (a) bananas are healthy and (b) bananas are eaten mainly because they taste good. In item II, the second statement is not equivalent to the first statement. An equivalent statement to the first statement would be "Either Dr. Jones is not in or we should call at the office."

3. The CORRECT answer is D.
   In item I, given that a person works one shift, we cannot draw any conclusion about whether he/she is a millworker. It is possible that a millworker works one, two, or a number more than two shifts. In item II, the second statement is the inverse of the first statement; they are not logically equivalent.

4. The CORRECT answer is B.
   In item I, any statement in the form "P implies Q" is equivalent to "Not P or Q." In this case, P = A member of the swim team attends practice, and Q = He will compete in the next meet. In item II, "P implies Q" is equivalent to "all P belongs to Q." In this case, P = Engineer wears glasses, and Q = He will know how to use AutoCAD.

5. The CORRECT answer is D. Because the number of high school graduates is so much larger than the number of convicted child abusers, none of the additional pieces of evidence make it reasonably certain that there are convicted abusers within this group of parents.

6. The CORRECT answer is B.
   Statement II is equivalent to "If Mr. Cantwell is reelected to the school board, then school buses are not approved. Statement I assures us that Mr. Cantwell will vote for new school buses. The only logical conclusion is that in spite of Mr. Cantwell's reelection to the board and subsequent vote, approval of the buses was still defeated.

7. The CORRECT answer is B. From Statement II, we conclude that Francis is either a sergeant or a major. If we also know that Stern is a major, we can deduce that Francis is a sergeant. This means that the third person, Jackson, must be a lieutenant.

8. The CORRECT answer is C.
Given that a survival kit contains a gas mask, Statement I assures us that it also contains the anthrax vaccine. If the survival kit near the typist pool only contains two items, than we can conclude that the gas mask in this location cannot contain a third item, namely the anthrax vaccine.

9. The CORRECT answer is C.
The original statement can be written in "P implies Q" form, where P = the heating coil temperature drops below 400 during the twin cycle, and Q = the mechanism shuts itself off. The contrapositive (which must be true) would be "If the mechanism did not shut itself off then the heating coil temperature did not drop below 400." We would then conclude that the temperature was too high and, therefore, the machine did not operate properly.

READING COMPREHENSION
UNDERSTANDING AND INTERPRETING WRITTEN MATERIAL
EXAMINATION SECTION
TEST 1

DIRECTIONS: Each question or incomplete statement is followed by several suggested answers or completions. Select the one that BEST answers the question or completes the statement. *PRINT THE LETTER OF THE CORRECT ANSWER IN THE SPACE AT THE RIGHT.*

Questions 1-3.

DIRECTIONS: Questions 1 through 3 are to be answered SOLELY on the basis of the following paragraph.

The final step in an accident investigation is the making out of the police report. In the case of a traffic accident, the officer should go right from the scene to his office to write up the report. However, if a person was injured in the accident and taken to a hospital, the officer should visit him there before going to his office to prepare his report. This personal visit to the injured person does not mean that the office must make a physical examination; but he should make an effort to obtain a statement from the injured person or persons. If this is not possible, information should be obtained from the attending physician as to the extent of the injury. In any event, without fail, the name of the physician should be secured and the report should state the name of the physician and the fact that he told the officer that, at a certain stated time on a certain stated date, the injuries were of such and such a nature. If the injured person dies before the officer arrives at the hospital, it may be necessary to take the responsible person into custody at once.

1. When a person has been injured in a traffic accident, the one of the following actions which it is necessary for a police officer to take in connection with the accident report is to   1.____
    A. prepare the police report immediately after the accident, and then go to the hospital to speak to the victim
    B. do his utmost to verify the victim's story prior to preparing the official police report of the incident
    C. be sure to include the victim's statement in the police report in every case
    D. try to get the victim's version of the accident prior to preparing the police report

2. When one of the persons injured in a motor vehicle accident dies, the above paragraph provides that the police officer   2.____
    A. must immediately take the responsible person into custody, if the injured person is already dead when the officer appears at the scene of the accident
    B. must either arrest the responsible person or get a statement from him, if the injured person dies after arrival at the hospital

C. may have to immediately arrest the responsible person, if the injured person dies in the hospital prior to the officer's arrival there
D. may refrain from arresting the responsible person, but only if the responsible person is also seriously injured

3. When someone has been injured in a collision between two automobiles and is given medical treatment shortly thereafter by a physician, the one of the following actions which the police officer MUST take with regard to the physician is to 3.____
   A. obtain his name and his diagnosis of the injuries, regardless of the place where treatment was given
   B. obtain his approval of the portion of the police report relating to the injured person and the treatment given him prior to and after his arrival at the hospital
   C. obtain his name, his opinion of the extent of the person's injuries, and his signed statement of the treatment he gave the injured person
   D. set a certain stated time on a certain stated date for interviewing him, unless he is an attending physician in a hospital

Questions 4-7.

DIRECTIONS: Questions 4 through 7 are to be answered SOLELY on the basis of the following paragraph.

Because of the importance of preserving physical evidence, the patrolman should not enter a scene of a crime if it can be examined visually from one position and if no other pressing duty requires his presence there. However, there are some responsibilities that take precedence over preservation of evidence. Some examples are: rescue work, disarming dangerous persons, quelling a disturbance. However, the patrolman should learn how to accomplish these more vital tasks, while at the same time preserving as much evidence as possible. If he finds it necessary to enter upon the scene, he should quickly study the place of entry to learn if any evidence will suffer by his contact; then he should determine the routes to be used in walking to the spot where his presence is required. Every place where a foot will fall or where a hand or other part of his body will touch, should be examined with the eye. Objects should not be touched or moved unless there is a definite and compelling reason. For identification of most items of physical evidence at the initial investigation, it is seldom necessary to touch or move them.

4. The one of the following titles which is the MOST appropriate for the above paragraph is: 4.____
   A. Determining the Priority of Tasks at the Scene of a Crime
   B. The Principal Reasons for Preserving Evidence at the Scene of a Crime
   C. Precautions to Take at the Scene of a Crime
   D. Evidence to be Examined at the Scene of a Crime

5. When a patrolman feels that it is essential for him to enter the immediate area where a crime has been committed, he should
   A. quickly but carefully glance around to determine whether his entering the area will damage any evidence present
   B. remove all objects of evidence from his predetermined route in order to avoid stepping on them
   C. carefully replace any object immediately if it is moved or touched by his hands or any other part of his body
   D. use only the usual place of entry to the scene in order to avoid disturbing any possible clues left on rear doors and windows by the criminal

6. The one of the following which is the LEAST urgent duty of a police officer who has just reported to the scene of a crime is to
   A. disarm the hysterical victim of the crime who is wildly waving a loaded gun in all directions
   B. give first aid to a possible suspect who has been injured while attempting to leave the scene of the crime
   C. prevent observers from attacking and injuring the persons suspected of having committed the crime
   D. preserve from damage or destruction any evidence necessary for the proper prosecution of the case against the criminals

7. A police officer has just reported to the scene of a crime in response to a phone call.
   The BEST of the following actions for him to take with respect to objects of physical evidence present at the scene is to
   A. make no attempt to enter the crime scene if his entry will disturb any vital physical evidence
   B. map out the shortest straight path to follow in walking to the spot where the physical evidence may be found
   C. move such objects of physical evidence as are necessary to enable him to assist the wounded victim of the crime
   D. quickly examine all objects of physical evidence in order to determine which objects may be touched and which may not

Questions 8-11.

DIRECTIONS: Questions 8 through 11 are to be answered SOLELY on the basis of the following paragraph.

After examining a document and comparing the characters with specimens of other specimens of other handwritings, the laboratory technician may conclude that a certain individual did write the questioned document. This opinion could be based on a large number of similar, as well as a small number of dissimilar but explainable characteristics. On the other hand, if the laboratory technician concludes that the person in question did not write the questioned document, such an opinion could be based on the large number of characteristics which are dissimilar, or even on a small number which are dissimilar provided that these are of overriding significance, and despite the presence of explainable similarities. The laboratory expert is not always able to give a positive opinion. He may state that a certain individual probably did or did not write the questioned document. Such an opinion is usually the result of insufficient material, either in the questioned document or in the specimens submitted for comparison. Finally, the expert may be unable to come to any conclusion at all because of insufficient material submitted for comparison or because of improper specimens.

8. The one of the following which is the MOST appropriate title for the above paragraph is:
   A. Similar and Dissimilar Characteristics in Handwriting
   B. The Limitations of Handwriting Analysis in Identifying the Writer
   C. The Positive Identification of Suspects Through Their Handwriting
   D. The Inability to Identify an Individual Through His Handwriting

8._____

9. When a handwriting expert compares the handwriting on two separate documents and decides that they were written by the same person, his conclusions are generally based on the fact that
   A. a large number of characteristics in both documents are dissimilar but the few similar characteristics are more important
   B. all the characteristics are alike in both documents
   C. similar characteristics need to be examined as to the cause for their similarity
   D. most of the characteristics in both documents are alike and their few differences are readily explainable

9._____

10. If a fingerprint technician carefully examines a handwritten threatening letter and compares it with specimens of handwriting made by a suspect, he would be MOST likely to decide that the suspect did NOT write the threatening letter when the handwriting specimens and the letter have
    A. a small number of dissimilarities
    B. a small number of dissimilar but explainable characteristics
    C. important dissimilarities despite the fact that these may be few
    D. some similar characteristics that are easily imitated or disguised

10._____

11. There are instances when even a trained handwriting expert cannot decide definitely whether or not a certain document and a set of handwriting specimens were written by the same person.
    This inability to make a positive decision generally arises in situations where
    A. only one document of considerable length is available for comparison with a sufficient supply of handwriting specimens
    B. the limited nature of the handwriting specimens submitted restricts their comparability with the questioned document
    C. the dissimilarities are not explainable
    D. the document submitted for comparison does not include all the characteristics included in the handwriting specimens

11._____

Questions 12-14.

DIRECTIONS: Questions 12 through 14 are to be answered SOLELY on the basis of the following paragraph.

In cases of drunken driving, or of disorderly conduct while intoxicated, too many times some person who had been completely under the influence of alcoholic liquor at the time of his arrest has walked out of court without any conviction just because an officer failed to make the proper observation. Many of the larger cities and counties make use of various scientific methods to determine the degree of intoxication of a person, such as breath, urine, and blood tests. Many of the smaller cities, however, do not have the facilities to make these various tests, and must, therefore, rely on the observation tests given at the scene. These consist, among other things, of noticing how the subject walked, talked, and acted. One test that is usually given at night is the eye reaction to light, which the officer gives by shining his flashlight into the eyes of the subject. The manner in which the pupils of the eyes react to the light helps to determine the sobriety of a person. If he is intoxicated, the pupils of his eyes are dilated more at night than the eyes of a sober person. Also, when a light is flashed into the eyes of a sober person, his pupils contract instantly, but in the case of a person under the influence of liquor, the pupils contract very slowly.

12. Many persons who have been arrested on a charge of driving while completely intoxicated have been acquitted by a judge because the arresting officer had neglected to
    A. bring the driver to court while he was still under the influence of alcohol
    B. make the required scientific tests to fully substantiate his careful personal observations of the driver's intoxicated condition
    C. submit to the court any test results showing the driver's condition or degree of drunkenness
    D. watch the driver closely for some pertinent facts which would support the officer's suspicions of the driver's intoxicated condition

13. When a person is arrested for acting in a disorderly and apparently intoxicated manner in public, the kind of test which would fit in BEST with the thought of the above statement is:
    A. In many smaller cities, a close watch on his behavior and of his reactions to various blood and body tests
    B. In many smaller cities, having him walk a straight line
    C. In most larger counties, close watch of the speed of his reactions to the flashlight test
    D. In most cities of all sizes, the application of the latest scientific techniques in the analysis of his breath

14. When a person suspected of driving a motor vehicle while intoxicated is being examined to determine whether or not he actually is intoxicated, one of the methods used is to shine the light of a flashlight into his eyes.

When this method is used, the NORMAL result is that the pupils of the suspect's eyes will
- A. expand instantly if he is fully intoxicated, and remain unchanged if he is completely sober
- B. expand very slowly if he has had only a small amount of alcohol, and very rapidly if he has had a considerable amount of alcohol
- C. grow smaller at once if he is sober, and grow smaller more slowly if he is intoxicated
- D. grow smaller very slowly if he is fully sober, and grow smaller instantaneously if he is fully intoxicated

Questions 15-17.

DIRECTIONS: Questions 15 through 17 are to be answered SOLELY on the basis of the following paragraph.

Where an officer has personal knowledge of facts, sufficient to constitute reasonable grounds to believe that a person has committed or is committing a felony, he may arrest him, and, after having lawfully placed him under arrest, may search and take into his possession any incriminating evidence. The right of an officer to make an arrest and search is not limited to cases where the officer has personal knowledge of the commission of a felony, because he may act upon information conveyed to him by third persons which he believes to be reliable. Where an officer, charged with the duty of enforcing the law, receives information from apparently reliable sources, which would induce in the mind of the prudent person a belief that a felony was being or had been committed, he may make an arrest and search the person of a defendant, but he is not justified in acting on anonymous information alone.

15. When a felony has been committed, an officer would be acting MOST properly if he arrested a man
    - A. when he, the officer, has a police report that the man is suspected of having been involved in several minor offenses
    - B. when he, the officer, has received information from a usually reliable source that the man was involved in the crime
    - C. only when he, the officer, has personal knowledge that the man has committed the felony
    - D. when he, the officer, knows for a fact that the man has associated in the past with several persons who had been seen near the scene of the felony

15.____

16. An officer would be acting MOST properly if he searched a suspect for incriminating evidence
    - A. when he has received detailed information concerning the fact that the suspect is going to commit a felony
    - B. only after having lawfully arrested the suspect and charged him with having committed a felony
    - C. when he has just received an anonymous tip that the suspect had just committed a felony and is in illegal possession of stolen goods

16.____

D. in order to find in his possession legally admissible evidence on the basis of which the officer could then proceed to arrest the suspect for having committed a felony

17. A police officer has received information from an informant that a crime has been committed. The informant has also named two persons who he says committed the crime.
 The officer's decision to both arrest and search the two suspects would be
 A. *correct*, if it would not be unreasonable to assume that the crime committed is a felony, and if the informant has been trustworthy in the past
 B. *incorrect*, if the informant has no proof but his own word to offer that a felony has been committed, although he has always been trustworthy in the past
 C. *correct*, if it would be logical and prudent to assume that the information is accurate regardless of whether the offense committed is a felony or a less serious crime
 D. *incorrect*, even if the informant produces objective and seemingly convincing proof that a felony has been committed, but has a reputation of occasional past unreliability

17.____

Questions 18-20.

DIRECTIONS: Questions 18 through 20 are to be answered SOLELY on the basis of the following paragraph.

If there are many persons at the scene of a hit-and-run accident, it would be a waste of time to question all of them; the witness needed is the one who can best describe the missing auto. Usually the person most qualified to do this is a youth of fifteen or sixteen years of age. He is more likely to be able to tell the make and year of a car than most other persons. A woman may be a good witness as to how the accident occurred, but usually will be unable to tell the make of the car. As soon as any information with regard to the missing car or its description is obtained, the police officer should call or radio headquarters and have the information put on the air. This should be done without waiting for further details, for time is an important factor. If a good description of the wanted car is obtained, then the next task is to get a description of the driver. In this hunt, it is found that a woman is often a more accurate witness than a man. Usually she will be able to state the color of clothes worn by the driver. If the wanted driver is a woman, another woman will often be able to tell the color and sometimes even the material of the clothing worn.

18. A hit-and-run accident has occurred and a police officer is attempting to obtain information from persons who had witnessed the incident.
 It would generally be BEST for him to question a
 A. boy in his late teens, when the officer is seeking an accurate description of the age, coloring, and physical build of the driver of the car
 B. man, when the officer is seeking an accurate description of the driver of the car and the color and material of his coat, suit, and hat

18.____

C. woman, when the officer is seeking an accurate description of the driver of the car
D. young teenage girl, when the officer is seeking an accurate description of the style and color of the clothes worn by the driver of the car

19. Time is an important factor when an attempt is being made to apprehend the guilty driver in a hit-and-run accident.
However, the EARLIEST moment when the police should broadcast a radio announcement of the crime is when a(n)
   A. description of the missing car or any facts concerning it have been obtained
   B. tentative identification of the driver of the missing car has been made
   C. detailed description of the missing car and its occupant has been obtained
   D. eyewitness account has been obtained of the accident, including the identity of the victim, the extent of injuries, and the make and license number of the car

20. The time when it would be MOST desirable to get a description of the driver of the hit-and-run car is
   A. after getting a description of the car itself
   B. before transmitting information concerning the car to headquarters for broadcasting
   C. as soon as the officer arrives at the scene of the accident
   D. as soon as the victim of the accident has been given needed medical assistance

KEY (CORRECT ANSWERS)

1.	D	11.	B
2.	C	12.	D
3.	A	13.	B
4.	C	14.	C
5.	A	15.	B
6.	D	16.	B
7.	C	17.	A
8.	B	18.	C
9.	D	19.	A
10.	C	20.	A

TEST 2

DIRECTIONS: Each question or incomplete statement is followed by several suggested answers or completions. Select the one that BEST answers the question or completes the statement. *PRINT THE LETTER OF THE CORRECT ANSWER IN THE SPACE AT THE RIGHT.*

Questions 1-4.

DIRECTIONS: Questions 1 through 4 are to be answered SOLELY on the basis of the following paragraph.

    Automobile tire tracks found at the scene of a crime constitute an important link in the chain of physical evidence. In many cases, these are the only clues available. In some areas, unpaved ground adjoins the highway or paved streets. A suspect will often park his car off the paved portion of the street when committing a crime, sometimes leaving excellent tire tracks. Comparison of the tire track impressions with the tires is possible only when the vehicle has been found. However, the initial problem facing the police is the task of determining what kind of car probably made the impressions found at the scene of the crime. If the make, model, and year of the car which made the impressions can be determined, it is obvious that the task of elimination is greatly lessened.

1. The one of the following which is the MOST appropriate title for the above paragraph is:
    A. The Use of Automobiles in the Commission of Crimes
    B. The Use of Tire Tracks in Police Work
    C. The Capture of Criminals by Scientific Police Work
    D. The Positive Identification of Criminals Through Their Cars

    1.____

2. When searching for clear signs left by the car used in the commission of a crime, the MOST likely place for the police to look would be on the
    A. highway adjoining unpaved streets
    B. highway adjacent to paved street
    C. paved street adjacent to the highway
    D. unpaved ground adjacent to a highway

    2.____

3. Automobile tire tracks found at the scene of a crime are of value as evidence in that they are
    A. generally sufficient to trap and convict a suspect
    B. the most important link in the chain of physical evidence
    C. often the only evidence at hand
    D. circumstantial rather than direct

    3.____

4. The PRIMARY reason for the police to try to find out which make, model, and year of car was involved in the commission of a crime is to
    A. compare the tire tracks left at the scene of the crime with the type of tires used on cars of that make
    B. determine if the mud on the tires of the suspected car matches the mud in the unpaved road near the scene of the crime

    4.____

C. reduce to a large extent the amount of work involved in determining the particular car used in the commission of a crime
D. alert the police patrol forces to question the occupants of all automobiles of this type

Questions 5-8.

DIRECTIONS: Questions 5 through 8 are to be answered SOLELY on the basis of the following paragraph.

When stopping vehicles on highways to check for suspects or fugitives, the police use an automobile roadblock whenever possible. This consists of three cars placed in prearranged positions. Car number one is parked across the left lane of the roadway with the front diagonally facing toward the center line. Car number two is parked across the right lane, with the front of the vehicle also toward the center line, in a position perpendicular to car number one and approximately twenty feet to the rear. Continuing another twenty feet to the rear along the highway, car number three is parked in an identical manner to car number one. The width of the highway determines the angle or position in which the autos should be placed. In addition to the regular roadblock signs and the uses of flares at night only, there is an officer located at both the entrance and exit to direct and control traffic from both directions. This type of roadblock forces all approaching autos to reduce speed and zigzag around the police cars. Officers standing behind the parked cars can most safely and carefully view all passing motorists. Once a suspect is inside the block, it becomes extremely difficult to crash out.

5. Of the following, the MOST appropriate title for this paragraph is:
   A. The Construction of an Escape-Proof Roadblock
   B. Regulation of Automobile Traffic Through a Police Roadblock
   C. Safety Precautions Necessary in Making an Automobile Roadblock
   D. Structure of a Roadblock to Detain Suspects or Fugitives

6. When setting up a three-car roadblock, the *relative* positions of the cars should be such that
   A. the front of car number one is placed diagonally to the center line and faces car number three
   B. car number three is placed parallel to the center line and its front faces the right side of the road
   C. car number two is placed about 20 feet from car number one and its front faces the left side of the road
   D. car number three is parallel to and about 20 feet away from car number one

7. Officers can observe occupants of all cars passing through the roadblock with GREATEST safety when
   A. warning flares are lighted to illuminate the area sufficiently at night
   B. warning signs are put up at each end of the roadblock
   C. they are stationed at both the exit and the entrance of the roadblock
   D. they take up positions behind cars in the roadblock

8. The type of automobile roadblock described in the above paragraph is of value in police work because
   A. a suspect is unable to escape its confines by using force
   B. it is frequently used to capture suspects with no danger to the police
   C. it requires only two officers to set up and operate
   D. vehicular traffic within its confines is controlled as to speed and direction

Questions 9-11.

DIRECTIONS: Questions 9 through 11 are to be answered SOLELY on the basis of the following paragraph.

A problem facing the police department in one area of the city was to try to reduce the number of bicycle thefts which had been increasing at an alarming rate in the past three or four years. A new program was adopted to get at the root of the problem. Tags were printed, reminding youngsters that bicycles left unlocked can be easily stolen. The police concentrated on such places as theaters, a municipal swimming pool, an athletic field, and the local high school, and tied tags on all bicycles which were not locked. The majority of bicycle thefts took place at the swimming pool. In 2019, during the first two weeks the pool was open, an average of 10 bicycle was stolen there daily. During the same two-week period, 30 bicycles a week were stolen at the athletic field, 15 at the high school, and 11 at all theaters combined. In 2020, after tagging the unlocked bicycles, it was found that 20 bicycles a week were stolen at the pool and 5 at the high school. It was felt that the police tags had helped the most, although the school officials had helped to a great extent in this program by distributing "locking" notices to parents and children, and the use of the loudspeaker at the pool urging children to lock their bicycles had also been very helpful.

9. The one of the following which had the GREATEST effect in the campaign to reduce bicycle stealing was the
   A. distribution of "locking" notices by the school officials
   B. locking of all bicycles left in public places
   C. police tagging of bicycles left unlocked by youngsters
   D. use of the loudspeaker at the swimming pool

10. The tagging program was instituted by the police department CHIEFLY to
    A. determine the areas where most bicycle thieves operated
    B. instill in youngsters the importance of punishing bicycle thieves
    C. lessen the rising rate of bicycle thefts
    D. recover as many as possible of the stolen bicycles

11. The figures showing the number of bicycle thefts in the various areas surveyed indicate that in 2019
    A. almost as many thefts occurred at the swimming pool as at all theaters combined
    B. fewer thefts occurred at the athletic field than at both the high school and all theaters combined
    C. more than half the thefts occurred at the swimming pool
    D. twice as many thefts occurred at the high school as at the athletic field

Questions 12-13.

DIRECTIONS: Questions 12 and 13 are to be answered SOLELY on the basis of the following paragraph.

A survey has shown that crime prevention work is most successful if the officers are assigned on rotating shifts to provide for around-the-clock coverage. An officer may work days for a time and then be switched to nights. The prime object of the night work is to enable the officer to spot conditions inviting burglars. Complete lack of, or faulty locations of, night lights and other conditions that may invite burglars, which might go unnoticed during daylight hours, can be located and corrected more readily through night work. Night work also enables the officer to check local hangouts of juvenile, such as bus and railway depots, certain cafes or pool halls, the local roller rink, and the building where a juvenile dance is held every Friday night. Detectives also join patrolmen cruising in radio patrol cars to check on juveniles loitering late at night and to spot-check local bars for juveniles.

12. The MOST important purpose of assigning officers to night shifts is to make it possible for them to 12.____
    A. correct conditions which may not be readily noticed during the day
    B. discover the locations of, and replace, missing and faulty night lights
    C. locate criminal hangouts
    D. notice things at night which cannot be noticed during the daytime

13. The type of shifting of officers which BEST prevents crime is to have 13.____
    A. day-shift officers rotated to night work
    B. rotating shifts provide sufficient officers for coverage 24 hours daily
    C. an officer work around the clock on a 24-hour basis as police needs arise
    D. rotating shifts to give the officers varied experience

Questions 14-15.

DIRECTIONS: Questions 14 and 15 are to be answered SOLELY on the basis of the following paragraph.

Proper firearms training is one phase of law enforcement which cannot be ignored. No part of the training of a police officer is more important or more valuable. The officer's life and often the lives of his fellow officers depend directly upon his skill with the weapon he is carrying. Proficiency with the revolver is not attained exclusively by the volume of ammunition used and the number of hours spent on the firing line. Supervised practice and the use of training aids and techniques help make the shooter. It is essential to have a good firing range where new officers are trained and older personnel practice in scheduled firearms sessions. The fundamental points to be stressed are grip, stance, breathing, sight alignment and trigger squeeze. Coordination of thought, vision, and motion must be achieved before the officer gains confidence in his shooting ability. Attaining this ability will make the student a better officer and enhance his value to the force.

14. A police officer will gain confidence in his shooting ability only after he has
    A. spent the required number of hours on the firing line
    B. been given sufficient supervised practice
    C. learned the five fundamental points
    D. learned to coordinate revolver movement with his sight and thought

15. Proper training in the use of firearms is one aspect of law enforcement which must be given serious consideration CHIEFLY because it is the
    A. most useful and essential single factor in the training of a police officer
    B. one phase of police officer training which stresses mental and physical coordination
    C. costliest aspect of police officer training involving considerable expense for the ammunition used in target practice
    D. most difficult part of police officer training, involving the expenditure of many hour on the firing line

Questions 16-20.

DIRECTIONS: Questions 16 through 20 are to be answered SOLELY on the basis of the following paragraph.

Lifting consists of transferring a print that has been dusted with powder to a transfer medium in order to preserve the print. Chemically developed prints cannot be lifted. Proper lifting of fingerprints is difficult and should be undertaken only when other means of recording the print are neither available nor suitable. Lifting should not be attempted from a porous surface. There are two types of commercial lifting tape which are good transfer mediums: rubber adhesive lift, one side of which is gummed and covered with thin, transparent celluloid; and transparent lifting tape, made of cellophane, one side of which is gummed. A package of acetate covers, frosted on one side and used to cover and protect the lifted print, accompanies each roll. If commercial tape is not available, transparent scotch tape may be used. The investigator should remove the celluloid or acetate cover from the lifting tape; smooth the tape, gummy side down, firmly and evenly over the entire print; gently peel the tape off the surface; replace the cover; and attach pertinent identifying data to the tape. All parts of the print should come in contact with the tape; air pockets should be avoided. The print will adhere to the lifting tape. The cover permits the print to be viewed and protects it from damage. Transparent lifting tape does not reverse the print. If a rubber adhesive lift is utilized, the print is reversed. Before a direct comparison can be made, the lifted print must be photographed, the negative reversed and a positive made.

16. An investigator wishing to preserve a record of fingerprints on a highly porous surface should
    A. develop them chemically before attempting to lift them
    B. lift them with scotch tape only when no other means of recording the prints are available
    C. employ some method other than lifting
    D. dust them with powder before attempting to lift them with rubber adhesive lift

17. Disregarding all other considerations, the SIMPLEST process to use in lifting a fingerprint from a window pane is that involving the use of
    A. rubber adhesive lift, because it gives a positive print in one step
    B. dusting powder and a camera, because the photograph is less likely to break than the window pane
    C. a chemical process, because it both develops and preserves the print at the same time
    D. transparent lifting tape, because it does not reverse the print

17._____

18. When a piece of commercial lifting tape is being used by an investigator wishing to lift a clear fingerprint from a smoothly-finished metal safe-door, he should
    A. prevent the ends of the tape from getting stuck to the metal surface because of the danger of forming air-pockets and thus damaging the print
    B. make certain that the tape covers all parts of the print and no air-pocket are formed
    C. carefully roll the tape over the most significant parts of the print only to avoid forming air-pockets
    D. be especially cautious not to destroy the air-pockets since this would tend to blur the print

18._____

19. When fingerprints lifted from an object found at the scene of a crime are to be compared with the fingerprints of a suspect, the lifted print
    A. can be compared directly only if a rubber adhesive lift was used
    B. cannot be compared directly if transparent scotch tape was used
    C. can be compared directly if transparent scotch tape was used
    D. must be photographed first and a positive made if any commercial lifting tape was used

19._____

20. When a rubber adhesive lift is to be used to lift a fingerprint, the one of the following which must be gently peeled off FIRST is the
    A. acetate cover   B. celluloid strip
    C. dusted surface   D. tape off the print surface

20._____

KEY (CORRECT ANSWERS)

1.	B	11.	C
2.	D	12.	A
3.	C	13.	B
4.	C	14.	D
5.	D	15.	A
6.	C	16.	C
7.	D	17.	D
8.	D	18.	B
9.	C	19.	C
10.	C	20.	B

PREPARING WRITTEN MATERIAL

PARAGRAPH REARRANGEMENT
COMMENTARY

The sentences that follow are in scrambled order. You are to rearrange them in proper order and indicate the letter choice containing the correct answer at the space at the right.

Each group of sentences in this section is actually a paragraph presented in scrambled order. Each sentence in the group has a place in that paragraph; no sentence is to be left out. You are to read each group of sentences and decide upon the best order in which to put the sentences so as to form a well-organized paragraph.

The questions in this section measure the ability to solve a problem when all the facts relevant to its solution are not given.

More specifically, certain positions of responsibility and authority require the employee to discover connection between events sometimes, apparently, unrelated. In order to do this, the employee will find it necessary to correctly infer that unspecified events have probably occurred or are likely to occur. This ability becomes especially important when action must be taken on incomplete information.

Accordingly, these questions require competitors to choose among several suggested alternatives, each of which presents a different sequential arrangement of the events. Competitors must choose the MOST logical of the suggested sequences.

In order to do so, they may be required to draw on general knowledge to infer missing concepts or events that are essential to sequencing the given events. Competitors should be careful to infer only what is essential to the sequence. The plausibility of the wrong alternatives will always require the inclusion of unlikely events or of additional chains of events which are NOT essential to sequencing the given events.

It's very important to remember that you are looking for the best of the four possible choices, and that the best choice of all may not even be one of the answers you're given to choose from.

There is no one right way to solve these problems. Many people have found it helpful to first write out the order of the sentences, as they would have arranged them, on their scrap paper before looking at the possible answers. If their optimum answer is there, this can save them some time. If it isn't, this method can still give insight into solving the problem. Others find it most helpful to just go through each of the possible choices, contrasting each as they go along. You should use whatever method feels comfortable and works for you.

While most of these types of questions are not that difficult, we've added a higher percentage of the difficult type, just to give you more practice. Usually there are only one or two questions on this section that contain such subtle distinctions that you're unable to answer confidently. And you then may find yourself stuck deciding between two possible choices, neither of which you're sure about.

PREPARING WRITTEN MATERIAL
PARAGRAPH REARRANGEMENT
EXAMINATION SECTION
TEST 1

DIRECTIONS: The sentences that follow are in scrambled order. You are to rearrange them in proper order and indicate the letter choice containing the CORRECT answer. *PRINT THE LETTER OF THE CORRECT ANSWER IN THE SPACE AT THE RIGHT.*

1. Police Officer Jenner responds to the scene of a burglary at 2106 La Vista Boulevard. He is approached by an elderly man named Richard Jenkins, whose account of the incident includes the following five sentences:
   I. I saw that the lock on my apartment door had been smashed and the door was open.
   II. My apartment was a shambles; my belongings were everywhere and my television set was missing.
   III. As I walked down the hallway toward the bedroom, I heard someone opening a window.
   IV. I left work at 5:30 P.M. and took the bus home.
   V. At that time, I called the police.
   The MOST logical order for the above sentence to appear in the report is
   A. I, V, IV, II, III   B. IV, I, II, III, V   C. I, V, II, III, IV   D. IV, III, II, V, I

   1.____

2. Police Officer LaJolla is writing an Incident Report in which back-up assistance was required. The report will contain the following five sentences:
   I. The radio dispatcher asked what my location was and he then dispatched patrol cars for back-up assistance.
   II. At approximately 9:30 P.M., while I was walking my assigned footpost, a gunman fired three shots at me.
   III. I quickly turned around and saw a white male, approximately 5'10", with black hair, wearing blue jeans, a yellow T-shirt, and white sneaker, running across the avenue carrying a handgun.
   IV. When the back-up officers arrived, we searched the area but could not find the suspect.
   V. I advised the radio dispatcher that a gunman had just fired a gun at me, and then I gave the dispatcher a description of the man
   The MOST logical order for the above sentences to appear in the report is:
   A. III, V, II, IV, I   B. II, III, V, I, IV   C. III, II, IV, I, V   D. II, V, I, III, IV

   2.____

3. Police Officer Durant is completing a report of a robbery and assault. The report will contain the following five sentences:
   I. I went to Mount Snow Hospital to interview a man who was attacked and robbed of his wallet earlier that night.
   II. An ambulance arrived at 82nd Street and 3rd Avenue and took an intoxicated, wounded man to Mount Snow Hospital
   III. Two youths attacked the man and stole his wallet.

   3.____

IV. A well-dressed man left Hanratty's Bar very drunk, with his wallet hanging out of his back pocket.
V. A passerby dialed 911 and requested police and ambulance assistance.
The MOST logical order for the above sentences to appear in the report is
   A. I, II, IV, III, V   B. IV, III, V, II, I   C. IV, V, II, III, I   D. V, IV, III, II, I

4. Police Officer Boswell is preparing a report of an armed robbery and assault which will contain the following five sentences:
  I. Both men approached the bartender and one of them drew a gun.
  II. The bartender immediately went to grab the phone at the bar.
  III. One of the men leaped over the counter and smashed a bottle over the bartender's head.
  IV. Two men in a blue Buick drove up to the bar and went inside.
  V. I found the cash register empty and the bartender unconscious on the floor, with the phone still dangling off the hook.
The MOST logical order for the above sentences to appear in the report is
   A. IV, I, II, III, V   B. V, IV, III, I, II   C. IV, III, II, V, I   D. II, I, III, IV, V

5. Police Officer Mitzler is preparing a report of a bank robbery, which will contain the following five sentences:
  I. The teller complied with the instructions on the note, but also hit the silent alarm.
  II. The perpetrator then fled south on Broadway.
  III. A suspicious male entered the bank at approximately 10:45 A.M.
  IV. At this time, an undetermined amount of money has been taken.
  V. He approached the teller on the far right side and handed her a note.
The MOST logical order for the above sentences to appear in the report is:
   A. III, V, I, II, IV   B. I, III, V, II, IV   C. III, V, IV, I, II   D. III, V, II, IV, I

6. A Police Officer is preparing an Accident Report for an accident which occurred at the intersection of East 119th Street and Lexington Avenue. The report will include the following five sentences:
  I. On September 18, while driving ten children to school, a school bus driver passed out.
  II. Upon arriving at the scene, I notified the dispatcher to send an ambulance.
  III. I notified the parents of each child once I got to the station house.
  IV. He said the school bus, while traveling west on East 119th Street, struck a parked Ford which was on the southwest corner of East 119th Street.
  V. A witness by the name of John Ramos came up to me to describe what happened.
The MOST logical order for the above sentences to appear in the Accident Report is:
   A. I, II, V, III, IV   B. I, II, V, IV, III   C. II, V, I, III, IV   D. II, V, I, IV, III

7. A Police Officer is preparing a report concerning a dispute. The report will contain the following five sentences:
  I. The passenger got out of the back of the taxi and leaned through the front window to complain to the driver about the fare.

II. The driver of the taxi caught up with the passenger and knocked him to the ground; the passenger then kicked the driver and a scuffle ensued.
III. The taxi drew up in front of the high-rise building and stopped.
IV. The driver got out of the taxi and followed the passenger into the lobby of the apartment building.
V. The doorman tried but was unable to break up the fight, at which point he called the precinct.
The MOST logical order for the above sentences to appear in the report is
   A. III, I, IV, II, V   B. III, IV, I, II, V   C. III, IV, II, V, I   D. V, I, III, IV, II

8. Police Officer Morrow is writing an Incident Report. The report will include the following four sentences:
    I. The man reached into his pocket and pulled out a gun.
    II. While on foot patrol, I identified a suspect, who was wanted for six robberies in the area, from a wanted picture I was carrying.
    III. I drew my weapon and fired six rounds at the suspect, killing him instantly.
    IV. I called for back-up assistance and told the man to put his hands up.
    The MOST logical order for the above sentences to appear in the report is
       A. II, III, IV, I   B. IV, I, III, II   C. IV, I, II, III   D. II, IV, I, III

9. Sergeant Allen responds to a call at 16 Grove Street regarding a missing child. At the scene, the Sergeant is met by Police Officer Samuels, who gives a brief account of the incident consisting of the following five sentences:
    I. I transmitted the description and waited for you to arrive before I began searching the area.
    II. Mrs. Banks, the mother, reports that she last saw her daughter Julie about 7:30 A.M. when she took her to school.
    III. About 6 P.M., my partner and I arrived at this location to investigate a report of a missing 8-year-old girl.
    IV. When Mrs. Banks left her, Julie was wearing a red and white striped T-shirt, blue jeans, and white sneakers.
    V. Mrs. Banks dropped her off in front of the playground of P.S. 11.
    The MOST logical order for the above sentences to appear in the report is
       A. III, V, IV, II, I   B. III, II, V, IV, I   C. III, IV, I, II, V   D. III, II, IV, I, V

10. Police Officer Franco is completing a report of an assault. The report will contain the following five sentences:
    I. In the park I observed an elderly man lying on the ground, bleeding from a back wound.
    II. I applied first aid to control the bleeding and radioed for an ambulance to respond.
    III. The elderly man stated that he was sitting on the park bench when he was attacked from behind by two males.
    IV. I received a report of a man's screams coming from inside the park, and I went to investigate.
    V. The old man could not give a description of his attackers.
    The MOST logical order for the above sentences to appear in the report is
       A. IV, I, II, III, V   B. V, III, I, IV, II   C. IV, III, V, II, I   D. II, I, V, IV, III

11. Police Officer Williams is completing a Crime Report. The report contains the following five sentences:
    I. As Police Officer Hanson and I approached the store, we noticed that the front door was broken.
    II. After determining that the burglars had fled, we notified the precinct of the burglary.
    III. I walked through the front door as Police Officer Hanson walked around to the back.
    IV. At approximately midnight, an alarm was heard at the Apex Jewelry Store.
    V. We searched the store and found no one.
    The MOST logical order for the above sentences to appear in the report is
    A. I, IV, II, III, V   B. I, IV, III, V, II   C. IV, I, III, II, V   D. IV, I, III, V, II

12. Police Officer Clay is giving a report to the news media regarding someone who has jumped from the Empire State Building. His report will include the following five sentences:
    I. I responded to the 86th floor, where I found the person at the edge of the roof.
    II. A security guard at the building had reported that a man was on the roof at the 86th floor.
    III. At 5:30 P.M., the person jumped from the building.
    IV. I received a call from the radio dispatcher at 4:50 P.M. to respond to the Empire State Building.
    V. I tried to talk to the person and convince him not to jump.
    The MOST logical order for the above sentences to appear in the report is
    A. I, II, IV, III, V   B. III, IV, I, II, V   C. II, IV, I, III, V   D. IV, II, I, V, III

13. The following five sentences are part of a report of a burglary written by Police Officer Reed:
    I. When I arrived at 2400 1st Avenue, I noticed that the door was slightly open.
    II. I yelled out, *Police, don't move!*
    III. As I entered the apartment, I saw a man with a TV set passing through a window to another man standing on a fire escape.
    IV. While on foot patrol, I was informed by the radio dispatcher that a burglary was in progress at 2400 1st Avenue.
    V. However, the burglars quickly ran down the fire escape.
    The MOST logical order for the above sentences to appear in the report is
    A. I, III, IV, V, II   B. IV, I, III, V, II   C. IV, I, III, II, V   D. I, IV, III, II, V

14. Police Officer Jenkins is preparing a report for Lost or Stolen Property. The report will include the following five sentences:
    I. On the stairs, Mr. Harris slipped on a wet leaf and fell on the landing.
    II. It wasn't until he got to the token booth that Mr. Harris realized his wallet was no longer in his back pants pocket.
    III. A boy wearing a football jersey helped him up and brushed off the back of Mr. Harris' pants.
    IV. Mr. Harris states he was walking up the stairs to the elevated subway at Queensborough Plaza.
    V. Before Mr. Harris could thank him, the boy was running down the stairs to the street.

The MOST logical order for the above sentences to appear in the report is
A. IV, III, V, I, II B. IV, I, III, V, II C. I, IV, II, III, V D. I, II, IV, III, V

15. Police Officer Hubbard is completing a report of a missing person. The report will contain the following five sentences:
    I. I visited the store at 7:55 P.M. and asked the employees if they had seen a girl fitting the description I had been given.
    II. She gave me a description and said she had gone into the local grocery store at about 6:15 P.M.
    III. I asked the woman for a description of her daughter.
    IV. The distraught woman called the precinct to report that her daughter, aged 12, had not returned from an errand.
    V. The storekeeper said a girl matching the description had been in the store earlier, but he could not give an exact time.
    The MOST logical order for the above sentences to appear in the report is
    A. I, III, II, V, IV B. IV, III, II, I, V C. V, I, II, III, IV D. III, I, II, IV, V

16. A police officer is completing an entry in his Daily Activity Log regarding traffic summonses which he issued. The following five sentences will be included in the entry:
    I. I was on routine patrol parked 16 yards west of 170th Street and Clay Avenue.
    II. The summonses were issued for unlicensed operator and disobeying a steady red light.
    III. At 8 A.M. hours, I observed an auto traveling westbound on 170th Street not stop for a steady red light at the intersection of Clay Avenue and 170th Street.
    IV. I stopped the driver of the auto and determined that he did not have a valid driver's license.
    V. After a brief conversation, I informed the motorist that he was receiving two summonses.
    The MOST logical order for the above sentences to appear in the report is
    A. I, III, IV, V, II B. III, IV, II, V, I C. V, II, I, III, IV D. IV, V, II, I, III

17. The following sentences appeared on an Incident Report:
    I. Three teenagers who had been ejected from the theater were yelling at patrons who were now entering.
    II. Police Officer Dixon told the teenagers to leave the area.
    III. The teenager said that they were told by the manager to leave the theater because they were talking during the movie.
    IV. The theater manager called the precinct at 10:20 P.M. to report a disturbance outside the theater.
    V. A patrol car responded to the theater at 10:42 P.M. and two police officers went over to the teenagers.
    The MOST logical order for the above sentences to appear in the Incident Report is
    A. I, V, IV, III, II B. IV, I, V, III, II C. IV, I, III, V, II D. IV, III, I, V, II

18. Activity Log entries are completed by police officers. Police Officer Samuels has written an entry concerning vandalism and part of it contains the following five sentences:
    I. The man, in his early twenties, ran down the block and around the corner.
    II. A man passing the store threw a brick through a window of the store.
    III. I arrived on the scene and began to question the witnesses about the incident.
    IV. Malcolm Holmes, the owner of the Fast Service Shoe Repair Store, was working in the back of the store at approximately 3 P.M.
    V. After the man fled, Mr. Holmes called the police.
    The MOST logical order for the above sentences to appear in the Activity Log is
    A. IV, II, I, V, III   B. II, IV, I, III, V   C. II, I, IV, III, V   D. IV, II, V, III, I

18.____

19. Police Officer Buckley is preparing a report concerning a dispute in a restaurant. The report will contain the following five sentences:
    I. The manager, Charles Chin, and a customer, Edward Green, were standing near the register arguing over the bill.
    II. The manager refused to press any charges providing Green pay the check and leave.
    III. While on foot patrol, I was informed by a passerby of a disturbance in the Dragon Flame Restaurant.
    IV. Green paid the $15.00 check and left the restaurant.
    V. According to witnesses, the customer punched the owner in the face when Chin asked him for the amount due.
    The MOST logical order for the above sentences to appear in the report is
    A. III, I, V, II, IV   B. I, II, III, IV, V   C. V, I, III, II, IV   D. III, V, II, IV, I

19.____

20. Police Officer Wilkins is preparing a report for leaving the scene of an accident. The report will include the following five sentences:
    I. The Dodge struck the right rear fender of Mrs. Smith's 2010 Ford and continued on its way.
    II. Mrs. Smith stated she was making a left turn from 40th Street onto Third Avenue.
    III. As the car passed, Mrs. Smith noticed the dangling rear license plate #412AEJ.
    IV. Mrs. Smith complained to police of back pains and was removed by ambulance to Bellevue Hospital.
    V. An old green Dodge traveling up Third Avenue went through the red light at 40th Street and Third Avenue.
    The MOST logical order for the above sentences to appear in the report is
    A. V, III, I, II, IV   B. I, III, II, V, IV   C. IV, V, I, II, III   D. II, V, I, III, IV

20.____

21. Detective Simon is completing a Crime Report. The report contains the following five sentences:
    I. Police Officer Chin, while on foot patrol, heard the yelling and ran in the direction of the man.
    II. The man, carrying a large hunting knife, left the High Sierra Sporting Goods Store at approximately 10:30 A.M.

21.____

III. When the man heard Police Officer Chin, he stopped, dropped the knife, and began to cry.
IV. As Police Officer Chin approached the man, he drew his gun and yelled, *Police, freeze.*
V. After the man left the store, he began yelling, over and over, *I am going to kill myself!*

The MOST logical order for the above sentences to appear in the report is
   A. V, II, I, IV, III   B. II, V, I, IV, III   C. II, V, IV, I, III   D. II, I, V, IV, III

22. Police Officer Miller is preparing a Complaint Report which will include the following five sentences:
    I. From across the lot, he yelled to the boys to get away from his car.
    II. When he came out of the store, he noticed two teenage boys trying to break into his car.
    III. The boys fled as Mr. Johnson ran to his car.
    IV. Mr. Johnson stated that he parked his car in the municipal lot behind Tams Department Store.
    V. Mr. Johnson saw that the door lock had been broken, but nothing was missing from inside the auto.

    The MOST logical order for the above sentences to appear in the report is
       A. IV, I, II, V, III   B. II, III, I, V, IV   C. IV, II, I, III, V   D. I, II, III, V, IV

23. Police Officer O'Hara completes a Universal Summons for a motorist who has just passed a red traffic light. The Universal Summons includes the following five sentences:
    I. As the car passed the light, I followed in the patrol car.
    II. After the driver stopped the car, he stated that the light was yellow, not red.
    III. A blue Cadillac sedan passed the red light on the corner of 79th Street and 3rd Avenue at 11:25 P.M.
    IV. As a result, the driver was informed that he did pass a red light and that his brake lights were not working.
    V. The driver in the Cadillac stopped his car as soon as he saw the patrol car, and I noticed that the brake lights were not working.

    The MOST logical order for the above sentences to appear in the Universal Summons is
       A. I, III, V, II, IV   B. III, I, V, II, IV   C. III, I, V, IV, II   D. I, III, IV, II, V

24. Detective Egan is preparing a follow-up report regarding a homicide on 170th Street and College Avenue. An unknown male was found at the scene. The report will contain the following five sentences:
    I. Police Officer Gregory wrote down the names, addresses, and phone numbers of the witnesses.
    II. A 911 operator received a call of a man shot and dispatched Police Officers Worth and Gregory to the scene.
    III. They discovered an unidentified male dead on the street.
    IV. Police Officer Worth notified the Precinct Detective Unit immediately.
    V. At approximately 9:00 A.M., an unidentified male shot another male in the chest during an argument.

The MOST logical order for the above sentences to appear in the report is
A. V, II, III, IV, I   B. II, III, V, IV, I   C. IV, I, V, II, III   D. V, III, II, IV, I

25. Police Officer Tracey is preparing a Robbery Report which will include the following five sentences:
    I. I ran around the corner and observe a man pointing a gun at a taxidriver.
    II. I informed the man I was a police officer and that he should not move.
    III. I was on the corner of 125th Street and Park Avenue when I heard a scream coming from around the corner.
    IV. The man turned around and fired one shot at me.
    V. I fired once, shooting him in the arm and causing him to fall to the ground.
    The MOST logical order for the above sentences to appear in the report is
    A. I, III, IV, II, V   B. IV, V, II, I, III   C. III, I, II, IV, V   D. III, I, V, II, IV

KEY (CORRECT ANSWERS)

1.	B	11.	D
2.	B	12.	D
3.	B	13.	C
4.	A	14.	B
5.	A	15.	B
6.	B	16.	A
7.	A	17.	B
8.	D	18.	A
9.	B	19.	A
10.	A	20.	D

21.	B
22.	C
23.	B
24.	A
25.	C

TEST 2

DIRECTIONS: The sentences that follow are in scrambled order. You are to rearrange them in proper order and indicate the letter choice containing the CORRECT answer. *PRINT THE LETTER OF THE CORRECT ANSWER IN THE SPACE AT THE RIGHT*

1. Police Officer Weiker is completing a Complaint Report which will contain the following five sentences:
    I. Mr. Texlor was informed that the owner of the van would receive a parking ticket and that the van would be towed away.
    II. The police tow truck arrived approximately one half hour after Mr. Texlor complained.
    III. While on foot patrol on West End Avenue, I saw the owner of Rand's Restaurant arrive to open his business.
    IV. Mr. Texlor, the owner, called to me and complained that he could not receive deliveries because a van was blocking his driveway.
    V. The van's owner later reported to the precinct that his van had been stolen, and he was then informed that it had been towed.
    The MOST logical order for the above sentences to appear in the report is
    A. III, V, I, II, IV   B. III, IV, I, II, V   C. IV, III, I, II, V   D. IV, III, II, I, V

    1.____

2. Police Officer Ames is completing an entry in his Activity Log. The entry contains the following five sentences:
    I. Mr. Sands gave me a complete description of the robber.
    II. Alvin Sands, owner of the Star Delicatessen, called the precinct to report he had just been robbed.
    III. I then notified all police patrol vehicles to look for a white male in his early twenties wearing brown pants and shirt, a black leather jacket, and black and white sneakers.
    IV. I arrived on the scene after being notified by the precinct that a robbery had just occurred at the Star Delicatessen.
    V. Twenty minutes later, a man fitting the description was arrested by a police officer on patrol six blocks from the delicatessen.
    The MOST logical order for the above sentences to appear in the Activity Log is
    A. II, I, IV, III, V   B. II IV, III, I, V   C. II, IV, I, III, V   D. II, IV, I, V, III

    2.____

3. Police Officer Benson is completing a Complaint Report concerning a stolen taxicab, which will include the following five sentences:
    I. Police Officer Benson noticed that a cab was parked next to a fire hydrant.
    II. Dawson *borrowed* the cab for transportation purposes since he was in a hurry.
    III. Ed Dawson got into his car and tried to start it, but the battery was dead.
    IV. When he reached his destination, he parked the cab by a fire hydrant and placed the keys under the seat.
    V. He looked around and saw an empty cab with the engine running.
    The MOST logical order for the above sentences to appear in the report is
    A. I, III, II, IV, V   B. III, I, II, V, IV   C. III, V, II, IV, I   D. V, II, IV, III, I

    3.____

C-794   CAREER EXAMINATION SERIES

This is your
PASSBOOK for...

Sheriff

Test Preparation Study Guide
Questions & Answers

15. A driver headed east on Union strikes a car that is pulling out from between two parked cars, and then continues east.

    15._____

16. A driver headed north on Post strikes a car that is pulling out from in front of a parked car, then veers into the oncoming lane and collides head-on with a car that is parked in the southbound lane of Post.

    16._____

17. A driver headed east on Union strikes a car that is pulling out from two parked cars, travels through the intersection, and makes a sudden right turn onto Cherry, where he strikes a parked car in the rear.

    17._____

18. A driver headed west on Union strikes a car that is pulling out from between two parked cars, and then swerves to the left. He cuts the corner and travels over the sidewalk at the intersection of Cherry and Post, and then strikes a car that is parked in the northbound lane on Post.

    18._____

19. A driver headed east on Union strikes a car that is pulling out from between two parked cars, and then swerves to the left. He cuts the corner and travels over the sidewalk at the intersection of Oak and Post, and then flees north on Post.

    19._____

Questions 20-22.

DIRECTIONS: In Questions 20 through 22, choose the word or phrase CLOSEST in meaning to the word or phrase printed in capital letters.

20. TITLE
    A. danger   B. ownership   C. description   D. treatise

    20._____

21. REVOKE
    A. cancel   B. imagine   C. solicit   D. cause

    21._____

22. BRIEF
    A. summary   B. ruling   C. plea   D. motion

    22._____

Questions 23-25.

DIRECTIONS: Questions 23 through 25 measure your ability to do fieldwork-related arithmetic. Each question presents a separate arithmetic problem for you to solve.

23. An investigator plans to drive from his home to Los Angeles, a trip of 2,800 miles. His car has a 24-gallon tank and gets 18 miles to the gallon. If he starts out with a full tank of gasoline, what is the FEWEST number of stops he will have to make for gasoline to complete his trip to Los Angeles?
    A. 4   B. 5   C. 6   D. 7

    23._____

24. A caseworker has 24 home visits to schedule for a week. She will visit three homes on Sunday, and on every day that follows she will visit one more home than she visited on the previous day.
At the end of the day on _____, the caseworker will have completed all of her home visits.
   A. Wednesday   B. Thursday   C. Friday   D. Saturday

25. Ms. Langhorn takes a cab from her house to the airport. The cab company charges $3.00 to start the meter and $.50 per mile after that. It's 15 miles from Ms. Langhorn's house to the airport.
How much will she have to pay for a cab?
   A. $10.50   B. $11.50   C. $14.00   D. $15.50

KEY (CORRECT ANSWERS)

1.	B		11.	D
2.	A		12.	A
3.	D		13.	B
4.	B		14.	C
5.	D		15.	A
6.	B		16.	E
7.	B		17.	C
8.	C		18.	D
9.	C		19.	B
10.	C		20.	B

21. A
22. A
23. C
24. B
25. A

14) Do not be afraid to admit an error in judgment if you are shown to be wrong

The board knows that you are forced to reply without any opportunity for careful consideration. Your answer may be demonstrably wrong. If so, admit it and get on with the interview.

15) Do not dwell at length on your present job

The opening question may relate to your present assignment. Answer the question but do not go into an extended discussion. You are being examined for a *new* job, not your present one. As a matter of fact, try to phrase ALL your answers in terms of the job for which you are being examined.

Basis of Rating

Probably you will forget most of these "do's" and "don'ts" when you walk into the oral interview room. Even remembering them all will not ensure you a passing grade. Perhaps you did not have the qualifications in the first place. But remembering them will help you to put your best foot forward, without treading on the toes of the board members.

Rumor and popular opinion to the contrary notwithstanding, an oral board wants you to make the best appearance possible. They know you are under pressure – but they also want to see how you respond to it as a guide to what your reaction would be under the pressures of the job you seek. They will be influenced by the degree of poise you display, the personal traits you show and the manner in which you respond.

ABOUT THIS BOOK

This book contains tests divided into Examination Sections. Go through each test, answering every question in the margin. We have also attached a sample answer sheet at the back of the book that can be removed and used. At the end of each test look at the answer key and check your answers. On the ones you got wrong, look at the right answer choice and learn. Do not fill in the answers first. Do not memorize the questions and answers, but understand the answer and principles involved. On your test, the questions will likely be different from the samples. Questions are changed and new ones added. If you understand these past questions you should have success with any changes that arise. Tests may consist of several types of questions. We have additional books on each subject should more study be advisable or necessary for you. Finally, the more you study, the better prepared you will be. This book is intended to be the last thing you study before you walk into the examination room. Prior study of relevant texts is also recommended. NLC publishes some of these in our Fundamental Series. Knowledge and good sense are important factors in passing your exam. Good luck also helps. So now study this Passbook, absorb the material contained within and take that knowledge into the examination. Then do your best to pass that exam.

4) Do not exaggerate your experience or abilities

In the first place, from information in the application or other interviews and sources, the board may know more about you than you think. Secondly, you probably will not get away with it. An experienced board is rather adept at spotting such a situation, so do not take the chance.

5) If you know a board member, do not make a point of it, yet do not hide it

Certainly you are not fooling him, and probably not the other members of the board. Do not try to take advantage of your acquaintanceship – it will probably do you little good.

6) Do not dominate the interview

Let the board do that. They will give you the clues – do not assume that you have to do all the talking. Realize that the board has a number of questions to ask you, and do not try to take up all the interview time by showing off your extensive knowledge of the answer to the first one.

7) Be attentive

You only have 20 minutes or so, and you should keep your attention at its sharpest throughout. When a member is addressing a problem or question to you, give him your undivided attention. Address your reply principally to him, but do not exclude the other board members.

8) Do not interrupt

A board member may be stating a problem for you to analyze. He will ask you a question when the time comes. Let him state the problem, and wait for the question.

9) Make sure you understand the question

Do not try to answer until you are sure what the question is. If it is not clear, restate it in your own words or ask the board member to clarify it for you. However, do not haggle about minor elements.

10) Reply promptly but not hastily

A common entry on oral board rating sheets is "candidate responded readily," or "candidate hesitated in replies." Respond as promptly and quickly as you can, but do not jump to a hasty, ill-considered answer.

11) Do not be peremptory in your answers

A brief answer is proper – but do not fire your answer back. That is a losing game from your point of view. The board member can probably ask questions much faster than you can answer them.

12) Do not try to create the answer you think the board member wants

He is interested in what kind of mind you have and how it works – not in playing games. Furthermore, he can usually spot this practice and will actually grade you down on it.

13) Do not switch sides in your reply merely to agree with a board member

Frequently, a member will take a contrary position merely to draw you out and to see if you are willing and able to defend your point of view. Do not start a debate, yet do not surrender a good position. If a position is worth taking, it is worth defending.

hesitate. But do not quibble about insignificant matters. Also, he will usually ask you some question about your education, experience or your present job – partly to get you to start talking and to establish the interviewing "rapport." He may start the actual questioning, or turn it over to one of the other members. Frequently, each member undertakes the questioning on a particular area, one in which he is perhaps most competent, so you can expect each member to participate in the examination. Because time is limited, you may also expect some rather abrupt switches in the direction the questioning takes, so do not be upset by it. Normally, a board member will not pursue a single line of questioning unless he discovers a particular strength or weakness.

After each member has participated, the chairman will usually ask whether any member has any further questions, then will ask you if you have anything you wish to add. Unless you are expecting this question, it may floor you. Worse, it may start you off on an extended, extemporaneous speech. The board is not usually seeking more information. The question is principally to offer you a last opportunity to present further qualifications or to indicate that you have nothing to add. So, if you feel that a significant qualification or characteristic has been overlooked, it is proper to point it out in a sentence or so. Do not compliment the board on the thoroughness of their examination – they have been sketchy, and you know it. If you wish, merely say, "No thank you, I have nothing further to add." This is a point where you can "talk yourself out" of a good impression or fail to present an important bit of information. Remember, *you close the interview yourself*.

The chairman will then say, "That is all, Mr. _____, thank you." Do not be startled; the interview is over, and quicker than you think. Thank him, gather your belongings and take your leave. Save your sigh of relief for the other side of the door.

How to put your best foot forward

Throughout this entire process, you may feel that the board individually and collectively is trying to pierce your defenses, seek out your hidden weaknesses and embarrass and confuse you. Actually, this is not true. They are obliged to make an appraisal of your qualifications for the job you are seeking, and they want to see you in your best light. Remember, they must interview all candidates and a non-cooperative candidate may become a failure in spite of their best efforts to bring out his qualifications. Here are 15 suggestions that will help you:

1) Be natural – Keep your attitude confident, not cocky

If you are not confident that you can do the job, do not expect the board to be. Do not apologize for your weaknesses, try to bring out your strong points. The board is interested in a positive, not negative, presentation. Cockiness will antagonize any board member and make him wonder if you are covering up a weakness by a false show of strength.

2) Get comfortable, but don't lounge or sprawl

Sit erectly but not stiffly. A careless posture may lead the board to conclude that you are careless in other things, or at least that you are not impressed by the importance of the occasion. Either conclusion is natural, even if incorrect. Do not fuss with your clothing, a pencil or an ashtray. Your hands may occasionally be useful to emphasize a point; do not let them become a point of distraction.

3) Do not wisecrack or make small talk

This is a serious situation, and your attitude should show that you consider it as such. Further, the time of the board is limited – they do not want to waste it, and neither should you.

involves supervisory responsibilities, the announcement will usually indicate that knowledge of modern supervisory methods and the qualifications of the candidate as a supervisor will be tested. If so, you can expect such questions, frequently in the form of a hypothetical situation which you are expected to solve. NEVER go into an oral without knowledge of the duties and responsibilities of the job you seek.

3) Think through each qualification required

Try to visualize the kind of questions you would ask if you were a board member. How well could you answer them? Try especially to appraise your own knowledge and background in each area, *measured against the job sought*, and identify any areas in which you are weak. Be critical and realistic – do not flatter yourself.

4) Do some general reading in areas in which you feel you may be weak

For example, if the job involves supervision and your past experience has NOT, some general reading in supervisory methods and practices, particularly in the field of human relations, might be useful. Do NOT study agency procedures or detailed manuals. The oral board will be testing your understanding and capacity, not your memory.

5) Get a good night's sleep and watch your general health and mental attitude

You will want a clear head at the interview. Take care of a cold or any other minor ailment, and of course, no hangovers.

What should be done on the day of the interview?

Now comes the day of the interview itself. Give yourself plenty of time to get there. Plan to arrive somewhat ahead of the scheduled time, particularly if your appointment is in the fore part of the day. If a previous candidate fails to appear, the board might be ready for you a bit early. By early afternoon an oral board is almost invariably behind schedule if there are many candidates, and you may have to wait. Take along a book or magazine to read, or your application to review, but leave any extraneous material in the waiting room when you go in for your interview. In any event, relax and compose yourself.

The matter of dress is important. The board is forming impressions about you – from your experience, your manners, your attitude, and your appearance. Give your personal appearance careful attention. Dress your best, but not your flashiest. Choose conservative, appropriate clothing, and be sure it is immaculate. This is a business interview, and your appearance should indicate that you regard it as such. Besides, being well groomed and properly dressed will help boost your confidence.

Sooner or later, someone will call your name and escort you into the interview room. *This is it.* From here on you are on your own. It is too late for any more preparation. But remember, you asked for this opportunity to prove your fitness, and you are here because your request was granted.

What happens when you go in?

The usual sequence of events will be as follows: The clerk (who is often the board stenographer) will introduce you to the chairman of the oral board, who will introduce you to the other members of the board. Acknowledge the introductions before you sit down. Do not be surprised if you find a microphone facing you or a stenotypist sitting by. Oral interviews are usually recorded in the event of an appeal or other review.

Usually the chairman of the board will open the interview by reviewing the highlights of your education and work experience from your application – primarily for the benefit of the other members of the board, as well as to get the material into the record. Do not interrupt or comment unless there is an error or significant misinterpretation; if that is the case, do not

X. HOW TO PASS THE INTERVIEW TEST

The examination for which you applied requires an oral interview test. You have already taken the written test and you are now being called for the interview test – the final part of the formal examination.

You may think that it is not possible to prepare for an interview test and that there are no procedures to follow during an interview. Our purpose is to point out some things you can do in advance that will help you and some good rules to follow and pitfalls to avoid while you are being interviewed.

What is an interview supposed to test?

The written examination is designed to test the technical knowledge and competence of the candidate; the oral is designed to evaluate intangible qualities, not readily measured otherwise, and to establish a list showing the relative fitness of each candidate – as measured against his competitors – for the position sought. Scoring is not on the basis of "right" and "wrong," but on a sliding scale of values ranging from "not passable" to "outstanding." As a matter of fact, it is possible to achieve a relatively low score without a single "incorrect" answer because of evident weakness in the qualities being measured.

Occasionally, an examination may consist entirely of an oral test – either an individual or a group oral. In such cases, information is sought concerning the technical knowledges and abilities of the candidate, since there has been no written examination for this purpose. More commonly, however, an oral test is used to supplement a written examination.

Who conducts interviews?

The composition of oral boards varies among different jurisdictions. In nearly all, a representative of the personnel department serves as chairman. One of the members of the board may be a representative of the department in which the candidate would work. In some cases, "outside experts" are used, and, frequently, a businessman or some other representative of the general public is asked to serve. Labor and management or other special groups may be represented. The aim is to secure the services of experts in the appropriate field.

However the board is composed, it is a good idea (and not at all improper or unethical) to ascertain in advance of the interview who the members are and what groups they represent. When you are introduced to them, you will have some idea of their backgrounds and interests, and at least you will not stutter and stammer over their names.

What should be done before the interview?

While knowledge about the board members is useful and takes some of the surprise element out of the interview, there is other preparation which is more substantive. It *is* possible to prepare for an oral interview – in several ways:

1) Keep a copy of your application and review it carefully before the interview

This may be the only document before the oral board, and the starting point of the interview. Know what education and experience you have listed there, and the sequence and dates of all of it. Sometimes the board will ask you to review the highlights of your experience for them; you should not have to hem and haw doing it.

2) Study the class specification and the examination announcement

Usually, the oral board has one or both of these to guide them. The qualities, characteristics or knowledges required by the position sought are stated in these documents. They offer valuable clues as to the nature of the oral interview. For example, if the job

2. *Considering only one side of a situation* – Wherever possible, indicate several alternatives and then point out the reasons you selected the best one
3. *Failing to indicate follow up* – Whenever your answer indicates action on your part, make certain that you will take proper follow-up action to see how successful your recommendations, procedures or actions turn out to be
4. *Taking too long in answering any single question* – Remember to time your answers properly

IX. AFTER THE TEST

Scoring procedures differ in detail among civil service jurisdictions although the general principles are the same. Whether the papers are hand-scored or graded by machine we have described, they are nearly always graded by number. That is, the person who marks the paper knows only the number – never the name – of the applicant. Not until all the papers have been graded will they be matched with names. If other tests, such as training and experience or oral interview ratings have been given, scores will be combined. Different parts of the examination usually have different weights. For example, the written test might count 60 percent of the final grade, and a rating of training and experience 40 percent. In many jurisdictions, veterans will have a certain number of points added to their grades.

After the final grade has been determined, the names are placed in grade order and an eligible list is established. There are various methods for resolving ties between those who get the same final grade – probably the most common is to place first the name of the person whose application was received first. Job offers are made from the eligible list in the order the names appear on it. You will be notified of your grade and your rank as soon as all these computations have been made. This will be done as rapidly as possible.

People who are found to meet the requirements in the announcement are called "eligibles." Their names are put on a list of eligible candidates. An eligible's chances of getting a job depend on how high he stands on this list and how fast agencies are filling jobs from the list.

When a job is to be filled from a list of eligibles, the agency asks for the names of people on the list of eligibles for that job. When the civil service commission receives this request, it sends to the agency the names of the three people highest on this list. Or, if the job to be filled has specialized requirements, the office sends the agency the names of the top three persons who meet these requirements from the general list.

The appointing officer makes a choice from among the three people whose names were sent to him. If the selected person accepts the appointment, the names of the others are put back on the list to be considered for future openings.

That is the rule in hiring from all kinds of eligible lists, whether they are for typist, carpenter, chemist, or something else. For every vacancy, the appointing officer has his choice of any one of the top three eligibles on the list. This explains why the person whose name is on top of the list sometimes does not get an appointment when some of the persons lower on the list do. If the appointing officer chooses the second or third eligible, the No. 1 eligible does not get a job at once, but stays on the list until he is appointed or the list is terminated.

5. Note and underline key words – *all, most, fewest, least, best, worst, same, opposite,* etc.
6. Pay particular attention to negatives
7. Note unusual option, e.g., unduly long, short, complex, different or similar in content to the body of the question
8. Observe the use of "hedging" words – *probably, may, most likely,* etc.
9. Make sure that your answer is put next to the same number as the question
10. Do not second-guess unless you have good reason to believe the second answer is definitely more correct
11. Cross out original answer if you decide another answer is more accurate; do not erase until you are ready to hand your paper in
12. Answer all questions; guess unless instructed otherwise
13. Leave time for review

b. Essay questions
1. Read each question carefully
2. Determine exactly what is wanted. Underline key words or phrases.
3. Decide on outline or paragraph answer
4. Include many different points and elements unless asked to develop any one or two points or elements
5. Show impartiality by giving pros and cons unless directed to select one side only
6. Make and write down any assumptions you find necessary to answer the questions
7. Watch your English, grammar, punctuation and choice of words
8. Time your answers; don't crowd material

8) Answering the essay question

Most essay questions can be answered by framing the specific response around several key words or ideas. Here are a few such key words or ideas:

M's: manpower, materials, methods, money, management
P's: purpose, program, policy, plan, procedure, practice, problems, pitfalls, personnel, public relations

a. Six basic steps in handling problems:
1. Preliminary plan and background development
2. Collect information, data and facts
3. Analyze and interpret information, data and facts
4. Analyze and develop solutions as well as make recommendations
5. Prepare report and sell recommendations
6. Install recommendations and follow up effectiveness

b. Pitfalls to avoid
1. *Taking things for granted* – A statement of the situation does not necessarily imply that each of the elements is necessarily true; for example, a complaint may be invalid and biased so that all that can be taken for granted is that a complaint has been registered

3) If the examination is of the objective or multiple-choice type – that is, each question will also give a series of possible answers: A, B, C or D, and you are called upon to select the best answer and write the letter next to that answer on your answer paper – it is advisable to start answering each question in turn. There may be anywhere from 50 to 100 such questions in the three or four hours allotted and you can see how much time would be taken if you read through all the questions before beginning to answer any. Furthermore, if you come across a question or group of questions which you know would be difficult to answer, it would undoubtedly affect your handling of all the other questions.

4) If the examination is of the essay type and contains but a few questions, it is a moot point as to whether you should read all the questions before starting to answer any one. Of course, if you are given a choice – say five out of seven and the like – then it is essential to read all the questions so you can eliminate the two that are most difficult. If, however, you are asked to answer all the questions, there may be danger in trying to answer the easiest one first because you may find that you will spend too much time on it. The best technique is to answer the first question, then proceed to the second, etc.

5) Time your answers. Before the exam begins, write down the time it started, then add the time allowed for the examination and write down the time it must be completed, then divide the time available somewhat as follows:
   - If 3-1/2 hours are allowed, that would be 210 minutes. If you have 80 objective-type questions, that would be an average of 2-1/2 minutes per question. Allow yourself no more than 2 minutes per question, or a total of 160 minutes, which will permit about 50 minutes to review.
   - If for the time allotment of 210 minutes there are 7 essay questions to answer, that would average about 30 minutes a question. Give yourself only 25 minutes per question so that you have about 35 minutes to review.

6) The most important instruction is to *read each question* and make sure you know what is wanted. The second most important instruction is to *time yourself properly* so that you answer every question. The third most important instruction is to *answer every question*. Guess if you have to but include something for each question. Remember that you will receive no credit for a blank and will probably receive some credit if you write something in answer to an essay question. If you guess a letter – say "B" for a multiple-choice question – you may have guessed right. If you leave a blank as an answer to a multiple-choice question, the examiners may respect your feelings but it will not add a point to your score. Some exams may penalize you for wrong answers, so in such cases *only*, you may not want to guess unless you have some basis for your answer.

7) Suggestions
   a. Objective-type questions
      1. Examine the question booklet for proper sequence of pages and questions
      2. Read all instructions carefully
      3. Skip any question which seems too difficult; return to it after all other questions have been answered
      4. Apportion your time properly; do not spend too much time on any single question or group of questions

5) Do not linger over difficult questions

If you come across a difficult question, mark it with a paper clip (useful to have along) and come back to it when you have been through the booklet. One caution if you do this – be sure to skip a number on your answer sheet as well. Check often to be sure that you have not lost your place and that you are marking in the row numbered the same as the question you are answering.

6) Read the questions

Be sure you know what the question asks! Many capable people are unsuccessful because they failed to *read* the questions correctly.

7) Answer all questions

Unless you have been instructed that a penalty will be deducted for incorrect answers, it is better to guess than to omit a question.

8) Speed tests

It is often better NOT to guess on speed tests. It has been found that on timed tests people are tempted to spend the last few seconds before time is called in marking answers at random – without even reading them – in the hope of picking up a few extra points. To discourage this practice, the instructions may warn you that your score will be "corrected" for guessing. That is, a penalty will be applied. The incorrect answers will be deducted from the correct ones, or some other penalty formula will be used.

9) Review your answers

If you finish before time is called, go back to the questions you guessed or omitted to give them further thought. Review other answers if you have time.

10) Return your test materials

If you are ready to leave before others have finished or time is called, take ALL your materials to the monitor and leave quietly. Never take any test material with you. The monitor can discover whose papers are not complete, and taking a test booklet may be grounds for disqualification.

VIII. EXAMINATION TECHNIQUES

1) Read the general instructions carefully. These are usually printed on the first page of the exam booklet. As a rule, these instructions refer to the timing of the examination; the fact that you should not start work until the signal and must stop work at a signal, etc. If there are any *special* instructions, such as a choice of questions to be answered, make sure that you note this instruction carefully.

2) When you are ready to start work on the examination, that is as soon as the signal has been given, read the instructions to each question booklet, underline any key words or phrases, such as *least, best, outline, describe* and the like. In this way you will tend to answer as requested rather than discover on reviewing your paper that you *listed without describing*, that you selected the *worst* choice rather than the *best* choice, etc.

- Leave excess paraphernalia at home – Shopping bags and odd bundles will get in your way. You need bring only the items mentioned in the official notice you received; usually everything you need is provided. Do not bring reference books to the exam. They will only confuse those last minutes and be taken away from you when in the test room.
- Arrive somewhat ahead of time – If because of transportation schedules you must get there very early, bring a newspaper or magazine to take your mind off yourself while waiting.
- Locate the examination room – When you have found the proper room, you will be directed to the seat or part of the room where you will sit. Sometimes you are given a sheet of instructions to read while you are waiting. Do not fill out any forms until you are told to do so; just read them and be prepared.
- Relax and prepare to listen to the instructions
- If you have any physical problem that may keep you from doing your best, be sure to tell the test administrator. If you are sick or in poor health, you really cannot do your best on the exam. You can come back and take the test some other time.

VII. AT THE TEST

The day of the test is here and you have the test booklet in your hand. The temptation to get going is very strong. Caution! There is more to success than knowing the right answers. You must know how to identify your papers and understand variations in the type of short-answer question used in this particular examination. Follow these suggestions for maximum results from your efforts:

1) Cooperate with the monitor

The test administrator has a duty to create a situation in which you can be as much at ease as possible. He will give instructions, tell you when to begin, check to see that you are marking your answer sheet correctly, and so on. He is not there to guard you, although he will see that your competitors do not take unfair advantage. He wants to help you do your best.

2) Listen to all instructions

Don't jump the gun! Wait until you understand all directions. In most civil service tests you get more time than you need to answer the questions. So don't be in a hurry. Read each word of instructions until you clearly understand the meaning. Study the examples, listen to all announcements and follow directions. Ask questions if you do not understand what to do.

3) Identify your papers

Civil service exams are usually identified by number only. You will be assigned a number; you must not put your name on your test papers. Be sure to copy your number correctly. Since more than one exam may be given, copy your exact examination title.

4) Plan your time

Unless you are told that a test is a "speed" or "rate of work" test, speed itself is usually not important. Time enough to answer all the questions will be provided, but this does not mean that you have all day. An overall time limit has been set. Divide the total time (in minutes) by the number of questions to determine the approximate time you have for each question.

Since the answer sheet will be dropped in a slot in the scoring machine, be careful not to bend the corners or get the paper crumpled.

The answer sheet normally has five vertical columns of numbers, with 30 numbers to a column. These numbers correspond to the question numbers in your test booklet. After each number, going across the page are four or five pairs of dotted lines. These short dotted lines have small letters or numbers above them. The first two pairs may also have a "T" or "F" above the letters. This indicates that the first two pairs only are to be used if the questions are of the true-false type. If the questions are multiple choice, disregard the "T" and "F" and pay attention only to the small letters or numbers.

Answer your questions in the manner of the sample that follows:

32. The largest city in the United States is
    A. Washington, D.C.
    B. New York City
    C. Chicago
    D. Detroit
    E. San Francisco

1) Choose the answer you think is best. (New York City is the largest, so "B" is correct.)
2) Find the row of dotted lines numbered the same as the question you are answering. (Find row number 32)
3) Find the pair of dotted lines corresponding to the answer. (Find the pair of lines under the mark "B.")
4) Make a solid black mark between the dotted lines.

VI. BEFORE THE TEST

Common sense will help you find procedures to follow to get ready for an examination. Too many of us, however, overlook these sensible measures. Indeed, nervousness and fatigue have been found to be the most serious reasons why applicants fail to do their best on civil service tests. Here is a list of reminders:

- Begin your preparation early – Don't wait until the last minute to go scurrying around for books and materials or to find out what the position is all about.
- Prepare continuously – An hour a night for a week is better than an all-night cram session. This has been definitely established. What is more, a night a week for a month will return better dividends than crowding your study into a shorter period of time.
- Locate the place of the exam – You have been sent a notice telling you when and where to report for the examination. If the location is in a different town or otherwise unfamiliar to you, it would be well to inquire the best route and learn something about the building.
- Relax the night before the test – Allow your mind to rest. Do not study at all that night. Plan some mild recreation or diversion; then go to bed early and get a good night's sleep.
- Get up early enough to make a leisurely trip to the place for the test – This way unforeseen events, traffic snarls, unfamiliar buildings, etc. will not upset you.
- Dress comfortably – A written test is not a fashion show. You will be known by number and not by name, so wear something comfortable.

- It can be in the form of a problem – again you select the best answer.

Here is an example of a multiple-choice question with a discussion which should give you some clues as to the method for choosing the right answer:

When an employee has a complaint about his assignment, the action which will *best* help him overcome his difficulty is to
    A. discuss his difficulty with his coworkers
    B. take the problem to the head of the organization
    C. take the problem to the person who gave him the assignment
    D. say nothing to anyone about his complaint

In answering this question, you should study each of the choices to find which is best. Consider choice "A" – Certainly an employee may discuss his complaint with fellow employees, but no change or improvement can result, and the complaint remains unresolved. Choice "B" is a poor choice since the head of the organization probably does not know what assignment you have been given, and taking your problem to him is known as "going over the head" of the supervisor. The supervisor, or person who made the assignment, is the person who can clarify it or correct any injustice. Choice "C" is, therefore, correct. To say nothing, as in choice "D," is unwise. Supervisors have and interest in knowing the problems employees are facing, and the employee is seeking a solution to his problem.

2) True/False Questions

The "true/false" or "right/wrong" form of question is sometimes used. Here a complete statement is given. Your job is to decide whether the statement is right or wrong.

SAMPLE: A roaming cell-phone call to a nearby city costs less than a non-roaming call to a distant city.

This statement is wrong, or false, since roaming calls are more expensive.

This is not a complete list of all possible question forms, although most of the others are variations of these common types. You will always get complete directions for answering questions. Be sure you understand *how* to mark your answers – ask questions until you do.

V. RECORDING YOUR ANSWERS

Computer terminals are used more and more today for many different kinds of exams.
For an examination with very few applicants, you may be told to record your answers in the test booklet itself. Separate answer sheets are much more common. If this separate answer sheet is to be scored by machine – and this is often the case – it is highly important that you mark your answers correctly in order to get credit.

An electronic scoring machine is often used in civil service offices because of the speed with which papers can be scored. Machine-scored answer sheets must be marked with a pencil, which will be given to you. This pencil has a high graphite content which responds to the electronic scoring machine. As a matter of fact, stray dots may register as answers, so do not let your pencil rest on the answer sheet while you are pondering the correct answer. Also, if your pencil lead breaks or is otherwise defective, ask for another.

3) Numerical ability

Number skills can be tested by the familiar arithmetic problem, by checking paired lists of numbers to see which are alike and which are different, or by interpreting charts and graphs. In the latter test, a graph may be printed in the test booklet which you are asked to use as the basis for answering questions.

4) Observation

A popular test for law-enforcement positions is the observation test. A picture is shown to you for several minutes, then taken away. Questions about the picture test your ability to observe both details and larger elements.

5) Following directions

In many positions in the public service, the employee must be able to carry out written instructions dependably and accurately. You may be given a chart with several columns, each column listing a variety of information. The questions require you to carry out directions involving the information given in the chart.

6) Skills and aptitudes

Performance tests effectively measure some manual skills and aptitudes. When the skill is one in which you are trained, such as typing or shorthand, you can practice. These tests are often very much like those given in business school or high school courses. For many of the other skills and aptitudes, however, no short-time preparation can be made. Skills and abilities natural to you or that you have developed throughout your lifetime are being tested.

Many of the general questions just described provide all the data needed to answer the questions and ask you to use your reasoning ability to find the answers. Your best preparation for these tests, as well as for tests of facts and ideas, is to be at your physical and mental best. You, no doubt, have your own methods of getting into an exam-taking mood and keeping "in shape." The next section lists some ideas on this subject.

IV. KINDS OF QUESTIONS

Only rarely is the "essay" question, which you answer in narrative form, used in civil service tests. Civil service tests are usually of the short-answer type. Full instructions for answering these questions will be given to you at the examination. But in case this is your first experience with short-answer questions and separate answer sheets, here is what you need to know:

1) Multiple-choice Questions

Most popular of the short-answer questions is the "multiple choice" or "best answer" question. It can be used, for example, to test for factual knowledge, ability to solve problems or judgment in meeting situations found at work.

A multiple-choice question is normally one of three types—

- It can begin with an incomplete statement followed by several possible endings. You are to find the one ending which *best* completes the statement, although some of the others may not be entirely wrong.
- It can also be a complete statement in the form of a question which is answered by choosing one of the statements listed.

check the description of duties. Will you be working under very close supervision, or will you have responsibility for independent decisions in this work?

4) Choose appropriate study materials

Now that you know the subjects to be examined and the relative amount of each subject to be covered, you can choose suitable study materials. For beginning level jobs, or even advanced ones, if you have a pronounced weakness in some aspect of your training, read a modern, standard textbook in that field. Be sure it is up to date and has general coverage. Such books are normally available at your library, and the librarian will be glad to help you locate one. For entry-level positions, questions of appropriate difficulty are chosen – neither highly advanced questions, nor those too simple. Such questions require careful thought but not advanced training.

If the position for which you are applying is technical or advanced, you will read more advanced, specialized material. If you are already familiar with the basic principles of your field, elementary textbooks would waste your time. Concentrate on advanced textbooks and technical periodicals. Think through the concepts and review difficult problems in your field.

These are all general sources. You can get more ideas on your own initiative, following these leads. For example, training manuals and publications of the government agency which employs workers in your field can be useful, particularly for technical and professional positions. A letter or visit to the government department involved may result in more specific study suggestions, and certainly will provide you with a more definite idea of the exact nature of the position you are seeking.

III. KINDS OF TESTS

Tests are used for purposes other than measuring knowledge and ability to perform specified duties. For some positions, it is equally important to test ability to make adjustments to new situations or to profit from training. In others, basic mental abilities not dependent on information are essential. Questions which test these things may not appear as pertinent to the duties of the position as those which test for knowledge and information. Yet they are often highly important parts of a fair examination. For very general questions, it is almost impossible to help you direct your study efforts. What we can do is to point out some of the more common of these general abilities needed in public service positions and describe some typical questions.

1) General information

Broad, general information has been found useful for predicting job success in some kinds of work. This is tested in a variety of ways, from vocabulary lists to questions about current events. Basic background in some field of work, such as sociology or economics, may be sampled in a group of questions. Often these are principles which have become familiar to most persons through exposure rather than through formal training. It is difficult to advise you how to study for these questions; being alert to the world around you is our best suggestion.

2) Verbal ability

An example of an ability needed in many positions is verbal or language ability. Verbal ability is, in brief, the ability to use and understand words. Vocabulary and grammar tests are typical measures of this ability. Reading comprehension or paragraph interpretation questions are common in many kinds of civil service tests. You are given a paragraph of written material and asked to find its central meaning.

II. HOW TO PASS THE WRITTEN TEST

A. NATURE OF THE EXAMINATION

To prepare intelligently for civil service examinations, you should know how they differ from school examinations you have taken. In school you were assigned certain definite pages to read or subjects to cover. The examination questions were quite detailed and usually emphasized memory. Civil service exams, on the other hand, try to discover your present ability to perform the duties of a position, plus your potentiality to learn these duties. In other words, a civil service exam attempts to predict how successful you will be. Questions cover such a broad area that they cannot be as minute and detailed as school exam questions.

In the public service similar kinds of work, or positions, are grouped together in one "class." This process is known as *position-classification*. All the positions in a class are paid according to the salary range for that class. One class title covers all of these positions, and they are all tested by the same examination.

B. FOUR BASIC STEPS

1) Study the announcement

How, then, can you know what subjects to study? Our best answer is: "Learn as much as possible about the class of positions for which you've applied." The exam will test the knowledge, skills and abilities needed to do the work.

Your most valuable source of information about the position you want is the official exam announcement. This announcement lists the training and experience qualifications. Check these standards and apply only if you come reasonably close to meeting them.

The brief description of the position in the examination announcement offers some clues to the subjects which will be tested. Think about the job itself. Review the duties in your mind. Can you perform them, or are there some in which you are rusty? Fill in the blank spots in your preparation.

Many jurisdictions preview the written test in the exam announcement by including a section called "Knowledge and Abilities Required," "Scope of the Examination," or some similar heading. Here you will find out specifically what fields will be tested.

2) Review your own background

Once you learn in general what the position is all about, and what you need to know to do the work, ask yourself which subjects you already know fairly well and which need improvement. You may wonder whether to concentrate on improving your strong areas or on building some background in your fields of weakness. When the announcement has specified "some knowledge" or "considerable knowledge," or has used adjectives like "beginning principles of…" or "advanced … methods," you can get a clue as to the number and difficulty of questions to be asked in any given field. More questions, and hence broader coverage, would be included for those subjects which are more important in the work. Now weigh your strengths and weaknesses against the job requirements and prepare accordingly.

3) Determine the level of the position

Another way to tell how intensively you should prepare is to understand the level of the job for which you are applying. Is it the entering level? In other words, is this the position in which beginners in a field of work are hired? Or is it an intermediate or advanced level? Sometimes this is indicated by such words as "Junior" or "Senior" in the class title. Other jurisdictions use Roman numerals to designate the level – Clerk I, Clerk II, for example. The word "Supervisor" sometimes appears in the title. If the level is not indicated by the title,

HOW TO TAKE A TEST

I. YOU MUST PASS AN EXAMINATION

A. *WHAT EVERY CANDIDATE SHOULD KNOW*

Examination applicants often ask us for help in preparing for the written test. What can I study in advance? What kinds of questions will be asked? How will the test be given? How will the papers be graded?

As an applicant for a civil service examination, you may be wondering about some of these things. Our purpose here is to suggest effective methods of advance study and to describe civil service examinations.

Your chances for success on this examination can be increased if you know how to prepare. Those "pre-examination jitters" can be reduced if you know what to expect. You can even experience an adventure in good citizenship if you know why civil service exams are given.

B. *WHY ARE CIVIL SERVICE EXAMINATIONS GIVEN?*

Civil service examinations are important to you in two ways. As a citizen, you want public jobs filled by employees who know how to do their work. As a job seeker, you want a fair chance to compete for that job on an equal footing with other candidates. The best-known means of accomplishing this two-fold goal is the competitive examination.

Exams are widely publicized throughout the nation. They may be administered for jobs in federal, state, city, municipal, town or village governments or agencies.

Any citizen may apply, with some limitations, such as the age or residence of applicants. Your experience and education may be reviewed to see whether you meet the requirements for the particular examination. When these requirements exist, they are reasonable and applied consistently to all applicants. Thus, a competitive examination may cause you some uneasiness now, but it is your privilege and safeguard.

C. *HOW ARE CIVIL SERVICE EXAMS DEVELOPED?*

Examinations are carefully written by trained technicians who are specialists in the field known as "psychological measurement," in consultation with recognized authorities in the field of work that the test will cover. These experts recommend the subject matter areas or skills to be tested; only those knowledges or skills important to your success on the job are included. The most reliable books and source materials available are used as references. Together, the experts and technicians judge the difficulty level of the questions.

Test technicians know how to phrase questions so that the problem is clearly stated. Their ethics do not permit "trick" or "catch" questions. Questions may have been tried out on sample groups, or subjected to statistical analysis, to determine their usefulness.

Written tests are often used in combination with performance tests, ratings of training and experience, and oral interviews. All of these measures combine to form the best-known means of finding the right person for the right job.

SHERIFF

DUTIES
Has responsibility for the serving of legal processes and the transporting and guarding of prisoners in court. Performs related work as required, including normal police duties and functions such as patrolling, arresting perpetrators and testifying in court.

SCOPE OF THE WRITTEN TEST
The written test will be designed to test for knowledge, skills, and/or abilities in such areas as:
1. Exercising good judgment in the police field;
2. Memory for facts and information;
3. Understanding and interpreting written material including legal passages;
4. Preparing written material; and
5. Arithmetic computations.

14. Police Officer Wendell is preparing an accident report for a 6-car accident that occurred at the intersection of Bath Avenue and Bay Parkway. The report will consist of the following five sentences:
   I. A 2016 Volkswagen Beetle, traveling east on Bath Avenue, swerved to the left to avoid the Impala, and struck a 2014 Ford station wagon which was traveling west on Bath Avenue.
   II. The Seville then mounted the curb on the northeast corner of Bath Avenue and Bay Parkway and struck a light pole.
   III. A 2013 Buick Lesabre, traveling northbound on Bay Parkway directly behind the Impala, struck the Impala, pushing it into the intersection of Bath Avenue and Bay Parkway.
   IV. A 2015 Chevy Impala, traveling northbound on Bay Parkway, had stopped for a red light at Bath Avenue.
   V. A 2017 Toyota, traveling westbound on Bath Avenue, swerved to the right to avoid hitting the Ford station wagon, and struck a 2017 Cadillac Seville double-parked near the corner.
   The MOST logical order for the above sentences to appear in the report is
   A. IV, III, V, II, I   B. III, IV, V, II, I   C. IV, III, I, V, II   D. III, IV, V, I, II

15. The following five sentences are part of an Activity Log entry Police Officer Rogers made regarding an explosion:
   I. I quickly treated the pedestrian for the injury.
   II. The explosion caused a glass window in an office building to shatter.
   III. After the pedestrian was treated, a call was placed to the precinct requesting additional police officers to evacuate the area.
   IV. After all the glass settled to the ground, I saw a pedestrian who was bleeding from the arm.
   V. While on foot patrol near 5th Avenue and 53rd Street, I heard a loud explosion.
   The MOST logical order for the above sentences to appear in the report is
   A. II, V, IV, I, III   B. V, II, IV, III, I   C. V, II, I, IV, III   D. V, II, IV, I, III

16. Police Officer David is completing a report regarding illegal activity near the entrance to Madison Square Garden during a recent rock concert. The report will obtain the following five sentences:
   I. As I came closer to the man, he placed what appeared to be tickets in his pocket and began to walk away.
   II. After the man stopped, I questioned him about *scalping* tickets.
   III. While on assignment near the Madison Square Garden entrance, I observed a man apparently selling tickets.
   IV. I stopped the man by stating that I was a police officer.
   V. The man was then given a summons, and he left the area.
   The MOST logical order for the above sentences to appear in the report is
   A. I, III, IV, II, V   B. III, I, IV, V, II   C. III, IV, I, II, V   D. III, I, IV, II, V

11. Police Officer Capalbo is preparing a report of a bank robbery. The report will contain the following five statements made by a witness:
    I. Initialing, all I could see were two men, dressed in maintenance uniforms, sitting in the area reserved for bank officers.
    II. I was passing the bank at 8 P.M. and noticed that all the lights were out, except in the rear section.
    III. Then I noticed two other men in the bank, coming from the direction of the vault, carrying a large metal box.
    IV. At this point, I decided to call the police.
    V. I knocked on the window to get the attention of the men in the maintenance uniforms, and they chased the two men carrying the box down a flight of steps.

    The MOST logical order for the above sentences to appear in the report is
    A. IV, I, II, V, III   B. I, III, II, V, IV   C. II, I, III, V, IV   D. II, III, I, V, IV

12. Police Officer Roberts is preparing a crime report concerning an assault and a stolen car. The report will contain the following five sentences:
    I. Upon leaving the store to return to his car, Winters noticed that a male unknown to him was sitting in his car.
    II. The man then re-entered Winters' car and drove away, fleeing north on 2nd Avenue.
    III. Mr. Winters stated that he parked his car in front of 235 East 25th Street and left the engine running while he went into the butcher shop at that location.
    IV. Mr. Robert Gering, a witness, stated that the male is known in the neighborhood as Bobby Rae and is believed to reside at 323 East 114th Street.
    V. When Winters approached the car and ordered the man to get out, the man got out of the auto and struck Winters with his fists, knocking him to the ground.

    The MOST logical order for the above sentences to appear in the report is
    A. III, II, V, I, IV   B. III, I, V, II, IV   C. I, IV, V, II, III   D. III, II, I, V, IV

13. Police Officer Robinson is preparing a crime report concerning the robbery of Mr. Edwards' store. The report will consist of the following five sentences:
    I. When the last customer left the store, the two men drew revolvers and ordered Mr. Edwards to give them all the money in the cash register.
    II. The men proceeded to the back of the store as if they were going to do some shopping.
    III. Janet Morley, a neighborhood resident, later reported that she saw the men enter a green Ford station wagon and flee northbound on Albany Avenue.
    IV. Edwards complied after which the gunmen ran from the store.
    V. Mr. Edwards states that he was stocking merchandise behind the store counter when two white males entered the store.

    The MOST logical order for the above sentences to appear in the report is
    A. V, II, III, I, IV   B. V, II, I, IV, III   C. II, I, V, IV, III   D. III, V, II, I, IV

V. I ordered the man to drop his gun, and he released the woman and was taken into custody.

The MOST logical order for the above sentences to appear in the report is
A. I, III, II, IV, V   B. IV, III, II, I, V   C. III, II, I, IV, V   D. V, I, II, III, IV

8. Police Officer Byrnes is preparing a crime report concerning a robbery. The report will consist of the following five sentences:
   I. Mr. White, following the man's instructions, opened the car's hood, at which time the man got out of the auto, drew a revolver, and ordered White to give him all the money in his pockets.
   II. Investigation has determined there were no witnesses to this incident.
   III. The man asked White to check the oil and fill the tank.
   IV. Mr. White, a gas attendant, states that he was working alone at the gas station when a black male pulled up to the gas pump in a white Mercury.
   V. White was then bound and gagged by the male and locked in the gas station's rest room.

   The MOST logical order for the above sentences to appear in the report is
   A. IV, I, III, II, V   B. III, I, II, V, IV   C. IV, III, I, V, II   D. I, III, IV, II, V

9. Police Officer Gale is preparing a report of a crime committed against Mr. Weston. The report will consist of the following five sentences:
   I. The man, who had a gun, told Mr. Weston not to scream for help and ordered him back into the apartment.
   II. With Mr. Weston disposed of in this fashion, the man proceeded to ransack the apartment.
   III. Opening the door to see who was there, Mr. Weston was confronted by a tall white male wearing a dark blue jacket and white pants.
   IV. Mr. Weston was at home alone in his living room when the doorbell rang.
   V. Once inside, the man bound and gagged Mr. Weston and locked him in the bathroom.

   The MOST logical order for the above sentences to appear in the report is
   A. III, V, II, I, IV   B. IV, III, I, V, II   C. III, V, IV, II, I   D. IV, III, V, I, II

10. A police officer is completing a report of a robbery, which will contain the following five sentences:
    I. Two police officers were about to enter the Red Rose Coffee Shop on 47th Street and 8th Avenue.
    II. They then noticed a male running up the street carrying a brown paper bag.
    III. They heard a woman standing outside the Broadway Boutique yelling that her store had just been robbed by a young man, and she was pointing up the street.
    IV. They caught up with him and made an arrest.
    V. The police officers pursued the male, who ran past them on 8th Avenue.

    The MOST logical order for the above sentences to appear in the report is
    A. I, III, II, V, IV   B. III, I, II, V, IV   C. IV, V, I, II, III   D. I, V, IV, III, II

4. Police Officer Hatfield is reviewing his Activity Log entry prior to completing a report. The entry contains the following five sentences:
   I. When I arrived at Zand's Jewelry Store, I noticed that the door was slightly open.
   II. I told the burglar I was a police officer and that he should stand still or he would be shot.
   III. As I entered the store, I saw a man wearing a ski mask attempting to open the safe in the back of the store.
   IV. On December 16, 2020, at 1:38 A.M., I was informed that a burglary was in progress at Zand's Jewelry Store on East 59th Street.
   V. The burglar quickly pulled a knife from his pocket when he saw me.
   The MOST logical order for the above sentences to appear in the report is
     A. IV, I, III, V, II   B. I, IV, III, V, II   C. IV, III, II, V, I   D. I, III, IV, V, II

4._____

5. Police Officer Lorenz is completing a report of a murder. The report will contain the following five statements made by a witness:
   I. I was awakened by the sound of a gunshot coming from the apartment next door and I decided to check.
   II. I entered the apartment and looked into the kitchen and the bathroom.
   III. I found Mr. Hubbard's body slumped in the bathtub.
   IV. The door to the apartment was open, but I didn't see anyone.
   V. He had been shot in the head.
   The MOST logical order for the above sentences to appear in the report is
     A. I, III, II, IV, V   B. I, IV, II, III, V   C. IV, II, I, III, V   D. III, I, II, IV, V

5._____

6. Police Officer Baldwin is preparing an accident report which will include the following five sentences:
   I. The old man lay on the ground for a few minutes, but was not physically hurt.
   II. Charlie Watson, a construction worker, was repairing some brick work at the top of a building at 54th Street and Madison Avenue.
   III. Steven Green, his partner, warned him that this could be dangerous, but Watson ignored him.
   IV. A few minutes later, one of the bricks thrown by Watson smashed to the ground in front of an old man, who fainted out of fright.
   V. Mr. Watson began throwing some of the bricks over the side of the building.
   The MOST logical order for the above sentences to appear in the report is
     A. II, V, III, IV, I   B. I, IV, II, V, III   C. III, II, IV, V, I   D. II, III, I, IV, V

6._____

7. Police Officer Porter is completing an Incident Report concerning her rescue of a woman being held hostage by a former boyfriend. Her report will contain the following five sentences:
   I. I saw a man holding .25 caliber gun to a woman's head, but he did not see me.
   II. I then broke a window and gained access to the house.
   III. As I approached the house on foot, a gunshot rang out and I heard a woman scream.
   IV. A decoy van brought me as close as possible to the house where the woman was being held hostage.

7._____

127

COPYRIGHT NOTICE

This book is SOLELY intended for, is sold ONLY to, and its use is RESTRICTED to individual, bona fide applicants or candidates who qualify by virtue of having seriously filed applications for appropriate license, certificate, professional and/or promotional advancement, higher school matriculation, scholarship, or other legitimate requirements of education and/or governmental authorities.

This book is NOT intended for use, class instruction, tutoring, training, duplication, copying, reprinting, excerption, or adaptation, etc., by:

1) Other publishers
2) Proprietors and/or Instructors of "Coaching" and/or Preparatory Courses
3) Personnel and/or Training Divisions of commercial, industrial, and governmental organizations
4) Schools, colleges, or universities and/or their departments and staffs, including teachers and other personnel
5) Testing Agencies or Bureaus
6) Study groups which seek by the purchase of a single volume to copy and/or duplicate and/or adapt this material for use by the group as a whole without having purchased individual volumes for each of the members of the group
7) Et al.

Such persons would be in violation of appropriate Federal and State statutes.

PROVISION OF LICENSING AGREEMENTS – Recognized educational, commercial, industrial, and governmental institutions and organizations, and others legitimately engaged in educational pursuits, including training, testing, and measurement activities, may address request for a licensing agreement to the copyright owners, who will determine whether, and under what conditions, including fees and charges, the materials in this book may be used them. In other words, a licensing facility exists for the legitimate use of the material in this book on other than an individual basis. However, it is asseverated and affirmed here that the material in this book CANNOT be used without the receipt of the express permission of such a licensing agreement from the Publishers. Inquiries re licensing should be addressed to the company, attention rights and permissions department.

All rights reserved, including the right of reproduction in whole or in part, in any form or by any means, electronic or mechanical, including photocopying, recording, or by any information storage and retrieval system, without permission in writing from the Publisher.

Copyright © 2024 by
National Learning Corporation

212 Michael Drive, Syosset, NY 11791
(516) 921-8888 • www.passbooks.com
E-mail: info@passbooks.com

PUBLISHED IN THE UNITED STATES OF AMERICA

PASSBOOK® SERIES

THE *PASSBOOK® SERIES* has been created to prepare applicants and candidates for the ultimate academic battlefield – the examination room.

At some time in our lives, each and every one of us may be required to take an examination – for validation, matriculation, admission, qualification, registration, certification, or licensure.

Based on the assumption that every applicant or candidate has met the basic formal educational standards, has taken the required number of courses, and read the necessary texts, the *PASSBOOK® SERIES* furnishes the one special preparation which may assure passing with confidence, instead of failing with insecurity. Examination questions – together with answers – are furnished as the basic vehicle for study so that the mysteries of the examination and its compounding difficulties may be eliminated or diminished by a sure method.

This book is meant to help you pass your examination provided that you qualify and are serious in your objective.

The entire field is reviewed through the huge store of content information which is succinctly presented through a provocative and challenging approach – the question-and-answer method.

A climate of success is established by furnishing the correct answers at the end of each test.

You soon learn to recognize types of questions, forms of questions, and patterns of questioning. You may even begin to anticipate expected outcomes.

You perceive that many questions are repeated or adapted so that you can gain acute insights, which may enable you to score many sure points.

You learn how to confront new questions, or types of questions, and to attack them confidently and work out the correct answers.

You note objectives and emphases, and recognize pitfalls and dangers, so that you may make positive educational adjustments.

Moreover, you are kept fully informed in relation to new concepts, methods, practices, and directions in the field.

You discover that you are actually taking the examination all the time: you are preparing for the examination by "taking" an examination, not by reading extraneous and/or supererogatory textbooks.

In short, this PASSBOOK®, used directedly, should be an important factor in helping you to pass your test.

17. Police Officer Sampson is preparing a report containing a dispute in a bar. The report will contain the following five sentences:
    I. John Evans, the bartender, ordered the two men out of the bar.
    II. Two men dressed in dungarees entered the C and D Bar at 5:30 P.M.
    III. The two men refused to leave and began to beat up Evans.
    IV. A customer in the bar saw me on patrol and yelled to me to come separate the three men.
    V. The two men became very drunk and loud within a short time.
    The MOST logical order for the above sentences to appear in the report is
    A. II, I, V, III, IV   B. II, III, IV, V, I   C. III, I, II, V, IV   D. II, V, I, III, IV

17.____

18. A police officer is completing a report concerning the response to a crime in progress. The report will include the following five sentences:
    I. The officers saw two armed men run out of the liquor store and into a waiting car.
    II. Police Officers Lunty and Duren received the call and responded to the liquor store.
    III. The robbers gave up without a struggle.
    IV. Lunty and Duren blocked the getaway car with their patrol car.
    V. A call came into the precinct concerning a robbery in progress at Jane's Liquor Store.
    The MOST logical order for the above sentence to appear in the report is
    A. V, II, I, IV, III   B. II, V, I, III, IV   C. V, I, IV, II, III   D. I, V, II, III, IV

18.____

19. Police Officers Jenkins is preparing a Crime Report which will consist of the following five sentences:
    I. After making inquirie in the vicinity, Smith found out that his next door neighbor, Viola Jones, had seen two local teenagers, Michael Heinz and Vincent Gaynor, smash his car's windshields with a crowbar.
    II. Jones told Smith that the teenagers live at 8700 19th Avenue.
    III. Mr. Smith heard a loud crash at approximately 11:00 P.M., looked out of his apartment window, and saw two white males running away from his car.
    IV. Smith then reported the incident to the precinct, and Heinz and Gaynor were arrested at the address given.
    V. Leaving his apartment to investigate further, Smith discovered that his car's front and rear windshields had been smashed.
    The MOST logical order for the above sentences to appear in the report is
    A. III, IV, V, I, II   B. III, V, I, II, IV   C. III, I, V, II, IV   D. V, III, I, II, IV

19.____

20. Sergeant Nancy Winston is reviewing a Gun Control Report which will contain the following five sentences:
    I. The man fell to the floor when hit in the chest with three bullets from 22 caliber gun.
    II. Merriam's 22 caliber gun was seized, and he was given a summons for not having a pistol permit.
    III. Christopher Merriam, the owner of A-Z Grocery, shot a man who attempted to rob him.
    IV. Police Officer Franks responded and asked Merriam for his pistol permit, which he could not produce.

20.____

V. Merriam phoned the police to report he had just shot a man who had attempted to rob him.

The MOST logical order for the above sentences to appear in the report is
A. III, I, V, IV, II   B. I, III, V, IV, II   C. III, I, V, II, IV   D. I, III, II, V, IV

21. Detective John Manville is completing a report for his superior regarding the murder of an unknown male who was shot in Central Park. The report will contain the following five sentences:
    I. Police Officers Langston and Cavers responded to the scene.
    II. I received the assignment to investigate the murder in Central Park from Detective Sergeant Rogers.
    III. Langston notified the Detective Bureau after questioning Jason.
    IV. An unknown male, apparently murdered, was discovered in Central Park by Howard Jason, a park employee, who immediately called the police.
    V. Langston and Cavers questioned Jason.

    The MOST logical order for the above sentences to appear in the report is
    A. I, IV, V, III, II   B. IV, I, V, II, III   C. IV, I, V, III, II   D. IV, V, I, III, II

21.____

22. A police officer is completing a report concerning the arrest of a juvenile. The report will contain the following five sentences:
    I. Sanders then telephoned Jay's parents from the precinct to inform them of their son's arrest.
    II. The store owner resisted, and Jay then shot him and ran from the store.
    III. Jay was transported directly to the precinct by Officer Sanders.
    IV. James Jay, a juvenile, walked into a candy store and announced a hold-up.
    V. Police Officer Sanders, while on patrol, arrested Jay a block from the candy store.

    The MOST logical order for the above sentences to appear in the report is
    A. IV, V, II, I, III   B. IV, II, V, III, I   C. II, IV, V, III, I   D. V, IV, II, I, III

22.____

23. Police Officer Olsen prepared a crime report for a robbery which contained the following five sentences:
    I. Mr. Gordon was approached by this individual who then produced a gun and demanded the money from the cash register.
    II. The man then fled from the scene on foot, southbound on 5th Avenue.
    III. Mr. Gordon was working at the deli counter when a white male, 5'6", 150-160 lbs., wearing a green jacket and blue pants, entered the store.
    IV. Mr. Gordon complied with the man's demands and handed him the daily receipts.
    V. Further investigation has determined there are no other witnesses to this robbery.

    The MOST logical order for the above sentences to appear in the report is
    A. I, III, IV, V, II   B. I, IV, II, III, V   C. III, IV, I, V, II   D. III, I, IV, II, V

23.____

24. Police Officer Bryant responded to 285 E. 31st Street to take a crime report of a burglary of Mr. Bond's home. The report will contain a brief description of the incident, consisting of the following five sentences:
   I. When Mr. Bond attempted to stop the burglar by grabbing him, he was pushed to the floor.
   II. The burglar had apparently gained access to the home by forcing open the 2nd floor bedroom window facing the fire escape.
   III. Mr. Bond sustained a head injury in the scuffle, and the burglar exited the home through the front door.
   IV. Finding nothing in the dresser, the burglar proceeded downstairs to the first floor, where he was confronted by Mr. Bond who was reading in the dining room.
   V. Once inside, he searched the drawers of the bedroom dresser.
   The MOST logical order for the above sentences to appear in the report is
      A. V, IV, I, II, III   B. II, V, IV, I, III   C. II, IV, V, III, I   D. III, II, I, V, IV

25. Police Officer Derringer responded to a call of a rape-homicide case in his patrol area and was ordered to prepare an incident report, which will contain the following five sentences:
   I. He pushed Miss Scott to the ground and forcibly raped her.
   II. Mary Scott was approached from behind by a white male, 5'7", 150-160 lbs. wearing dark pants and a white jacket.
   III. As Robinson approached the male, he ordered him to stop.
   IV. Screaming for help, Miss Scott alerted one John Robinson, a local grocer, who chased her assailant as he fled the scene.
   V. The male turned and fired two shots at Robinson, who fell to the ground mortally wounded.
   The MOST logical order for the above sentences to appear in the report is
      A. IV, III, I, II, V   B. II, IV, III, V, I   C. II, IV, I, V, III   D. II, I, IV, III, V

KEY (CORRECT ANSWERS)

1. B
2. C
3. C
4. A
5. B

6. A
7. B
8. C
9. B
10. A

11. C
12. B
13. B
14. C
15. D

16. D
17. D
18. A
19. B
20. A

21. C
22. B
23. D
24. B
25. D

PREPARING WRITTEN MATERIAL
EXAMINATION SECTION
TEST 1

DIRECTIONS: Each question or incomplete statement is followed by several suggested answers or completions. Select the one that BEST answers the question or completes the statement. *PRINT THE LETTER OF THE CORRECT ANSWER IN THE SPACE AT THE RIGHT.*

1. The one of the following sentences which is LEAST acceptable from the viewpoint of correct usage is:
    A. The police thought the fugitive to be him.
    B. The criminals set a trap for whoever would fall into it.
    C. It is ten years ago since the fugitive fled from the city.
    D. The lecturer argued that criminals are usually cowards.
    E. The police removed four bucketfuls of earth from the scene of the crime.

1.____

2. The one of the following sentences which is LEAST acceptable from the viewpoint of correct usage is:
    A. The patrolman scrutinized the report with great care.
    B. Approaching the victim of the assault, two bruises were noticed by the patrolman.
    C. As soon as I had broken down the door, I stepped into the room.
    D. I observed the accused loitering near the building, which was closed at the time.
    E. The storekeeper complained that his neighbor was guilty of violating a local ordinance.

2.____

3. The one of the following sentences which is LEAST acceptable from the viewpoint of correct usage is:
    A. I realized immediately that he intended to assault the woman, so I disarmed him.
    B. It was apparent that Mr. Smith's explanation contained many inconsistencies.
    C. Despite the slippery condition of the street, he managed to stop the vehicle before injuring the child.
    D. Not a single one of them wish, despite the damage to property, to make a formal complaint.
    E. The body was found lying on the floor.

3.____

4. The one of the following sentences which contains NO error in usage is:
    A. After the robbers left, the proprietor stood tied in his chair for about two hours before help arrived.
    B. In the cellar I found the watchman's hat and coat.
    C. The persons living in adjacent apartments stated that they had heard no unusual noises.

4.____

D. Neither a knife or any firearms were found in the room.
E. Walking down the street, the shouting of the crowd indicated that something was wrong.

5. The one of the following sentences which contains NO error in usage is:
   A. The policeman lay a firm hand on the suspect's shoulder.
   B. It is true that neither strength nor agility are the most important requirement for a good patrolman.
   C. Good citizens constantly strive to do more than merely comply the restraints imposed by society.
   D. No decision was made as to whom the prize should be awarded.
   E. Twenty years is considered a severe sentence for a felony.

6. Which of the following sentences is NOT expressed in standard English usage?
   A. The victim reached a pay-phone booth and manages to call police headquarters.
   B. By the time the call was received, the assailant had left the scene.
   C. The victim has been a respected member of the community for the past eleven years.
   D. Although the lighting was bad and the shadows were deep, the storekeeper caught sight of the attacker.
   E. Additional street lights have since been installed, and the patrols have been strengthened.

7. Which of the following sentences is NOT expressed in standard English usage?
   A. The judge upheld the attorney's right to question the witness about the missing glove.
   B. To be absolutely fair to all parties is the jury's chief responsibility.
   C. Having finished the report, a loud noise in the next room startled the sergeant.
   D. The witness obviously enjoyed having played a part in the proceedings.
   E. The sergeant planned to assign the case to whoever arrived first.

8. In which of the following sentences is a word misused?
   A. As a matter of principle, the captain insisted that the suspect's partner be brought for questioning.
   B. The principle suspect had been detained at the station house for most of the day.
   C. The principal in the crime had no previous criminal record, but his closest associate had been convicted of felonies on two occasions.
   D. The interest payments had been made promptly, but the firm had been drawing upon the principal for these payments.
   E. The accused insisted that his high school principal would furnish him a character reference.

9. Which of the following statements is ambiguous? 9._____
   A. Mr. Sullivan explained why Mr. Johnson had been dismissed from his job.
   B. The storekeeper told the patrolman he had made a mistake.
   C. After waiting three hours, the patients in the doctor's office were sent home.
   D. The janitor's duties were to maintain the building in good shape and to answer tenants' complaints.
   E. The speed limit should, in my opinion, be raised to sixty miles an hour on that stretch of road.

10. In which of the following is the punctuation or capitalization faulty? 10._____
    A. The accident occurred at an intersection in the Kew Gardens section of Queens, near the bus stop.
    B. The sedan, not the convertible, was struck in the side.
    C. Before any of the patrolmen had left the police car received an important message from headquarters.
    D. The dog that had been stolen was returned to his master, John Dempsey, who lived in East Village.
    E. The letter had been sent to 12 Hillside Terrace, Rutland, Vermont 05702.

Questions 11-25.

DIRECTIONS: Questions 11 through 25 are to be answered in accordance with correct English usage; that is, standard English rather than nonstandard or substandard. Nonstandard and substandard English includes words or expressions usually classified as slang, dialect, illiterate, etc., which are not generally accepted as correct in current written communication. Standard English also requires clarity, proper punctuation and capitalization and appropriate use of words. Write the letter of the sentence NOT expressed in standard English usage in the space at the right.

11. A. There were three witnesses to the accident. 11._____
     B. At least three witnesses were found to testify for the plaintiff.
     C. Three of the witnesses who took the stand was uncertain about the defendant's competence to drive.
     D. Only three witnesses came forward to testify for the plaintiff.
     E. The three witnesses to the accident were pedestrians.

12. A. The driver had obviously drunk too many martinis before leaving for home. 12._____
     B. The boy who drowned had swum in these same waters many times before.
     C. The petty thief had stolen a bicycle from a private driveway before he was apprehended.
     D. The detectives had brung in the heroin shipment they intercepted.
     E. The passengers had never ridden in a converted bus before.

13. A. Between you and me, the new platoon plan sounds like a good idea.
    B. Money from an aunt's estate was left to his wife and he.
    C. He and I were assigned to the same patrol for the first time in two months.
    D. Either you or he should check the front door of that store.
    E. The captain himself was not sure of the witness's reliability.

    13.____

14. A. The alarm had scarcely begun to ring when the explosion occurred.
    B. Before the firemen arrived at the scene, the second story had been destroyed.
    C. Because of the dense smoke and heat, the firemen could hardly approach the now-blazing structure.
    D. According to the patrolman's report, there wasn't nobody in the store when the explosion occurred.
    E. The sergeant's suggestion was not at all unsound, but no one agreed with him.

    14.____

15. A. The driver and the passenger they were both found to be intoxicated.
    B. The driver and the passenger talked slowly and not too clearly.
    C. Neither the driver nor his passengers were able to give a coherent account of the accident.
    D. In a corner of the room sat the passenger, quietly dozing.
    E. the driver finally told a strange and unbelievable story, which the passenger contradicted.

    15.____

16. A. Under the circumstances I decided not to continue my examination of the premises.
    B. There are many difficulties now not comparable with those existing in 1960.
    C. Friends of the accused were heard to announce that the witness had better been away on the day of the trial.
    D. The two criminals escaped in the confusion that followed the explosion.
    E. The aged man was struck by the considerateness of the patrolman's offer.

    16.____

17. A. An assemblage of miscellaneous weapons lay on the table.
    B. Ample opportunities were given to the defendant to obtain counsel.
    C. The speaker often alluded to his past experience with youthful offenders in the armed forces.
    D. The sudden appearance of the truck aroused my suspicions.
    E. Her studying had a good affect on her grades in high school.

    17.____

18. A. He sat down in the theater and began to watch the movie.
    B. The girl had ridden horses since she was four years old.
    C. Application was made on behalf of the prosecutor to cite the witness for contempt.
    D. The bank robber, with his two accomplices, were caught in the act.
    E. His story is simply not credible.

    18.____

19. A. The angry boy said that he did not like those kind of friends.
     B. The merchant's financial condition was so precarious that he felt he must avail himself of any offer of assistance.
     C. He is apt to promise more than he can perform.
     D. Looking at the messy kitchen, the housewife felt like crying.
     E. A clerk was left in charge of the stolen property.

20. A. His wounds were aggravated by prolonged exposure to sub-freezing temperatures.
     B. The prosecutor remarked that the witness was not averse to changing his story each time he was interviewed.
     C. The crime pattern indicated that the burglars were adapt in the handling of explosives.
     D. His rigid adherence to a fixed plan brought him into renewed conflict with his subordinates.
     E. He had anticipated that the sentence would be delivered by noon.

21. A. The whole arraignment procedure is badly in need of revision.
     B. After his glasses were broken in the fight, he would of gone to the optometrist if he could.
     C. Neither Tom nor Jack brought his lunch to work.
     D. He stood aside until the quarrel was over.
     E. A statement in the psychiatrist's report disclosed that the probationer vowed to have his revenge.

22. A. His fiery and intemperate speech to the striking employees fatally affected any chance of a future reconciliation.
     B. The wording of the statute has been variously construed.
     C. The defendant's attorney, speaking in the courtroom, called the official a demagogue who contempuously disregarded the judge's orders.
     D. The baseball game is likely to be the most exciting one this year.
     E. The mother divided the cookies among her two children.

23. A. There was only a bed and a dresser in the dingy room.
     B. John was one of the few students that have protested the new rule.
     C. It cannot be argued that the child's testimony is negligible; it is, on the contrary, of the greatest importance.
     D. The basic criterion for clearance was so general that officials resolved any doubts in favor of dismissal.
     E. Having just returned from a long vacation, the officer found the city unbearably hot.

24. A. The librarian ought to give more help to small children.
     B. The small boy was criticized by the teacher because he often wrote careless.
     C. It was generally doubted whether the women would permit the use of her apartment for intelligence operations.
     D. The probationer acts differently every time the officer visits him.
     E. Each of the newly appointed officers has 12 years of service.

25. A. The North is the most industrialized region in the country.
    B. L. Patrick Gray 3d, the bureau's acting director, stated that, while "rehabilitation is fine" for some convicted criminals, "it is a useless gesture for those who resist every such effort."
    C. Careless driving, faulty mechanism, narrow or badly kept roads all play their part in causing accidents.
    D. The childrens' books were left in the bus.
    E. It was a matter of internal security; consequently, he felt no inclination to rescind his previous order.

25.____

KEY (CORRECT ANSWERS)

1.	C		11.	C
2.	B		12.	D
3.	D		13.	B
4.	C		14.	D
5.	E		15.	A
6.	A		16.	C
7.	C		17.	E
8.	B		18.	D
9.	B		19.	A
10.	C		20.	C

21. B
22. E
23. B
24. B
25. D

TEST 2

DIRECTIONS: Each question or incomplete statement is followed by several suggested answers or completions. Select the one that BEST answers the question or completes the statement. *PRINT THE LETTER OF THE CORRECT ANSWER IN THE SPACE AT THE RIGHT.*

Questions 1-6.

DIRECTIONS: Each of Questions 1 through 6 consists of a statement which contains a word (one of those underlined) that is either incorrectly used because it is not in keeping with the meaning the quotation is evidently intended to convey, or is misspelled. There is only one INCORRECT word in each quotation. Of the four underlined words, determine if the first one should be replaced by the word lettered A, the second replaced by the word lettered B, the third replaced by the word lettered C, or the fourth replaced by the word lettered D.

1. Whether one depends on fluorescent or artificial light or both, adequate standards should be maintained by means of systematic tests.
   A. natural   B. safeguards   C. established   D. routine

2. A police officer has to be prepared to assume his knowledge as a social scientist in the community.
   A. forced   B. role   C. philosopher   D. street

3. It is practically impossible to indicate whether a sentence is too long simply by measuring its length.
   A. almost   B. tell   C. very   D. guessing

4. Strong leaders are required to organize a community for delinquency prevention and for dissemination of organized crime and drug addiction.
   A. tactics   B. important   C. control   D. meetings

5. The demonstrators who were taken to the Criminal Courts building in Manhattan (because it was large enough to accommodate them), contended that the arrests were unwarranted.
   A. demonstraters
   B. Manhatten
   C. accomodate
   D. unwarranted

6. They were guaranteed a calm atmosphere, free from harassment, which would be conducive to quiet consideration of the indictments.
   A. guarenteed
   B. atmspher
   C. harassment
   D. inditements

Questions 7-11.

DIRECTIONS: Each of Questions 7 through 11 consists of a statement containing four words in capital letters. One of these words in capital letters is not in keeping with the meaning which the statement is evidently intended to carry. The four words in capital letters in each statement are reprinted after the statement. Print the capital letter preceding the one of the four words which does MOST to spoil the true meaning of the statement in the space at the right.

7. Retirement and pension systems are essential not only to provide employees with with a means of support in the future, but also to prevent longevity and CHARITABLE considerations from UPSETTING the PROMOTIONAL opportunities RETIRED members of the career service. 7.____
   A. charitable   B. upsetting   C. promotional   D. retired

8. Within each major DIVISION in a properly set up public or private organization, provision is made so that each NECESSARY activity is CARED for and lines of authority and responsibility are clear-cut and INFINITE. 8.____
   A. division   B. necessary   C. cared   D. infinite

9. In public service, the scale of salaries paid must be INCIDENTAL to the services rendered, with due CONSIDERATION for the attraction of the desired MANPOWER and for the maintenance of a standard of living COMMENSURATE with the work to be performed. 9.____
   A. incidental   B. consideration
   C. manpower   D. commensurate

10. An understanding of the AIMS of an organization by the staff will AID greatly in increasing the DEMAND of the correspondence work of the office, and will to a large extent DETERMINE the nature of the correspondence. 10.____
    A. aims   B. aid   C. demand   D. determine

11. BECAUSE the Civil Service Commission strongly feels that the MERIT system is a key factor in the MAINTENANCE of democratic government, it has adopted as one of its major DEFENSES the progressive democratization of its own procedures in dealing with candidates for positions in the public service. 11.____
    A. Because   B. merit   C. maintenance   D. defenses

Questions 12-14.

DIRECTIONS: Questions 12 through 14 consist of one sentence each. Each sentence contains an incorrectly used word. First, decide which is the incorrectly used word. Then, from among the options given, decide which word, when substituted for the incorrectly used word, makes the meaning of the sentence clear.
EXAMPLE:
The U.S. national income exhibits a pattern of long term deflection.
   A. reflection   B. subjection   C. rejoicing   D. growth

The word *deflection* in the sentence does not convey the meaning the sentence evidently intended to convey. The word *growth* (Answer D), when substituted for the word *deflection*, makes the meaning of the sentence clear. Accordingly, the answer to the question is D.

12. The study commissioned by the joint committee fell compassionately short of the mark and would have to be redone.
    A. successfully
    B. insignificantly
    C. experimentally
    D. woefully

13. He will not idly exploit any violation of the provisions of the order.
    A. tolerate
    B. refuse
    C. construe
    D. guard

14. The defendant refused to be virile and bitterly protested service.
    A. irked
    B. feasible
    C. docile
    D. credible

Questions 15-25.

DIRECTIONS: Questions 15 through 25 consist of short paragraphs. Each paragraph contains one word which is INCORRECTLY used because it is NOT in keeping with the meaning of the paragraph. Find the word in each paragraph which is INCORRECTLY used and then select as the answer the suggested word which should be substituted for the incorrectly used word.

SAMPLE QUESTION:
In determining who is to do the work in your unit, you will have to decide just who does what from day to day. One of your lowest responsibilities is to assign work so that everybody gets a fair share and that everyone can do his part well.
    A. new
    B. old
    C. important
    D. performance

EXPLANATION:
The word which is NOT in keeping with the meaning of the paragraph is *lowest*. This is the INCORRECTLY used word. The suggested word *important* would be in keeping with the meaning of the paragraph and should be substituted for *lowest*. Therefore, the CORRECT answer is choice C.

15. If really good practice in the elimination of preventable injuries is to be achieved and held in any establishment, top management must refuse full and definite responsibility and must apply a good share of its attention to the task.
    A. accept
    B. avoidable
    C. duties
    D. problem

16. Recording the human face for identification is by no means the only service performed by the camera in the field of investigation. When the trial of any issue takes place, a word picture is sought to be distorted to the court of incidents, occurrences, or events which are in dispute.
    A. appeals
    B. description
    C. portrayed
    D. deranged

17. In the collection of physical evidence, it cannot be emphasized too strongly that a haphazard systematic search at the scene of the crime is vital. Nothing must be overlooked. Often the only leads in a case will come from the results of this search.
    A. important
    B. investigation
    C. proof
    D. thorough

18. If an investigator has reason to suspect that the witness is mentally stable, or a habitual drunkard, he should leave no stone unturned in his investigation to determine if the witness was under the influence of liquor or drugs, or was mentally unbalanced either at the time of the occurrence to which he testified or at the time of the trial.
    A. accused
    B. clue
    C. deranged
    D. question

19. The use of records is a valuable step in crime investigation and is the main reason every department should maintain accurate reports. Crimes are not committed through the use of departmental records alone but from the use of all records, of almost every type, wherever they may be found and whenever they give any incidental information regarding the criminal.
    A. accidental
    B. necessary
    C. reported
    D. solved

20. In the years since passage of the Harrison Narcotic Act of 1914, making the possession of opium amphetamines illegal in most circumstances, drug use has become a subject of considerable scientific interest and investigation. There is at present a voluminous literature on drug use of various kinds.
    A. ingestion
    B. derivatives
    C. addiction
    D. opiates

21. Of course, the fact that criminal laws are extremely patterned in definition does not mean that the majority of persons who violate them are dealt with as criminals. Quite the contrary, for a great many forbidden acts are voluntarily engaged in within situations of privacy and go unobserved and unreported.
    A. symbolic
    B. casual
    C. scientific
    D. broad-gauged

22. The most punitive way to study punishment is to focus attention on the pattern of punitive action: to study how a penalty is applied, too study what is done to or taken from an offender.
    A. characteristic
    B. degrading
    C. objective
    D. distinguished

23. The most common forms of punishment in times past have been death, physical torture, mutilation, branding, public humiliation, fines, forfeits of property, banishment, transportation, and imprisonment. Although this list is by no means differentiated, practically every form of punishment has had several variations and applications.
    A. specific
    B. simple
    C. exhaustive
    D. characteristic

24. There is another important line of inference between ordinary and professional criminals, and that is the source from which they are recruited. The professional criminal seems to be drawn from legitimate employment and, in many instances, from parallel vocations or pursuits.
    A. demarcation   B. justification   C. superiority   D. reference

24.____

25. He took the position that the success of the program was insidious on getting additional revenue.
    A. reputed   B. contingent   C. failure   D. indeterminate

25.____

KEY (CORRECT ANSWERS)

1.	A	11.	D
2.	B	12.	D
3.	B	13.	A
4.	C	14.	C
5.	D	15.	A
6.	C	16.	C
7.	D	17.	D
8.	D	18.	C
9.	A	19.	D
10.	C	20.	B

21.	D
22.	C
23.	C
24.	A
25.	B

TEST 3

DIRECTIONS: Each question or incomplete statement is followed by several suggested answers or completions. Select the one that BEST answers the question or completes the statement. *PRINT THE LETTER OF THE CORRECT ANSWER IN THE SPACE AT THE RIGHT.*

Questions 1-5.

DIRECTIONS: Questions 1 through 5 are to be answered on the basis of the following.

You are a supervising officer in an investigative unit. Earlier in the day, you directed Detectives Tom Dixon and Sal Mayo to investigate a reported assault and robbery in a liquor store within your area of jurisdiction.

Detective Dixon has submitted to you a preliminary investigative report containing the following information:

- At 1630 hours on 2/20, arrived at Joe's Liquor Store at 350 SW Avenue with Detective Mayo to investigate A & R.
- At store interviewed Rob Ladd, store manager, who stated that he and Joe Brown (store owner) had been stuck up about ten minutes prior to our arrival.
- Ladd described the robbers as male whites in their late teens or early twenties. Further stated that one of the robbers displayed what appeared to be an automatic pistol as he entered the store, and said, *Give us the money or we'll kill you.* Ladd stated that Brown then reached under the counter where he kept a loaded .38 caliber pistol. Several shots followed, and Ladd threw himself to the floor.
- The robbers fled, and Ladd didn't know if any money had been taken.
- At this point, Ladd realized that Brown was unconscious on the floor and bleeding from a head wound.
- Ambulance called by Ladd, and Brown was removed by same to General Hospital.
- Personally interviewed John White, 382 Dartmouth Place, who stated he was inside store at the time of occurrence. White states that he hid behind a wine display upon hearing someone say, *Give us the money.* He then heard shots and saw two young men run from the store to a yellow car parked at the curb. White was unable to further describe auto. States the taller of the two men drove the car away while the other sat on passenger side in front.
- Recovered three spent .38 caliber bullets from premises and delivered them to Crime Lab.
- To General Hospital at 1800 hours but unable to interview Brown, who was under sedation and suffering from shock and a laceration of the head.
- Alarm #12487 transmitted for car and occupants.
- Case Active.

Based solely on the contents of the preliminary investigation submitted by Detective Dixon, select one sentence from the following groups of sentences which is MOST accurate and is grammatically correct.

1. A. Both robbers were armed.
    B. Each of the robbers were described as a male white.
    C. Neither robber was armed.
    D. Mr. Ladd stated that one of the robbers was armed.

2. A. Mr. Brown fired three shots from his revolver.
    B. Mr. Brown was shot in the head by one of the robbers.
    C. Mr. Brown suffered a gunshot wound of the head during the course of the robbery.
    D. Mr. Brown was taken to General Hospital by ambulance.

3. A. Shots were fired after one of the robbers said, *Give us the money or we'll kill you.*
    B. After one of the robbers demanded the money from Mr. Brown, he fired a shot.
    C. The preliminary investigation indicated that although Mr. Brown did not have a license for the gun, he was justified in using deadly physical force.
    D. Mr. Brown was interviewed at General Hospital.

4. A. Each of the witnesses were customers in the store at the time of occurrence.
    B. Neither of the witnesses interviewed was the owner of the liquor store.
    C. Neither of the witnesses interviewed were the owner of the store.
    D. Neither of the witnesses was employed by Mr. Brown.

5. A. Mr. Brown arrived at General Hospital at about 5:00 P.M.
    B. Neither of the robbers was injured during the robbery.
    C. The robbery occurred at 3:30 P.M. on February 10.
    D. One of the witnesses called the ambulance.

Questions 6-10.

DIRECTIONS: Each of Questions 6 through 10 consists of information given in outline form and four sentences labeled A, B, C, and D. For each question, choose the one sentence which CORRECTLY expresses the information given in outline form and which also displays PROPER English usage.

6. Client's Name: Joanna Jones
    Number of Children: 3
    Client's Income: None
    Client's Marital Status: Single

    A. Joanna Jones is an unmarried client with three children who have no income.
    B. Joanna Jones, who is single and has no income, a client she has three children.
    C. Joanna Jones, whose three children are clients, is single and has no income.
    D. Joanna Jones, who has three children, is an unmarried client with no income.

7. Client's Name: Bertha Smith
   Number of Children: 2
   Client's Rent: $1050 per month
   Number of Rooms: 4

   A. Bertha Smith, a client, pays $1050 per month for her four rooms with two children.
   B. Client Bertha Smith has two children and pays $1050 per month for four rooms.
   C. Client Bertha Smith is paying $1050 per month for two children with four rooms.
   D. For four rooms and two children client Bertha Smith pays $1050 per month.

   7.____

8. Name of Employee: Cynthia Dawes
   Number of Cases Assigned: 9
   Date Cases were Assigned: 12/16
   Number of Assigned Cases Completed: 8

   A. On December 16, employee Cynthia Dawes was assigned nine cases; she has completed eight of these cases.
   B. Cynthia Dawes, employee on December 16, assigned nine cases, completed eight.
   C. Being employed on December 16, Cynthia Dawes completed eight of nine assigned cases.
   D. Employee Cynthia Dawes, she was assigned nine cases and completed eight, on December 16.

   8.____

9. Place of Audit: Broadway Center
   Names of Auditors: Paul Cahn, Raymond Perez
   Date of Audit: 11/20
   Number of Cases Audited: 41

   A. On November 20, at the Broadway Center 41 cases was audited by auditors Paul Cahn and Raymond Perez.
   B. Auditors Raymond Perez and Paul Cahn has audited 41 cases at the Broadway Center on November 20.
   C. At the Broadway Center, on November 20, auditors Paul Cahn and Raymond Perez audited 41 cases.
   D. Auditors Paul Cahn and Raymond Perez at the Broadway Center, on November 20, is auditing 41 cases.

   9.____

10. Name of Client: Barbra Levine
    Client's Monthly Income: $2100
    Client's Monthly Expenses: $4520

    A. Barbra Levine is a client, her monthly income is $2100 and her monthly expenses is $4520.
    B. Barbra Levine's monthly income is $2100 and she is a client, with whose monthly expenses are $4520.

    10.____

C. Barbra Levine is a client whose monthly income is $2100 and whose monthly expenses are $4520.
D. Barbra Levine, a client, is with a monthly income which is $2100 and monthly expenses which are $4520.

Questions 11-13.

DIRECTIONS: Questions 11 through 13 involve several statements of fact presented in a very simple way. These statements of fact are followed by 4 choices which attempt to incorporate all of the facts into one logical statement which is properly constructed and grammatically correct.

11. I. Mr. Brown was sweeping the sidewalk in front of his house. 11.____
    II. He was sweeping it because it was dirty.
    III. He swept the refuse into the street.
    IV. Police Officer gave him a ticket.

    Which one of the following BEST presents the information given above?
    A. Because his sidewalk was dirty, Mr. Brown received a ticket from Officer Green when he swept the refuse into the street.
    B. Police Officer Green gave Mr. Brown a ticket because his sidewalk was dirty and he swept the refuse into the street.
    C. Police Officer Green gave Mr. Brown a ticket for sweeping refuse into the street because his sidewalk was dirty.
    D. Mr. Brown, who was sweeping refuse from his dirty sidewalk into the street, was given a ticket by Police Officer Green.

12. I. Sergeant Smith radioed for help. 12.____
    II. The sergeant did so because the crowd was getting larger.
    III. It was 10:00 A.M. when he made his call.
    IV. Sergeant Smith was not in uniform at the time of occurrence.

    Which one of the following BEST presents the information given above?
    A. Sergeant Smith, although not on duty at the time, radioed for help at 10 o'clock because the crowd was getting uglier.
    B. Although not in uniform, Sergeant Smith called for help at 10:00 A.M. because the crowd was getting uglier.
    C. Sergeant Smith radioed for help at 10:00 A.M. because the crowd was getting larger.
    D. Although he was not in uniform, Sergeant Smith radioed for help at 10:00 A.M. because the crowd was getting larger.

13. I. The payroll office is open on Fridays. 13.____
    II. Paychecks are distributed from 9:00 A.M. to 12 Noon.
    III. The office is open on Fridays because that's the only day the payroll staff is available.
    IV. It is open for the specified hours in order to permit employees to cash checks at the bank during lunch hour.

The choice below which MOST clearly and accurately presents the above idea is:
- A. Because the payroll office is open on Fridays from 9:00 A.M. to 12 Noon, employees can cash their checks when the payroll staff is available.
- B. Because the payroll staff is only available on Fridays until noon, employees can cash their checks during their lunch hour.
- C. Because the payroll staff is available only on Fridays, the office is open from 9:00 A.M. to 12 Noon to allow employees to cash their checks.
- D. Because of payroll staff availability, the payroll office is open on Fridays. It is open from 9:00 A.M. to 12 Noon so that distributed paychecks can be cashed at the bank while employees are on their lunch hour.

Questions 14-16.

DIRECTIONS: In each of Questions 14 through 6, the four sentences are from a paragraph in a report. They are not in the right order. Which of the following arrangements is the BEST one?

14. I. An executive may answer a letter by writing his reply on the face of the letter itself instead of having a return letter typed.
    II. This procedure is efficient because it saves the executive's time, the typist's time, and saves office file space.
    III. Copying machines are used in small offices as well as large offices to save time and money in making brief replies to business letters.
    IV. A copy is made on a copy machine to go into the company files, while the original is mailed back to the sender.

   The CORRECT answer is:
   A. I, II, IV, III   B. I, IV, II, III   C. III, I, IV, II   D. III, IV, II, I

15. I. Most organizations favor one of the types but always include the others to a lesser degree.
    II. However, we can detect a definite trend toward greater use of symbolic control.
    III. We suggest that our local police agencies are today primarily utilizing material control.
    IV. Control can be classified into three types: physical, material, and symbolic.

   The CORRECT answer is:
   A. IV, II, III, I   B. II, I, IV, III   C. III, IV, II, I   D. IV, I, III, II

16. I. They can and do take advantage of ancient political and geographical boundaries, which often give them sanctuary from effective policy activity.
    II. This country is essentially a country of small police forces, each operating independently within the limits of its jurisdiction.
    III. The boundaries that define and limit police operations do not hinder the movement of criminals, of course.
    IV. The machinery of law enforcement in America is fragmented, complicated, and frequently overlapping.

The CORRECT answer is:
A. III, I, IV   B. II, IV, I, III   C. IV, II, III, I   D. IV, III, II, I

17. Examine the following sentence, and then choose from below the words which should be inserted in the blank spaces to produce the best sentence.
The unit has exceeded _____ goals and the employees are satisfied with _____ accomplishments.
A. their, it's   B. it's; it's   C. its, there   D. its, their

18. Examine the following sentence, and then choose from below the words which should be inserted in the blank spaces to produce the best sentence.
Research indicates that employees who _____ no opportunity for close social relationships often find their work unsatisfying, and this _____ of satisfaction often reflects itself in low production.
A. have; lack   B. have; excess   C. has; lack   D. has; excess

19. Words in a sentence must be arranged properly to make sure that the intended meaning of the sentence is clear.
The sentence below that does NOT make sense because a clause has been separated from the word on which its meaning depends is:
A. To be a good writer, clarity is necessary.
B. To be a good writer, you must write clearly.
C. You must write clearly to be a good writer.
D. Clarity is necessary to good writing.

Questions 20-21.

DIRECTIONS: Each of Questions 20 and 21 consists of a statement which contains a word (one of those underlined) that is either incorrectly used because it is not in keeping with the meaning the quotation is evidently intended to convey, or is misspelled. There is only one INCORRECT word in each quotation. Of the four underlined words, determine if the first one should be replaced by the word lettered A, the second one replaced by the word lettered B, the third one replaced by the word lettered C, or the fourth one replaced by the word lettered D.

20. The alleged killer was occasionally permitted to excercise in the corridor.
A. alledged   B. ocasionally   C. permited   D. exercise

21. Defense counsel stated, in affect, that their conduct was permissible under the First Amendment.
A. council   B. effect   C. there   D. permissable

Question 22.

DIRECTIONS: Question 22 consists of one sentence. This sentence contains an incorrectly used word. First, decide which is the incorrectly used word. Then, from among the options given, decide which word, when substituted for the incorrectly used word, makes the meaning of the sentence clear.

22. As today's violence has no single cause, so its causes have no single scheme. 22.____
    A. deference   B. cure   C. flaw   D. relevance

23. In the sentence, *A man in a light-grey suit waited thirty-five minutes in the ante-room for the all-important document*, the word IMPROPERLY hyphenated is 23.____
    A. light-grey
    B. thirty-five
    C. ante-room
    D. all-important

24. In the sentence, *The candidate wants to file his application for preference before it is too late*, the word *before* is used as a(n) 24.____
    A. preposition
    B. subordinating conjunction
    C. pronoun
    D. adverb

25. In the sentence, *The perpetrators ran from the scene*, the word *from* is a 25.____
    A. preposition   B. pronoun   C. verb   D. conjunction

KEY (CORRECT ANSWERS)

1.	D	11.	D
2.	D	12.	D
3.	A	13.	D
4.	B	14.	C
5.	D	15.	D
6.	D	16.	C
7.	B	17.	D
8.	A	18.	A
9.	C	19.	A
10.	C	20.	D

21. B
22. B
23. C
24. B
25. A

INTERPRETING STATISTICAL DATA GRAPHS, CHARTS AND TABLES
EXAMINATION SECTION
TEST 1

DIRECTIONS: Each question or incomplete statement is followed by several suggested answers or completions. Select the one that BEST answers the question or completes the statement. *PRINT THE LETTER OF THE CORRECT ANSWER IN THE SPACE AT THE RIGHT.*

Questions 1-4.

DIRECTIONS: Questions 1 through 4 are to be answered SOLELY on the basis of the following table.

STOLEN AND RECOVERED PROPERTY IN COMMUNITY X
2018-2019

Type of Property	Value of Property Stolen		Value of Property Recovered	
	2018	2019	2018	2019
Currency	$264,925	$204,534	$10,579	$13,527
Jewelry	165,317	106,885	20,913	20,756
Furs	10,007	24,028	105	1,620
Clothing	62,265	49,219	4,322 7	15,821
Automobiles	740,719	606,062	36,701	558,442
Miscellaneous	356,901	351,064	62,077	103,117
TOTAL	$1,600,134	$1,341,792	$834,697	$713,283

1. Of the following types of property, the one which shows the HIGHEST ratio of *value of property recovered* to *value of property stolen* is

   A. clothing for 2018
   B. currency for 2018
   C. jewelry for 2019
   D. miscellaneous for 2019

1.____

2. Of the types of property which show a decrease from 2018 to 2019 in the value of property stolen, the one which shows the GREATEST percentage decrease in the value of the property recovered is

   A. automobiles
   B. currency
   C. furs
   D. jewelry

2.____

3. According to the above table, the total value of currency and jewelry stolen in 2019, as compared to 2018, decreased APPROXIMATELY by

   A. 3%   B. 20%   C. 28%   D. 38%

3.____

4. According to the above table, the TOTAL value of all types of property recovered was 4._____
   A. a slightly lower percentage of the value of property stolen for 2018 than for 2019
   B. less for the year 2018 than the value of any individual type of property recovered for the year 2019
   C. approximately 60% of the value of all property stolen in 2018 and approximately 70% in 2019
   D. greater for the year 2019 than the value of any individual type of property recovered for the year 2018

KEY (CORRECT ANSWERS)

1. D
2. A
3. C
4. A

TEST 2

Questions 1-6.

DIRECTIONS: Questions 1 through 6 are to be answered SOLELY on the basis of the information supplied in the chart below.

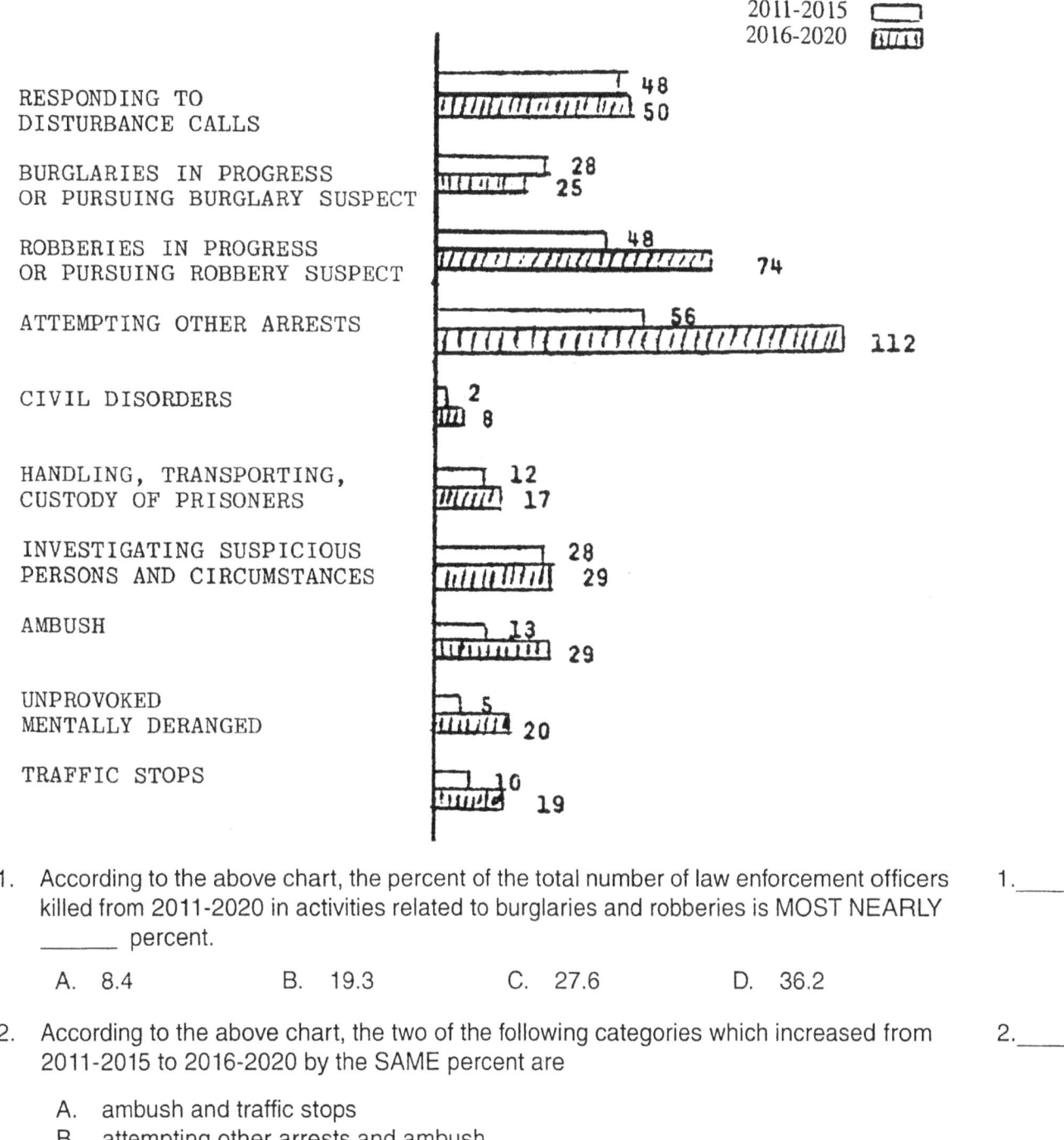

LAW ENFORCEMENT OFFICERS KILLED
(By Type of Activity)
2011-2020

2011-2015
2016-2020

RESPONDING TO DISTURBANCE CALLS: 48 / 50
BURGLARIES IN PROGRESS OR PURSUING BURGLARY SUSPECT: 28 / 25
ROBBERIES IN PROGRESS OR PURSUING ROBBERY SUSPECT: 48 / 74
ATTEMPTING OTHER ARRESTS: 56 / 112
CIVIL DISORDERS: 2 / 8
HANDLING, TRANSPORTING, CUSTODY OF PRISONERS: 12 / 17
INVESTIGATING SUSPICIOUS PERSONS AND CIRCUMSTANCES: 28 / 29
AMBUSH: 13 / 29
UNPROVOKED MENTALLY DERANGED: 5 / 20
TRAFFIC STOPS: 10 / 19

1. According to the above chart, the percent of the total number of law enforcement officers killed from 2011-2020 in activities related to burglaries and robberies is MOST NEARLY _____ percent.

    A. 8.4   B. 19.3   C. 27.6   D. 36.2

2. According to the above chart, the two of the following categories which increased from 2011-2015 to 2016-2020 by the SAME percent are

    A. ambush and traffic stops
    B. attempting other arrests and ambush

155

C. civil disorders and unprovoked mentally deranged
D. response to disturbance calls and investigating suspicious persons and circumstances

3. According to the above chart, the percentage increase in law enforcement officers killed from the 2011-2015 period to the 2016-2020 period is MOST NEARLY _____ percent.

 A. 34 B. 53 C. 65 D. 100

4. According to the above chart, in which one of the following activities did the number of law enforcement officers killed increase by 100 percent?

 A. Ambush
 B. Attempting other arrests
 C. Robberies in progress or pursuing robbery suspect
 D. Traffic stops

5. According to the above chart, the two of the following activities during which the total number of law enforcement officers killed from 2011 to 2020 was the SAME are

 A. burglaries in progress or pursuing burglary suspect and investigating suspicious persons and circumstances
 B. handling, transporting, custody of prisoners and traffic stops
 C. investigating suspicious persons and circumstances and ambush
 D. responding to disturbance calls and robberies in progress or pursuing robbery suspect

6. According to the categories in the above chart, the one of the following statements which can be made about law enforcement officers killed from 2011 to 2015 is that

 A. the number of law enforcement officers killed during civil disorders equals one-sixth of the number killed responding to disturbance calls
 B. the number of law enforcement officers killed during robberies in progress or pursuing robbery suspect equals 25 percent of the number killed while handling or transporting prisoners
 C. the number of law enforcement officers killed during traffic stops equals one-half the number killed for unprovoked reasons or by the mentally deranged
 D. twice as many law enforcement officers were killed attempting other arrests as were killed during burglaries in progress or pursuing burglary suspect

KEY (CORRECT ANSWERS)

1. C
2. C
3. B
4. B
5. B
6. D

TEST 3

Questions 1-6.

DIRECTIONS: Questions 1 through 6 are to be answered SOLELY on the basis of the graph below.

YEARLY INCIDENCE OF MAJOR CRIMES FOR COMMUNITY Z
2017-2019

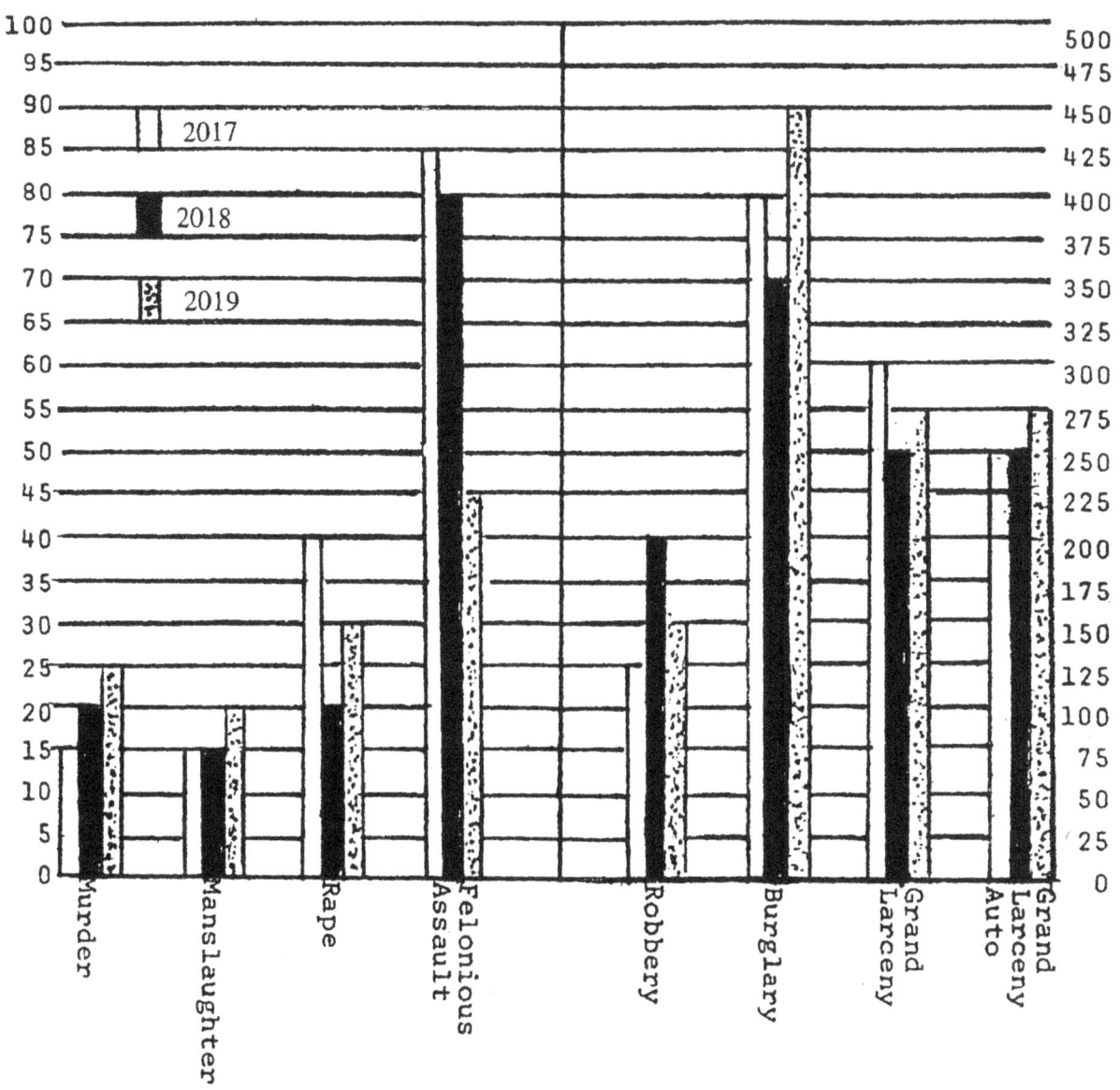

CRIMES AGAINST THE PERSON   CRIMES AGAINST PROPERTY

157

1. Of the following crimes, the one for which the 2019 figure was GREATER than the average of the previous two years was

   A. grand larceny
   B. manslaughter
   C. rape
   D. robbery

2. If the incidence of burglary in 2020 were to increase over 2019 by the same number as it increased in 2019 over 2018, then the average for this crime for the four-year period from 2017 through 2020 would be MOST NEARLY

   A. 100   B. 400   C. 415   D. 440

3. The above graph indicates that the percentage INCREASE in grand larceny auto over the previous year was

   A. greater in 2019 than in 2018
   B. greater in 2018 than in 2019
   C. greater in 2019 than in 2017
   D. the same in both 2018 and 2019

4. The one of the following which cannot be determined because there is not enough information in the above graph to do so is the

   A. percentage of Crimes Against Property for the three-year period which were committed in 2017
   B. percentage of Crimes Against the Person for the three-year period which were murders committed in 2018
   C. percentage of Major Crimes for the three-year period which were committed in the first six months of 2018
   D. major crimes which were following a pattern of continuing yearly increases for the three-year period

5. According to this graph, the ratio of Crimes Against Property to Crimes Against the Person for 2019, as compared to the ratio for 2018, is

   A. increasing
   B. decreasing
   C. about the same
   D. cannot be determined

6. Assume that it is desired to present information from the above graph to the public in a form most likely to gain their cooperation in a special police effort to reduce the incidence of grand larceny auto.
   The one of the following which is MOST likely to result in such cooperation is a public statement that

   A. in 2019, approximately .75 of an automobile was stolen every day
   B. in 2019, one automobile was stolen, on the average, about 32 hours hours
   C. the number of automobiles stolen per year will increase from year to year
   D. there were more crimes of grand larceny auto than crimes of robbery committed during the past three years

KEY (CORRECT ANSWERS)

1. B   4. C
2. D   5. A
3. B   6. B

TEST 4

Questions 1-7.

DIRECTIONS: Questions 1 through 7 are to be answered SOLELY on the basis of the information contained in the following tables and chart.

TABLE 1

Number of Murders by Region, United States: 2014 and 2015

Region	Year	
	2014	2015
Northeastern States	2,521	2,849
North Central States	3,427	3,697
Southern States	6,577	7,055
Western States	2,062	2,211

Number in each case for given year and region represents total number (100%) of murders in that region for that year.

TABLE 2

Murder by Circumstance, U.S. - 2015
(Percent distribution by category)

Region	Total	Spouse Killing spouse	Parent Killing child	Other family killings	Romantic triangle and lovers' quarrels	Other arguments	Known Felony type	Suspected felony type
Northeastern States	100.0	9.6	3.7	6.1	7.9	38.4	25.4	8.9
North Central States	100.0	11.3	3.0	8.9	5.0	39.5	22.4	9.9
Southern States	100.0	13.8	2.2	8.8	8.4	46.0	13.9	6.9
Western States	100.0	12.5	4.9	7.0	6.4	32.2	28.0	9.0

CHART 1

Murder by Type of Weapon Used, U.S. - 2015
(Percent Distribution)

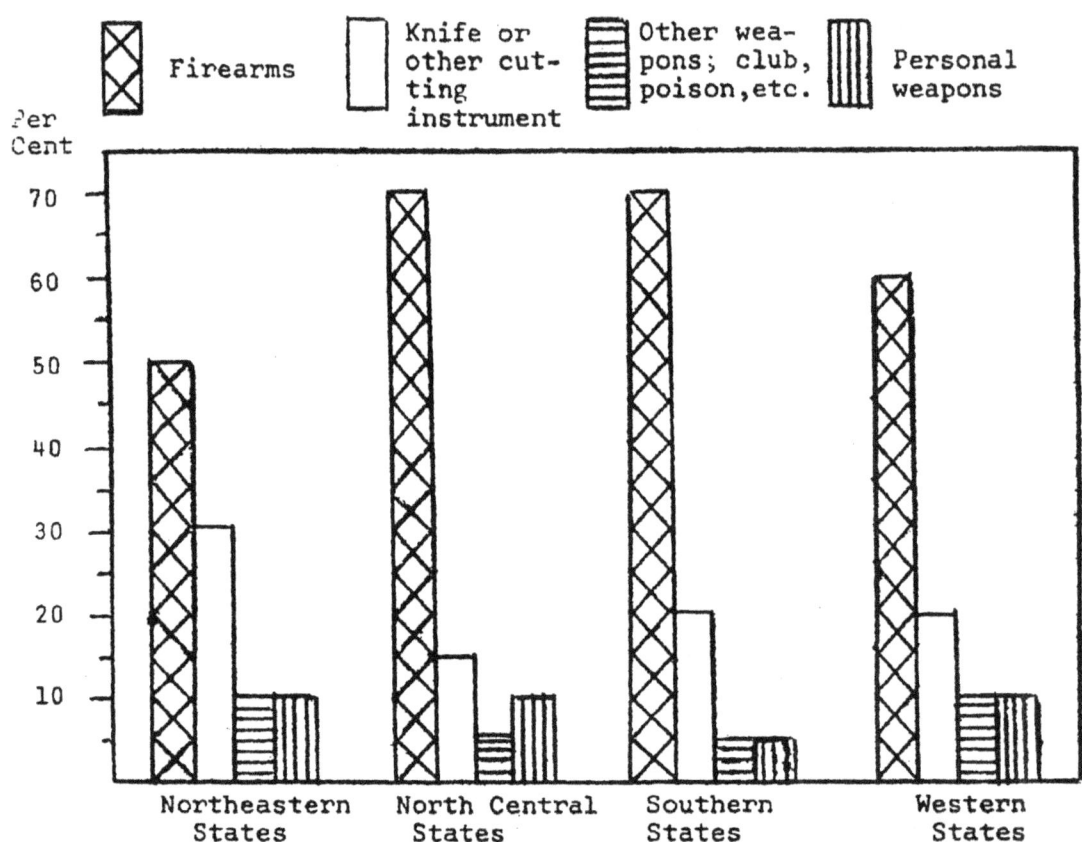

1. The number of persons murdered by firearms in the Western States in 2015 was MOST NEARLY

    A. 220   B. 445   C. 1235   D. 1325

2. In 2015, the number of murders in the category *Parent killing child* was GREATEST in the _____ States.

    A. Northeastern   B. North Central
    C. Southern   D. Western

3. The difference between the number of persons murdered with firearms and the number of persons murdered with other weapons (club, poison, etc.) in the North Central States in 2015 is MOST NEARLY

    A. 2200   B. 2400   C. 2600   D. 2800

4. In 2014, the ratio of the number of murders in the Western States to the total number of murders in the U.S. was MOST NEARLY

    A. 1 to 4   B. 1 to 5   C. 1 to 7   D. 1 to 9

5. The total number of murders in the U.S. in the category of *Romantic triangles and lovers' quarrels* in 2015 was MOST NEARLY

   A. 850   B. 950   C. 1050   D. 1150

6. Which of the following represents the GREATEST number of murders in 2015? Persons murdered by

   A. firearms in the Western States
   B. knives or other cutting instruments in the Southern States
   C. knives or other cutting instruments and persons murdered by other weapons (club, poison, etc.) in the Northeastern States
   D. knives or other cutting instruments, persons murdered by other weapons (club, poison, etc.) and persons murdered by personal weapons in the North Central States

7. From 2014 to 2015, the total number of murders increased by the GREATEST percentage in the _____ States.

   A. Northeastern   B. North Central
   C. Southern   D. Western

KEY (CORRECT ANSWERS)

1. D
2. C
3. B
4. C
5. D
6. B
7. A

TEST 5

Questions 1-5.

DIRECTIONS: Questions 1 through 5 are to be answered SOLELY on the basis of the following.

DISTRIBUTION OF CITIZENS' RESPONSES TO STATEMENTS CONCERNING SHERIFFS' ARRESTS
(Number of citizens responding = 1171)

		CATEGORIES				
		(A) Strongly Agree	(B) Agree	(C) Disagree	(D) Strongly Disagree	(E) Don't Know
I.	Sheriffs act improperly in arresting defendants, even when these persons are rude and ill-mannered	12%	37%	36%	9%	6%
II.	Sheriffs frequently use more force than necessary when making arrests	9%	19%	46%	19%	7%
III.	Any defendant who insults or physically abuses a sheriff has no complaint if he is sternly handled in return	13%	44%	32%	7%	4%

1. The total percentage of responses to Statement III OTHER THAN *Strongly Agree* and *Disagree* is

    A. 45%   B. 46%   C. 55%   D. 59%

2. The number of *Disagree* responses to Statement II is MOST NEARLY

    A. 71   B. 114   C. 539   D. 820

3. Assume that for Statement II the (B) percentage of responses were doubled and the (A) percentage increased one and a half times.
   If the (D) and (E) percentages remained the same, the (C) percentage would then MOST NEARLY be

   A. 23%   B. 26%   C. 39%   D. 52%

4. The total number of *Don't Know* responses is MOST NEARLY

   A. 17
   B. 188
   C. 200
   D. a figure which cannot be determined from the table

5. If the percentage of Disagree responses to Statement III were 35% less, the resulting percentage would MOST NEARLY be

   A. 11%   B. 14%   C. 15%   D. 21%

KEY (CORRECT ANSWERS)

1. C
2. C
3. A
4. C
5. D

TEST 6

Questions 1-3.

DIRECTIONS: Questions 1 through 3 are to be answered SOLELY on the basis of the statistical report given below.

The following is a statistical report of the activities of the bureau during the current year as compared with the previous year.

	Current Year	Previous Year
Memoranda of law prepared	68	83
Legal matters forwarded to Corporation Counsel	122	144
Letters requesting legal information	756	807
Letters requesting departmental records	139	111
Matters for publication	17	26
Court appearances of members of bureau	4,678	4,621
Conferences	94	103
Lectures at Police Academy	30	33
Reports on proposed legislation	194	255
Deciphering of codes	79	27
Expert testimony	31	16
Notices to court witnesses	55	81
Briefs prepared	22	18
Court papers prepared	258	

1. According to the report, the percentage of bills prepared and sponsored by the Legal Bureau which were passed by the State Legislature and sent to the Governor for approval was APPROXIMATELY   1.____

    A. 3.1%
    B. 2.6%
    C. .5%
    D. not capable of determination from the data given

2. According to the statistical report, the activity showing the GREATEST percentage of decrease in the current year as compared with the previous year was   2.____

    A. matters for publication
    B. reports on proposed legislation

C. notices to court witnesses
D. memoranda of law prepared

3. According to the statistical report, the activity showing the GREATEST percentage of *increase* in the current year as compared with the previous year was

    A. court appearances of members of the bureau
    B. giving expert testimony
    C. deciphering of codes
    D. letters requesting departmental records

KEY (CORRECT ANSWERS)

1. D
2. A
3. C

TEST 7

Questions 1-5.

DIRECTIONS: Questions 1 through 5 are to be answered SOLELY on the basis of the information contained in Tables I and II that appear below and on the following page.

TABLE I
NUMBER OF ARRESTS FOR VARIOUS CRIMES AND DISPOSITION

OFFENSES	TOTAL ARRESTED	INVESTIGATED AND RELEASED	HELD FOR PROSECUTION	GUILTY AS CHARGED	GUILTY OF LESSER OFFENSES	DISPOSITION OTHER THAN CONVICTION
Murder	48	10	38	12	9	17
Rape	41	10	31	8	3	20
Aggravated assault	241	106	135	36	32	67
Robbery	351	177	174	98	35	41
Burglary	890	371	519	322	88	109
Larceny	1,665	466	1,199	929	58	212
Auto theft	464	78	386	278	46	62
TOTAL	3,700	1,218	2,482	1,683	271	528

TABLE II

ARRESTS FOR LARCENY - PERCENTAGE OF SUCH ARRESTS BY AGE AND SEX

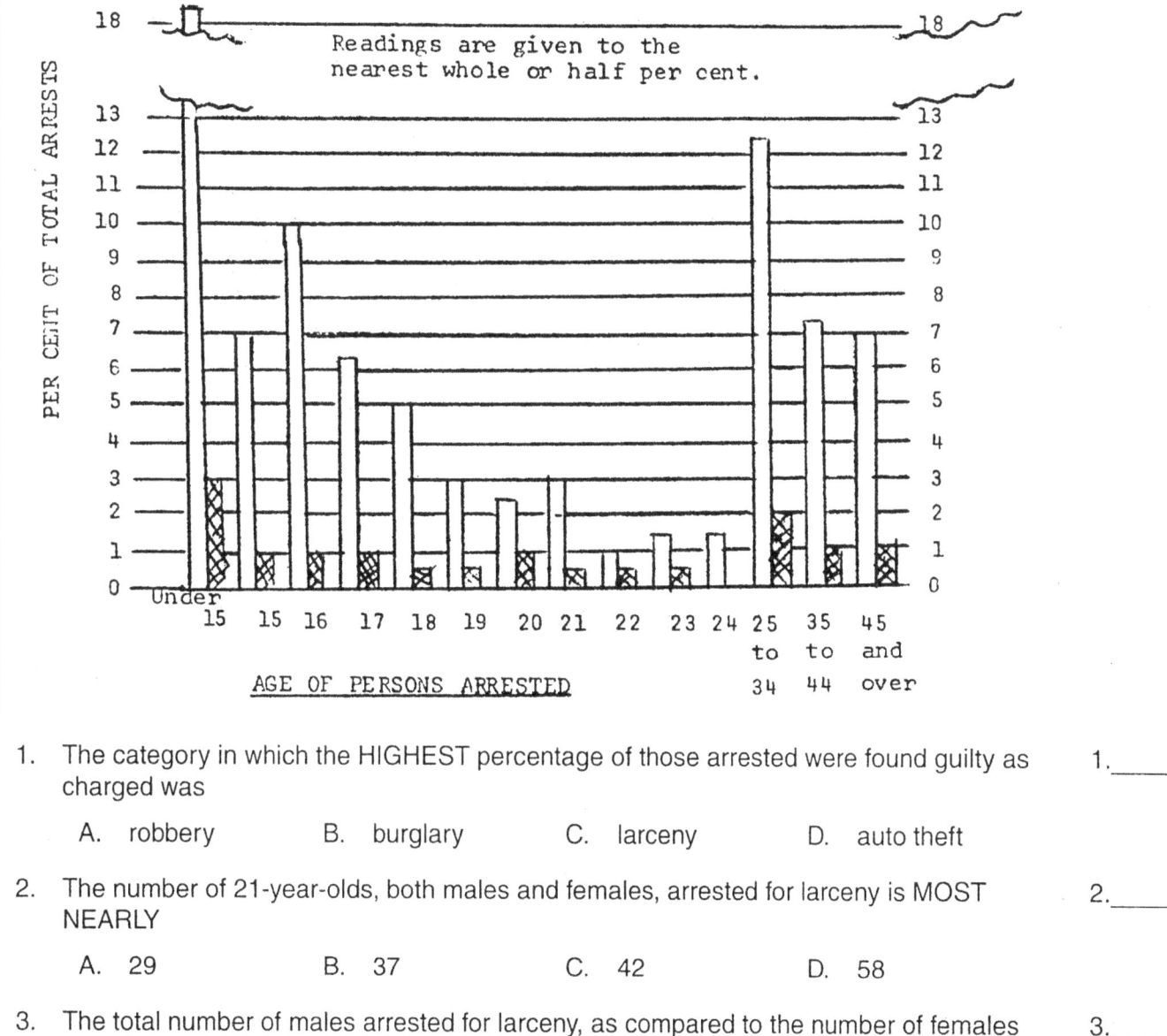

1. The category in which the HIGHEST percentage of those arrested were found guilty as charged was

    A. robbery   B. burglary   C. larceny   D. auto theft

2. The number of 21-year-olds, both males and females, arrested for larceny is MOST NEARLY

    A. 29   B. 37   C. 42   D. 58

3. The total number of males arrested for larceny, as compared to the number of females arrested for larceny, is _____ times as great.

    A. 5   B. 6   C. 8   D. 10

4. Considering only the category of larceny, the one of the following statements which is INCORRECT is:

    A. The percentage of 25-year-old males arrested cannot be determined
    B. Twice as many 16-year-old males were arrested as 18-year-old males

C. The percentage of 16-year-old males arrested was twice as high as the percentage of 18-year-old males
D. Persons 19 years of age and younger accounted for exactly half of the total arrests for larceny

5. The one of the following which is the MOST accurate statement with respect to the disposition of arrests in each category is that in

   A. no category was the number investigated and released greater than half the number arrested
   B. no category was the number investigated and released less than one-fifth of those arrested
   C. only two categories was the number found guilty of lesser offense greater than one-tenth of those arrested
   D. only one category was the number found guilty as charged less than one-fourth of those arrested

KEY (CORRECT ANSWERS)

1. D
2. D
3. B
4. D
5. C

TEST 8

Questions 1-5.

DIRECTIONS: Questions 1 through 5 are to be answered SOLELY on the basis of the table below.

VALUE OF PROPERTY STOLEN - 2017 AND 2018
LARCENY

Category	2017		2018	
	Number of Offenses	Value of Stolen Property	Number of Offense	Value of Stolen Property
Pocket-picking	20	$1,950	10	$ 950
Purse-snatching	175	5,750	20	12,500
Shoplifting	155	7,950	225	17,350
Automobile thefts	1,040	127,050	860	108,000
Thefts of auto accessories	1,135	34,950	970	24,400
Bicycle thefts	355	8,250	240	6,350
All other thefts	1,375	187,150	1,300	153,150

1. Of the total number of larcenies reported for 2017, automobile thefts accounted for MOST NEARLY

   A. 5%   B. 15%   C. 25%   D. 50%

2. The LARGEST percentage decrease in the value of the stolen property from 2017 to 2018 was in the category of

   A. pocket-picking
   B. automobile thefts
   C. thefts of automobile accessories
   D. bicycle thefts

3. In 2018, the average amount of each theft was LOWEST for the category of

   A. pocket-picking
   B. purse-snatching
   C. shoplifting
   D. thefts of auto accessories

4. The category which had the LARGEST numerical reduction in the number of offenses from 2017 to 2018 was

   A. pocket-picking
   B. automobile thefts
   C. thefts of auto accessories
   D. bicycle thefts

5. When the categories are ranked for each year according to the number of offenses committed in each category (largest number to rank first), the number of categories which will have the SAME rank in 2017 as in 2018 is

   A. 3   B. 4   C. 5   D. 6

5._____

KEY (CORRECT ANSWERS)

1. C
2. A
3. D
4. B
5. C

TEST 9

Questions 1-5.

DIRECTIONS: Questions 1 through 5 are to be answered SOLELY on the basis of the graphs below.

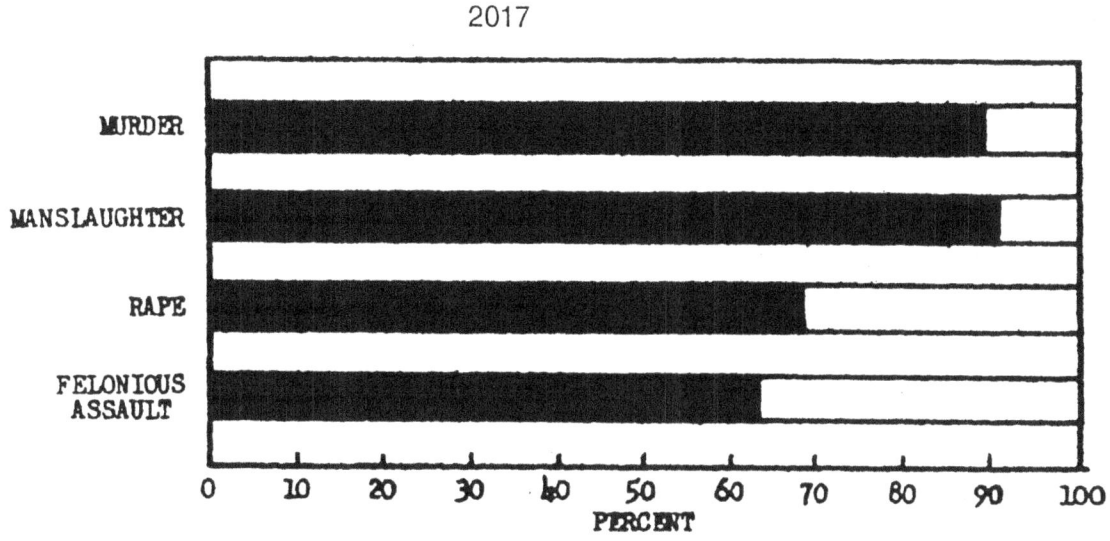

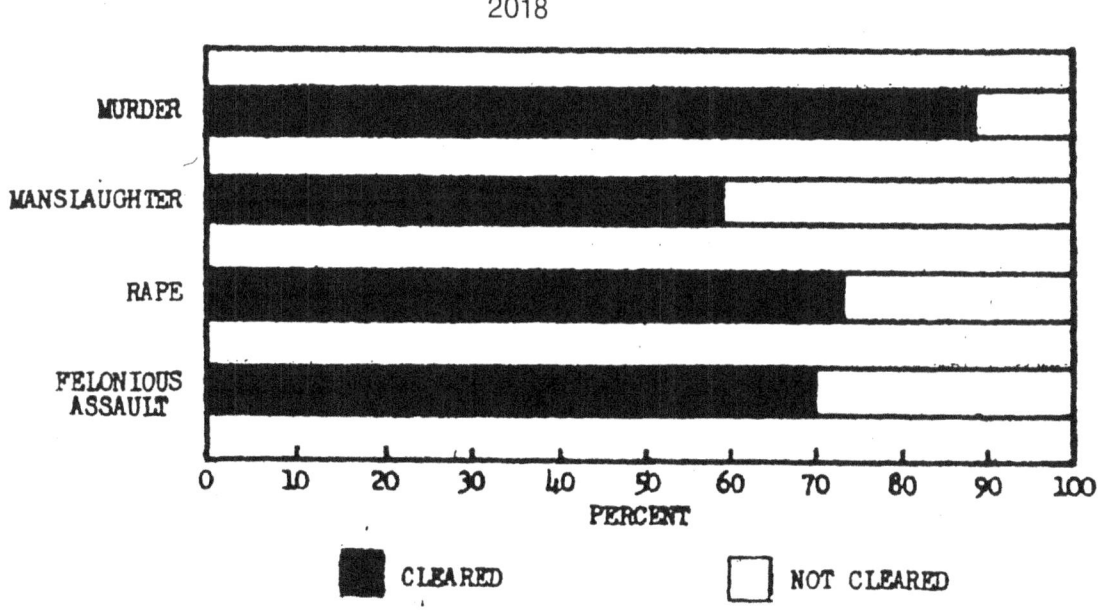

NOTE: The clearance rate is defined as the percentage of reported cases which were closed by the police through arrests or other means.

1. According to the above graphs, the AVERAGE clearance rate for all four crimes for 2018　　1.____
   A. was greater than in 2017
   B. was less than in 2017

C. was the same as in 2017
D. cannot properly be compared to the 2017 figures

2. According to the above graphs, the crimes which did NOT show an increasing clearance rate from 2017 to 2018 were

A. manslaughter and murder
B. rape and felonious assault
C. manslaughter and felonious assault
D. rape and murder

2._____

3. According to the above graphs, the average clearance rate for the two-year period 2017-2018 was SMALLEST for the crime of

A. murder
C. rape
B. manslaughter
D. felonious assault

3._____

4. If, in 2018, 63 cases of reported felonious assault remained *not cleared,* then the total number of felonious assault cases reported that year was MOST NEARLY

A. 90   B. 150   C. 210   D. 900

4._____

5. In comparing the graphs for 2017 and 2018, it would be MOST accurate to state that

A. it is not possible to compare the total number of crimes cleared in 2017 with the total number cleared in 2018
B. the total number of crimes reported in 2017 is greater than the number in 2018
C. there were fewer manslaughter cases cleared during 2017 than in 2018
D. there were more rape cases cleared during 2018 than manslaughter cases cleared in the same year

5._____

KEY (CORRECT ANSWERS)

1. B
2. A
3. D
4. C
5. A

TEST 10

Questions 1-5.

DIRECTIONS: Questions 1 through 5 are to be answered SOLELY on the basis of the following chart.

	FATAL HIGHWAY ACCIDENTS					
	Drivers Over 18 Years of Age			Drivers 18 Years of Age And Under		
2018	Auto	Other Vehicles	Total	Auto	Other Vehicles	Total
January	43	0	43	4	0	4
February	52	0	52	10	0	10
March	36	0	36	8	0	8
April	50	0	50	17	0	17
May	40	2	42	5	0	5
June	26	0	26	8	0	8
July	29	0	29	6	0	6
August	29	1	30	3	0	3
September	36	0	36	4	0	4
October	45	1	46	2	1	3
November	54	1	55	3	0	3
December	66	1	67	3	0	6
TOTALS	506	6	512	76	1	77

1. The average number of fatal auto accidents per month during 2018 involving drivers older than eighteen was MOST NEARLY

    A. 42   B. 43   C. 44   D. 45

2. The TOTAL number of fatal highway accidents during 2018 was

    A. 506   B. 512   C. 582   D. 589

3. The month during which the LOWEST number of fatal highway accidents occurred was

    A. March   B. June   C. July   D. August

4. Of the total number of fatal highway accidents during 2018 involving drivers older than eighteen, the percentage of accidents which took place during December is MOST NEARLY

   A. 10   B. 13   C. 16   D. 19

5. The GREATEST percentage drop in fatal highway accidents occurred from

   A. February to March
   B. April to May
   C. June to July
   D. July to Augus

KEY (CORRECT ANSWERS)

1. A
2. D
3. D
4. B
5. B

POLICE SCIENCE NOTES
DETENTION PROCEDURES

Introduction

Generally detention is thought of as confinement of a prisoner in a jail facility from his formal booking to his formal release. This includes a period of time when he is merely held for bail or court appearance, when he is held after trial for formal sentencing, and when he is actually serving time in a jail or prison. Actually his arrest restricts or removes his freedom and places him under official restraint; thus, it is at this point that his actual detention begins.

Responsibility for the prisoner before booking may be solely that of the arresting officer or it may be given over to jail personnel assigned to transport him to the detention facility. We are concerned, therefore, as a practical matter with the entire time the prisoner is in official custody beginning with his arrest and ending with his release from custody.

Security is the essence of detention and implies assurance against escape or rescue of the prisoner. It also implies a full measure of personal safety for the officers, the prisoner himself, other inmates and visitors and other citizens.

Although it has been implied, and is true in fact, that our concern is with persons arrested for the commission of crimes, our responsibility is a broader one. The more broad responsibility will be increasingly important in time of natural disaster or civil defense emergency. The latter includes the "holding" for safekeeping of the mentally and physically incompetent, children without parents or who are lost or abandoned, persons who are threatened by mobs or individuals, and those who must be held as material witnesses. While legal and procedural provisions must be made to handle each of the above, this is a local matter not detailed here.

Transportation

Usually an arresting officer makes a search of his prisoner at the time of arrest for dangerous weapons, means of self-destruction, and less frequently, for evidence of a crime. Officers should be trained and required to make this search. Nonetheless, since it is often made under unusual conditions of stress, transporting and booking officers should also conduct searches with final responsibility lying with the booking officer. Adequate search is a protection to police and jailers, to the prisoner and other inmates, and to visitors and other citizens.

The search, however, only removes one kind of danger; the security measure of adequate restraint must be provided to avoid loss of the prisoner by his own actions or those of others. The restraint is also provided, of course, as another means of preventing injury to the prisoner and to others.

Transportation should be considered as any means used to get the prisoner from one point to another which is usually considered to be from the location of arrest to the place of detention. Transportation, however, is also involved in taking the prisoner to court, in moving him from one place of detention to another, and in taking him to the site of work details or assignments. For our purposes we must assume that transportation may mean moving the prisoner on foot, in a special or regular police automobile, in a special prisoner vehicle (paddywagon or prisoner van) or by other means including aircraft or boats.

The same general precautions apply to all means of transport because the need for security and restraint exists in all. Transport by walking should only be considered in the absence of a proper vehicle, for very short distances, or when physical circumstances may require it, as in moving the prisoner from a detention facility to a court. The number of officers required varies according to apparent need but also according to prescribed regulations. Only one officer is required in the transport of noncriminal nonviolent persons in protective custody and these include children, the aged, minor offenders, and others. Two officers should be used normally for a person under criminal arrest if there is even a nominal possibility of escape or rescue. Three or more officers should be used in serious criminal cases, cases involving a violent prisoner, or where there is likely to be a serious attempt to escape, rescue, or attack the prisoner.

Two officers should almost always be used in prisoner transport by vehicle except in minor cases when the prisoner is placed in a separate, secure and specially designed section of the vehicle screened off from the driver. When a vehicle is used all doors should be locked and inside handles removed from the prisoner section, as in the rear of an automobile.

Minimal restraint is required when the prisoner is in a secure and separate section of the vehicle unless conflict among prisoners may develop. Reasonable restraint should be used otherwise and will usually involve the use of handcuffs. Whenever handcuffs and other restraining devices are required public display of their use should be avoided.

Special precautions should be used at the place of detention because this is the most likely point of escape or rescue. It is important that detention officers assist transporting officers in placing prisoners in the detention facility. Although the prisoner has been under restraint since his arrest, detention in a formal sense begins when he is placed in the detention facility. Properly booking and admitting the prisoner is of utmost importance and carefully prescribed admittance procedures should be established and followed. The latter, of course, must conform to State and local legal requirements. A prisoner's property, and evidence also, must be properly identified, receipted, and secured. Identification of property should be witnessed under most circumstances and especially when the prisoner is unable to sign for it. Securing property implies controlling it so that it may be returned intact on the prisoner's release.

Fingerprinting and photographing of each prisoner should be required in all criminal cases and in emergency conditions where accurate identification is important as when the prisoner is suffering from amnesia. Exceptions to this practice may be established, i.e., if the prisoner had been previously arrested and his identification established prior to the present arrest.

A final detailed and complete search must be made. The search should be for evidence if this is appropriate under the circumstances; however, the principal purpose at this point is probably to remove offensive weapons and means of self-destruction. Before a prisoner is placed in a cell it should be carefully searched also.

Capabilities for medical examination of incoming prisoners, especially those who are sick or injured, should be provided. This is not only humane but may prevent serious problems later including criticism for failure to provide proper care. Under some circumstances a detailed medical examination for all prisoners may be practicable. In this case, by formal regulation, prisoners falling in certain categories must be examined. Categories should include any person over 60 years of age as this age group will usually contain a much higher percentage of persons requiring care than would those who are younger; any person with a history of illness or disability known to the officers by prior acquaintance with the person or through medical records he carries on his person; any person who is apparently, although not necessarily obviously, ill or injured; any prisoner who complains of illness or injury; and any person who is unconscious or comatose.

It is standard practice in detention facilities to provide for separation of prisoners by age and sex. Quite obviously juveniles and adults should not be quartered together, nor should men be placed with women. Those who have communicable diseases or who may have been exposed to them should be placed in quarantine sections. Those who are perverts or who exhibit tendencies to perversion should be separated from others, particularly children. Those who are mentally deranged, or who apparently become so, must also be isolated. This may be an especially important consideration under emer-gency conditions. Less serious offenders should be separated from the more serious offenders to avoid recruiting prisoners to the ranks of major criminals. The use of psychiatrists and medical personnel is recommended to assist in determining necessary separation in the case of perversion and mental derangement.

Providing adequate security is essential. All offensive weapons and means of self-destruction must be physically protected and adequately guarded. None should be within reach of any prisoner. Guards should not carry firearms while in any prisoner section. Full control of all means of entrance and exit must be provided. No guard should have on his person a set of keys which would allow escape from or admittance to the full facility or a series of its sections. All tools require close control because they may be used as weapons, escape devices, or provide the means to make such items. Prisoners being returned to cells from corridors, shops, and dining rooms should be searched.

Medical supplies must be carefully controlled. Their possession by prisoners provide means of self-destruction and barter. Under some circumstances prisoners would maliciously destroy essential medical provisions.

On a frequent, intermittent basis, quarters and inmates must be inspected and prisoners counted.

To avoid emotional problems, provide exercise, and for other reasons prisoners who warrant the trust can be given some freedom in the facility and be put to minor but productive tasks. Classification of prisoners as "trusties" or available for light work must be carefully done to avoid escapes and other problems.

All security measures must be established on a basis that allows prompt implementation of plans for evacuation of prisoners in the event of fire or facility destruction by other means. Planning must also provide full means of protection against the consequences of riot and mob attempts at rescue or attack. This may require provisions to quickly and inconspicuously move key prisoners to other detention.

Detention When Jails Unavailable

Most shelters and relocation facilities are not designed for detention purposes. This will require imaginative improvisation of both quarters and procedures. Two things must be provided in spite of adverse circumstances: (1) Basic security for prisoners, officers, and other occupants; and (2) separation of various categories of prisoners.

Large rooms, of course, can be used for group detention if adequate security is provided and if the need for separation is minimal or absent. Such use of space, however, may require the use of additional guards constantly on the alert to avoid altercations or plotting for escape.

In shelters the problems of security and separation may require unusual use of restraining devices and materials. Individual prisoners can be handcuffed to pipes, doorknobs, stanchions, or window bars. If this is done, adequate free space around the prisoner should be provided to avoid improper and dangerous contact with other prisoners or occupants of the shelter. Two prisoners can be secured with a single set of handcuffs merely by passing the cuffs behind a pipe set close to a wall or the floor, or behind a bar in a barred window or door.

Ropes, belts, and similar material may be used in lieu of handcuffs, but require unusual care to avoid injury or escapes. Although it may be necessary to occasionally check handcuffs to see that they are not too tight for the comfort or safety of the prisoner, frequent inspection of rope and other nonmetallic material is essential. These may quickly become either too tight and thus cause injury, or too loose and thus permit escape. Restraints of material must also be checked if they become wet, or dry out after being wet.

Sedatives may be used under unusual circumstances by a doctor or by a nurse under his direction. Sedatives have a particular value when handling a violent person and may be used both as a restraint and treatment in many cases.

Expensive, but necessary on occasion, will be the use of guards or officers on the basis of one guard to a prisoner. This should be avoided if possible because of the excessive drain it puts on available personnel.

Conclusion

It should be said once again that security is the essence of detention. The safety of officers, prisoners, and others is dependent on strict adherence to carefully prepared procedures.

DISCIPLINE

INTRODUCTION

Inevitably, there are some prisoners who do not readily respond to positive staff attitudes and often refuse to cooperate with even the most understanding and patient jail officers. When this is the case, disciplinary measures must often be used. It is extremely important for the jail officer to understand what is meant by discipline and what must be involved in his decision to use discipline in controlling a prisoner. The rest of this chapter has been designed to help you:
- recognize what situations require disciplinary action
- choose the correct disciplinary action when needed

Before continuing, it is important for you to realize that this section will *not* be a discussion of punishment. Punishment is only a "last resort" and, as such, is only a small factor in the overall view of discipline. Actual punishment usually involves such *negative* actions as:
- taking away some of a prisoner's "good time"
- taking away a privilege
- assigning a prisoner to a solitary cell

The *positive* factors of discipline include:
- teaching self control
- setting standards of proper behavior
- correcting improper behavior consistently and fairly

For the benefit of jail personnel and prisoners it is desirable that officers constantly seek ways of treating disciplinary problems informally in a thoughtful, constructive manner rather than assuming that all misconduct must be punished.

Before continuing, it is important that you understand the definitions of DISCIPLINE and PUNISHMENT and that you keep the relationship between the two clearly in mind.
- DISCIPLINE is the training required to insure obedience to established rules.
- PUNISHMENT is a penalty for some offense—it is usually a denial of privileges rather than infliction of pain.

Effective discipline is designed to *correct* and *teach* rather than to punish or seek revenge. However, punishment *may* be appropriate in some cases as a method of encouraging proper behavior.

Every jail in the country must operate under a set of established regulations. Prisoners are expected to learn these rules and abide by them. And when prisoners break jail rules, it is the responsibility of the jail officer to determine the cause of the misconduct and decide whether he should make a formal report of the matter or try to informally correct the prisoner's behavior. This is often a difficult decision for the officer. He must use personal judgment to analyze the situation and determine the correct action. Not all circumstances require formal disciplinary action, and it would be unwise for an officer to be a "hard nose" and attempt to treat all cases of prisoner misconduct in the same way and with the same intensity.

When a prisoner breaks a rule and thereby endangers the safety of the personnel and prisoners, there is usually a clearcut need for some sort of punishment. The following actions by prisoners are considered dangerous to the security and well-being of the jail staff and prisoners and usually require punishment:
- interfering with a prisoner count
- attempting escape
- possession of a weapon
- attacking a jail officer
- attacking a prisoner
- destroying security equipment

In no case should an officer punish a prisoner. An officer who feels that punishment is in order has the duty to let someone else decide what to do. In a small jail, a higher ranking officer or the sheriff may be the one who should decide the action. And in a larger jail, there may be a disciplinary board or court available to decide these cases. Just as the police must allow a judge or court to decide the penalties for the persons they have arrested, you, the jail officer, must allow an impartial person or group of people to decide disciplinary action for the prisoners who you report. Read what happened to a jail officer who considered it his right to impose punishment on uncooperative prisoners:

> Recently a jail officer decided that, rather than reporting several prisoners for serious misconduct, he would punish the prisoners himself. He ordered the men to do 150 deepknee bends. One of the prisoners collapsed after the exercise and had to be helped to his cell. The following day, he was hospitalized for kidney failure. Because the officer had ignored the established procedure for formally reporting misconduct to the sheriff, the district attorny formally charged him with "assault, coercion, official misconduct, and reckless endangerment"

Note:

A jail officer may not always agree with the punishment that is assigned. Some prisoners will be given warnings; others not punished; and others, punished only lightly. The reporting officer should not interpret these decisions as a lack of support for him. The action taken on a formal report usually reflects the administrator's concern for factors that the jail officer may not have considered. These factors include the prisoner's overall adjustment, his personality, and the circumstances of the violation.

In most instances of misconduct, prisoners break jail rules that do *not* directly affect the safety of personnel and prisoners in the jail. These rules might deal with such things as:

- cleaning up their cells
- wasting food
- performing a job assignment
- making excess noise
- displaying insolence and lack of respect for authority

Prisoners may misbehave because they are purposely trying to cause trouble. In such cases, some sort of disciplinary action may be called for.

Can you think of any other reasons why prisoners may misbehave? Before turning the page, see if you can name some other reasons for misbehavior.

Prisoners often misbehave because they are under unusual emotional stress, because they have not thoroughly understood a jail regulation, or because lack of exercise and the monotony of jail life have resulted in excess energy and a desire to "blow off steam". They may also misbehave because jail officers have not indicated *what behavior is expected* of prisoners while in the jail. Naturally, it is the duty of jail officers to make these standards of behavior very clear and understandable for prisoners.

It is the jail officer who has the responsibility to decide whether a situation can be handled informally or if there is clearly a need to report the matter. He must reach his decision by using his own judgment concerning the personality and past behavior record of the prisoner and the circumstances in which the prisoner misbehaved.

Often an officer who has seen a prisoner break a jail rule can determine whether the misconduct was intentional or just a careless lapse. And the officer can often determine the cause of misconduct by quietly talking to a prisoner and finding out what is bothering him. In any case, it is a mistake to automatically treat all misconduct as an attempt by the prisoner to defy authority or cause trouble.

> "I won't get on that scaffold and paint no matter what you do to me!"
>
> Knowing that Prisoner Myron Jeffries was usually a willing and cooperative worker, Officer Chase was extremely surprised to hear Jeffries flatly refuse to follow his orders to paint the ceiling of the jail.
>
> Refusal to follow work orders in this jail constitutes an infraction of jail regulations and usually brings a punishment such as temporary suspension of the prisoner's recreation privileges. However, rather than automatically filing a formal report, Chase decided to talk privately with Jeffries to determine if anything was troubling him.
>
> *RESULT*: Officer Chase found that Jeffries had developed a great fear of scaffolds after seeing a friend badly injured in a fall from one. Chase promptly assigned Jeffries to another job. The officer also warned Jeffries that such a flat refusal to work, without an accompanying explanation, might have been interpreted as insolence and misconduct. He suggested ways that Jeffries could more constructively voice his complaints in the future.

After taking the time to talk privately with the prisoner, Officer Chase correctly recognized that formal disciplinary action would not be appropriate in this case. However, he also realized that *informal* discipline *was* appropriate. He pointed out to the prisoner that he must learn to rationally explain his complaints to officers if he expected to receive fair treatment from them.

In this case, the informal disciplinary action which Officer Chase took was:
___ 1) Changing Jeffries' work assignment to a harder one
___ 2) Threatening to punish Jeffries the next time he refuses to work in this way
___ 3) Telling Jeffries that his blunt way of refusing to work might result in punishment and suggesting better ways of voicing his complaints to officers

Turn page to check your answer . . .

Answer:
___ 1) Changing Jeffries' work assignment to a harder one
___ 2) Threatening to punish Jeffries the next time he refuses to work in this way
_X_ 3) Telling Jeffries that his blunt way of refusing to work might result in punishment and suggesting better ways of voicing his complaints to officers

---

All too many jail officers think that their only responsibility in disciplining prisoners is to see that all violations and infractions are reported. And, in smaller jails where there is no formal disciplinary procedure, many officers think that their only responsibility is punishing prisoners *after* they have committed a violation. This way of thinking can only bring trouble and conflict to the jail.

It is well known among experienced jail officers that the best and most effective among them are those officers who *seldom* file formal disciplinary reports. These are officers who consider it their responsibility to use positive discipline to *prevent* violations of the rules by closely observing prisoners and dealing with potential problems on an individual basis before they become serious. In the majority of cases, officers *can* avoid serious problems if they reason with individuals and explain correct behavior to them.

NOTES

Use of "silent insolence" by prisoners in order to annoy or harass jail officers is common. Staring sullenly at an officer, responding to an officer's orders in a deliberately slow and reluctant manner, and whispering and laughing with other prisoners while an officer passes by, are all methods of displaying "silent insolence". The purpose of such behavior, naturally, is to cause an officer to lose his temper, become angry and frustrated, and make himself ridiculous in the eyes of the prisoner population. Dealing with this type of insolence is far more difficult than dealing with a refusal to work, verbal disobedience, or other, more tangible methods of disobedience. And, since it is difficult to prove "silent insolence" or to stop it by warnings or punishment, the wisest, most proven course for the officer to follow when faced with the problem is to *ignore it* as long as no specific rules are being broken. When prisoners are unable to force an officer to "lose his cool" by using silent insolence, they often stop trying. But if prisoners succeed in making an officer lose his temper, they will undoubtedly be encouraged to continue their insolent behavior.

Naturally, not all cases of silent insolence can be handled by simply ignoring them. An officer should use his judgment to determine if a prisoner is merely trying to annoy him, or if a change in the prisoner's situation or a misunderstanding have made him depressed and difficult to handle. If the latter is the case, talking informally with the prisoner in an attempt to determine what is troubling him might be effective in relieving the problem.

> Robert Coles had been a cooperative and well-behaved prisoner until recently when he began to stare sullenly at Officer Dubinsky as he made his rounds past the cellblock. Coles had always made a practice of greeting the officer pleasantly as he passed but now only stared without speaking. Dubinsky usually made a practice of ignoring such practices since they were usually prisoner attempts to make him angry. However, in this case, Dubinsky became worried about the prisoner. He took an opportunity to speak privately with Coles and, after a long pause, the prisoner finally told him that he had been suffering from severe headaches and hadn't reported for sick call because he was convinced that the doctor would tell him he was dying of a brain tumor. Hearing this, the officer was able to reason with the prisoner and managed to convince him that the doctor would be able to help him and that brooding over his condition had probably made the headaches worse.

The majority of jail prisoners *do* respond to attempts by officers to teach them correct behavior and respect for jail rules. And, as we have already mentioned, the most effective officers are able to maintain discipline on an informal, individual, basis without relying on more formal disciplinary measures. However, there are prisoners who continually break rules and refuse to cooperate with officers on any terms. When dealing with these prisoners, it is vital that officers make a conscious effort to control themselves and not resort to impulsive force.

Edgar Lucas, a prisoner in a large jail, has consistently shown hostility toward jail officers. Usually his misbehavior is characterized by "silent insolence" and a slowness in following orders. Recently he did not appear for the morning prisoner count and was found sitting in a corner of his cell, refusing to move. The officer in charge attempted to talk to the prisoner in order to find out if he had a problem or complaint. However, Lucas swore at the officer and told him to, "Get off my back." Lucas then refused to clean up his cell or perform any of his assigned chores for the day.

Here is a case in which the uncooperative behavior of Lucas as well as his hostile remark might well have caused the officer to lose his temper and try to force Lucas to behave. But it is in the officer's best interest to control his temper, simply walk away from the prisoner and submit a formal report to the jail administrator concerning the situation. The officer has done his duty; dealing informally with the matter at first, and then submitting a formal report. Any further action must be decided by the administrator; it is he who bears the responsibility for deciding further action concerning the prisoner.

> In a large county jail, one experienced jail officer feels that he is able to "keep his cool" and still retain his "self-respect" in the eyes of his prisoners. Whenever a prisoner swears at him, calls him a name, or threatens him, the officer does the following:
>
> "I just put the keys in the cell door and say to the man, 'If you want to prove something, come with me to the end of the cell block; I'll take off my badge and uniform shirt and we'll fight it out to see who's boss. If you win, I'll throw the book at you.'"
>
> To this date, a prisoner has never accepted the officer's invitation.

What do you think of the officer's policy?

Be sure you think of your answer before turning the page . . .

Answer:
Although this officer *thinks* he retains control of prisoners by this method, he is far from correct. His offer to fight with prisoners is a clear indication that *they* control *him* with remarks and insolence. Removing a badge or uniform shirt does *not* remove an officer's responsibility to always remain in control of his emotions and actions in his relationship with prisoners. It is a serious mistake for a jail officer to feel that his professional responsibility can be so easily set aside while he satisfies a personal need to defend his manhood and establish his superiority.

NOTES

NOTES

Sometimes a prisoner will become violent and try to injure another prisoner or a jail officer. Although it is rare for this to happen, it is important for you to know how to respond to and subdue violent prisoners.

The following guidelines are suggested for handling violent prisoners:

- NEVER ATTEMPT TO SUBDUE A VIOLENT PRISONER ALONE

    Always seek the assistance of one or more officers. Struggling alone with a violent prisoner increases an officer's chances of being injured or overpowered. When two or more officers are involved, they have a better chance of subduing the prisoner quickly and without injury. Also, if more than one officer is involved, the prisoner can "allow" himself to be controlled without embarrassment. Losing a struggle with two officers is not the embarrassment that losing to only one officer is.

- AVOID STRIKING OR OTHERWISE HARMING THE PRISONER

    The officer's duty is to *contain* the prisoner; that is, to prevent him from further violent action. Your duty is *not* to injure the prisoner or "teach him lesson".

NOTES

Some jails are equipped with a protective shield which is used in handling violent prisoners. The pictures shown below demonstrate how the shield can be used to subdue a violent prisoner:

The officers using this shield are correctly following the two guidelines for controlling violent prisoners. Write the guidelines here in your own words:

1. _____

2. _____

When you are finished, turn page to check your answer . . .

Answer:
Your answer should include these two rules:
- NEVER ATTEMPT TO SUBDUE A VIOLENT PRISONER ALONE
- AVOID STRIKING OR OTHERWISE HARMING THE PRISONER (Notice that, by using the shield, the officers are able to contain the prisoner without struggling with him or hitting him.)

Not all jails are equipped with such things as protective shields and, unfortunately, not all violent incidents that occur are easily handled. A jail officer's judgment is always the important element in stopping violence. For instance, if he must subdue a prisoner where other prisoners are watching, his ability to handle the situation calmly, as quickly as possible, and in accordance with jail rules is extremely important.

What do you think would be the probable result of using too much roughness in front of a sympathetic prisoner audience?

Turn page for answer...

Answer:
It has been well established that a sympathetic prisoner audience can easily get out of control and cause more violence if officers are seen using unnecessary roughness against a prisoner and ignoring rules for their own official behavior.

Whether or not your jail has a formal procedure for handling discipline, there is one universal rule that applies to all jails, large or small. The rule is:

WHENEVER A PRISONER IS PUNISHED, A RECORD OF THE ACTION MUST BE KEPT

You may remember the previous discussion in the Supervision section concerning the importance of keeping medical records. You read examples in which jail officers had failed to keep medical records and thereby gave prisoners an opportunity to bring successful legal suits against the jail, charging improper medical treatment. The same principle applies whenever punishment is involved. In recent years, courts have been increasingly concerned with cases in which prisoners have charged that jail officers used "cruel and unusual punishment" to discipline them. If you do not keep careful jail records detailing each case in which punishment is used, it will be extremely difficult to prove that "cruel and unusual punishment" was *not* used. Good records are *particularly important* in cases where "good time" is taken away or a prisoner is placed in segregation. To avoid legal problems in your jail, you should make records that include the following:

- Previous warnings that prisoner has received
- Reason for punishment
- Time and date when punishment decided and begun (also names of persons deciding punishment)
- Details of the punishment decided upon (for instance, if punishment involves revocation of recreation privileges, the record should indicate how long this is to be enforced and how many recreation sessions the prisoner will miss during this time)

In many of the larger jails, officers are required to submit formal disciplinary reports to the person (or persons) who must make a judgment about the misconduct and suggest corrective action or punishment. If your jail is one that requires *you* to write these reports, you should read the next few pages carefully and study the ways in which you can write an effective and constructive report.

On the next few pages are the basic requirements for a good disciplinary report:
- Full name of the prisoner
- A complete description of the *prisoner's behavior leading to necessity for the report*, and a notation of warnings which he has received.

Here is an example of such a description:

> "Prisoner Adams was assigned to potwashing crew along with several others. He objected loudly to the assignment but then apologized to me explaining that he had not slept well last night. I suggested that he try harder to cooperate in the future or I would have to report him. Fifteen minutes later, the prisoner purposely started a fight with another prisoner, punching him and shouting, 'Next time you splatter water on me I'll kill you!'"

- *Time and place of the offense:* These are two important elements because they lend specific proof to your accusation of misconduct.
- *Location of officer* when offense occurred: For example:

> "I was passing the kitchen door when I observed the incident. Adams and the other prisoner, Sawyer, were standing at the sink, with their backs toward me when Adams started to hit Sawyer."

- If the offense is serious, such as a violation of a criminal statute, *information on witnesses should be included*. For instance, if a prisoner has been sexually assaulted, he should be required to identify his assailants and provide names of any prisoners who could testify in his behalf.

Note:

Prisoner witnesses should not be included for violations that are not particularly serious since they will undoubtedly be victimized and intimidated later when other prisoners find that he is a "stool pigeon". However, if other officers have observed the violation, their names should be included.

- The reporting officer should indicate *what actions he took in response to the prisoner's behavior*. For example:

> I called for Officer Dorsey to help me and, together, we backed the prisoner into a corner so that he could no longer reach Sawyer. At this point, with each of us holding one of the prisoner's arms, we escorted him back to his cell and locked him in.

- In the same description, the reporting officer should describe the *prisoner's response to any action taken*. For example:

> Adams did not struggle but said, "I'll get even with you jerks." When he was locked in his cell, he muttered some remarks that we couldn't hear well enough to quote.

- If the behavior has been consistent, the reporting officer should indicate *what warnings have been given in the past*. For example:

> Several weeks ago, prisoner Adams started to bully one of his cellmates for no apparent reason. He stopped immediately when I warned him that further misconduct like this could force me to make a formal disciplinary report.

The next time you are required to write a formal disciplinary report, use this page as a checklist to determine if you have left any important details out of your report.

- Prisoner's full name
- Complete description of prisoner's behavior leading to necessity for report
- Time and place of offense
- Location of reporting officer when offense occurred
- Information on witnesses
- Immediate actions taken by reporting officer in response to prisoner behavior
- Prisoner's response to reporting officer's actions
- Warnings given to prisoner previously (in case of persistent behavior)

GLOSSARY OF LEGAL TERMS

TABLE OF CONTENTS

	Page
Action ... Affiant	1
Affidavit ... At Bar	2
At Issue ... Burden of Proof	3
Business ... Commute	4
Complainant ... Conviction	5
Cooperative ... Demur (v.)	6
Demurrage ... Endorsement	7
Enjoin ... Facsimile	8
Factor ... Guilty	9
Habeas Corpus ... Incumbrance	10
Indemnify ... Laches	11
Landlord and Tenant ... Malice	12
Mandamus ... Obiter Dictum	13
Object (v.) ... Perjury	14
Perpetuity ... Proclamation	15
Proffered Evidence ... Referee	16
Referendum ... Stare Decisis	17
State ... Term	18
Testamentary ... Warrant (Warranty) (v.)	19
Warrant (n.) ... Zoning	20

GLOSSARY OF LEGAL TERMS

A

ACTION - "Action" includes a civil action and a criminal action.
A FORTIORI - A term meaning you can reason one thing from the existence of certain facts.
A POSTERIORI - From what goes after; from effect to cause.
A PRIORI - From what goes before; from cause to effect.
AB INITIO - From the beginning.
ABATE - To diminish or put an end to.
ABET - To encourage the commission of a crime.
ABEYANCE - Suspension, temporary suppression.
ABIDE - To accept the consequences of.
ABJURE - To renounce; give up.
ABRIDGE - To reduce; contract; diminish.
ABROGATE - To annul, repeal, or destroy.
ABSCOND - To hide or absent oneself to avoid legal action.
ABSTRACT - A summary.
ABUT - To border on, to touch.
ACCESS - Approach; in real property law it means the right of the owner of property to the use of the highway or road next to his land, without obstruction by intervening property owners.
ACCESSORY - In criminal law, it means the person who contributes or aids in the commission of a crime.
ACCOMMODATED PARTY - One to whom credit is extended on the strength of another person signing a commercial paper.
ACCOMMODATION PAPER - A commercial paper to which the accommodating party has put his name.
ACCOMPLICE - In criminal law, it means a person who together with the principal offender commits a crime.
ACCORD - An agreement to accept something different or less than that to which one is entitled, which extinguishes the entire obligation.
ACCOUNT - A statement of mutual demands in the nature of debt and credit between parties.
ACCRETION - The act of adding to a thing; in real property law, it means gradual accumulation of land by natural causes.
ACCRUE - To grow to; to be added to.
ACKNOWLEDGMENT - The act of going before an official authorized to take acknowledgments, and acknowledging an act as one's own.
ACQUIESCENCE - A silent appearance of consent.
ACQUIT - To legally determine the innocence of one charged with a crime.
AD INFINITUM - Indefinitely.
AD LITEM - For the suit.
AD VALOREM - According to value.
ADJECTIVE LAW - Rules of procedure.
ADJUDICATION - The judgment given in a case.
ADMIRALTY - Court having jurisdiction over maritime cases.
ADULT - Sixteen years old or over (in criminal law).
ADVANCE - In commercial law, it means to pay money or render other value before it is due.
ADVERSE - Opposed; contrary.
ADVOCATE - (v.) To speak in favor of;
    (n.) One who assists, defends, or pleads for another.
AFFIANT - A person who makes and signs an affidavit.

AFFIDAVIT - A written and sworn to declaration of facts, voluntarily made.
AFFINITY - The relationship between persons through marriage with the kindred of each other; distinguished from consanguinity, which is the relationship by blood.
AFFIRM - To ratify; also when an appellate court affirms a judgment, decree, or order, it means that it is valid and right and must stand as rendered in the lower court.
AFOREMENTIONED; AFORESAID - Before or already said.
AGENT - One who represents and acts for another.
AID AND COMFORT - To help; encourage.
ALIAS - A name not one's true name.
ALIBI - A claim of not being present at a certain place at a certain time.
ALLEGE - To assert.
ALLOTMENT - A share or portion.
AMBIGUITY - Uncertainty; capable of being understood in more than one way.
AMENDMENT - Any language made or proposed as a change in some principal writing.
AMICUS CURIAE - A friend of the court; one who has an interest in a case, although not a party in the case, who volunteers advice upon matters of law to the judge. For example, a brief amicus curiae.
AMORTIZATION - To provide for a gradual extinction of (a future obligation) in advance of maturity, especially, by periodical contributions to a sinking fund which will be adequate to discharge a debt or make a replacement when it becomes necessary.
ANCILLARY - Aiding, auxiliary.
ANNOTATION - A note added by way of comment or explanation.
ANSWER - A written statement made by a defendant setting forth the grounds of his defense.
ANTE - Before.
ANTE MORTEM - Before death.
APPEAL - The removal of a case from a lower court to one of superior jurisdiction for the purpose of obtaining a review.
APPEARANCE - Coming into court as a party to a suit.
APPELLANT - The party who takes an appeal from one court or jurisdiction to another (appellate) court for review.
APPELLEE - The party against whom an appeal is taken.
APPROPRIATE - To make a thing one's own.
APPROPRIATION - Prescribing the destination of a thing; the act of the legislature designating a particular fund, to be applied to some object of government expenditure.
APPURTENANT - Belonging to; accessory or incident to.
ARBITER - One who decides a dispute; a referee.
ARBITRARY - Unreasoned; not governed by any fixed rules or standard.
ARGUENDO - By way of argument.
ARRAIGN - To call the prisoner before the court to answer to a charge.
ASSENT - A declaration of willingness to do something in compliance with a request.
ASSERT - Declare.
ASSESS - To fix the rate or amount.
ASSIGN - To transfer; to appoint; to select for a particular purpose.
ASSIGNEE - One who receives an assignment.
ASSIGNOR - One who makes an assignment.
AT BAR - Before the court.

AT ISSUE - When parties in an action come to a point where one asserts something and the other denies it.

ATTACH - Seize property by court order and sometimes arrest a person.

ATTEST - To witness a will, etc.; act of attestation.

AVERMENT - A positive statement of facts.

B

BAIL - To obtain the release of a person from legal custody by giving security and promising that he shall appear in court; to deliver (goods, etc.) in trust to a person for a special purpose.

BAILEE - One to whom personal property is delivered under a contract of bailment.

BAILMENT - Delivery of personal property to another to be held for a certain purpose and to be returned when the purpose is accomplished.

BAILOR - The party who delivers goods to another, under a contract of bailment.

BANC (OR BANK) - Bench; the place where a court sits permanently or regularly; also the assembly of all the judges of a court.

BANKRUPT - An insolvent person, technically, one declared to be bankrupt after a bankruptcy proceeding.

BAR - The legal profession.

BARRATRY - Exciting groundless judicial proceedings.

BARTER - A contract by which parties exchange goods for other goods.

BATTERY - Illegal interfering with another's person.

BEARER - In commercial law, it means the person in possession of a commercial paper which is payable to the bearer.

BENCH - The court itself or the judge.

BENEFICIARY - A person benefiting under a will, trust, or agreement.

BEST EVIDENCE RULE, THE - Except as otherwise provided by statute, no evidence other than the writing itself is admissible to prove the content of a writing. This section shall be known and may be cited as the best evidence rule.

BEQUEST - A gift of personal property under a will.

BILL - A formal written statement of complaint to a court of justice; also, a draft of an act of the legislature before it becomes a law; also, accounts for goods sold, services rendered, or work done.

BONA FIDE - In or with good faith; honestly.

BOND - An instrument by which the maker promises to pay a sum of money to another, usually providing that upon performances of a certain condition the obligation shall be void.

BOYCOTT - A plan to prevent the carrying on of a business by wrongful means.

BREACH - The breaking or violating of a law, or the failure to carry out a duty.

BRIEF - A written document, prepared by a lawyer to serve as the basis of an argument upon a case in court, usually an appellate court.

BURDEN OF PRODUCING EVIDENCE - The obligation of a party to introduce evidence sufficient to avoid a ruling against him on the issue.

BURDEN OF PROOF - The obligation of a party to establish by evidence a requisite degree of belief concerning a fact in the mind of the trier of fact or the court. The burden of proof may require a party to raise a reasonable doubt concerning the existence of nonexistence of a fact or that he establish the existence or nonexistence of a fact by a preponderance of the evidence, by clear and convincing proof, or by proof beyond a reasonable doubt.

Except as otherwise provided by law, the burden of proof requires proof by a preponderance of the evidence.

BUSINESS, A - Shall include every kind of business, profession, occupation, calling or operation of institutions, whether carried on for profit or not.

BY-LAWS - Regulations, ordinances, or rules enacted by a corporation, association, etc., for its own government.

C

CANON - A doctrine; also, a law or rule, of a church or association in particular.

CAPIAS - An order to arrest.

CAPTION - In a pleading, deposition or other paper connected with a case in court, it is the heading or introductory clause which shows the names of the parties, name of the court, number of the case on the docket or calendar, etc.

CARRIER - A person or corporation undertaking to transport persons or property.

CASE - A general term for an action, cause, suit, or controversy before a judicial body.

CAUSE - A suit, litigation or action before a court.

CAVEAT EMPTOR - Let the buyer beware. This term expresses the rule that the purchaser of an article must examine, judge, and test it for himself, being bound to discover any obvious defects or imperfections.

CERTIFICATE - A written representation that some legal formality has been complied with.

CERTIORARI - To be informed of; the name of a writ issued by a superior court directing the lower court to send up to the former the record and proceedings of a case.

CHANGE OF VENUE - To remove place of trial from one place to another.

CHARGE - An obligation or duty; a formal complaint; an instruction of the court to the jury upon a case.

CHARTER - (n.) The authority by virtue of which an organized body acts;
  (v.) in mercantile law, it means to hire or lease a vehicle or vessel for transportation.

CHATTEL - An article of personal property.

CHATTEL MORTGAGE - A mortgage on personal property.

CIRCUIT - A division of the country, for the administration of justice; a geographical area served by a court.

CITATION - The act of the court by which a person is summoned or cited; also, a reference to legal authority.

CIVIL (ACTIONS)- It indicates the private rights and remedies of individuals in contrast to the word "criminal" (actions) which relates to prosecution for violation of laws.

CLAIM (n.) - Any demand held or asserted as of right.

CODICIL - An addition to a will.

CODIFY - To arrange the laws of a country into a code.

COGNIZANCE - Notice or knowledge.

COLLATERAL - By the side; accompanying; an article or thing given to secure performance of a promise.

COMITY - Courtesy; the practice by which one court follows the decision of another court on the same question.

COMMIT - To perform, as an act; to perpetrate, as a crime; to send a person to prison.

COMMON LAW - As distinguished from law created by the enactment of the legislature (called statutory law), it relates to those principles and rules of action which derive their authority solely from usages and customs of immemorial antiquity, particularly with reference to the ancient unwritten law of England. The written pronouncements of the common law are found in court decisions.

COMMUTE - Change punishment to one less severe.

COMPLAINANT - One who applies to the court for legal redress.
COMPLAINT - The pleading of a plaintiff in a civil action; or a charge that a person has committed a specified offense.
COMPROMISE - An arrangement for settling a dispute by agreement.
CONCUR - To agree, consent.
CONCURRENT - Running together, at the same time.
CONDEMNATION - Taking private property for public use on payment therefor.
CONDITION - Mode or state of being; a qualification or restriction.
CONDUCT - Active and passive behavior; both verbal and nonverbal.
CONFESSION - Voluntary statement of guilt of crime.
CONFIDENTIAL COMMUNICATION BETWEEN CLIENT AND LAWYER - Information transmitted between a client and his lawyer in the course of that relationship and in confidence by a means which, so far as the client is aware, discloses the information to no third persons other than those who are present to further the interest of the client in the consultation or those to whom disclosure is reasonably necessary for the transmission of the information or the accomplishment of the purpose for which the lawyer is consulted, and includes a legal opinion formed and the advice given by the lawyer in the course of that relationship.
CONFRONTATION - Witness testifying in presence of defendant.
CONSANGUINITY - Blood relationship.
CONSIGN - To give in charge; commit; entrust; to send or transmit goods to a merchant, factor, or agent for sale.
CONSIGNEE - One to whom a consignment is made.
CONSIGNOR - One who sends or makes a consignment.
CONSPIRACY - In criminal law, it means an agreement between two or more persons to commit an unlawful act.
CONSPIRATORS - Persons involved in a conspiracy.
CONSTITUTION - The fundamental law of a nation or state.
CONSTRUCTION OF GENDERS - The masculine gender includes the feminine and neuter.
CONSTRUCTION OF SINGULAR AND PLURAL - The singular number includes the plural; and the plural, the singular.
CONSTRUCTION OF TENSES - The present tense includes the past and future tenses; and the future, the present.
CONSTRUCTIVE - An act or condition assumed from other parts or conditions.
CONSTRUE - To ascertain the meaning of language.
CONSUMMATE - To complete.
CONTIGUOUS - Adjoining; touching; bounded by.
CONTINGENT - Possible, but not assured; dependent upon some condition.
CONTINUANCE - The adjournment or postponement of an action pending in a court.
CONTRA - Against, opposed to; contrary.
CONTRACT - An agreement between two or more persons to do or not to do a particular thing.
CONTROVERT - To dispute, deny.
CONVERSION - Dealing with the personal property of another as if it were one's own, without right.
CONVEYANCE - An instrument transferring title to land.
CONVICTION - Generally, the result of a criminal trial which ends in a judgment or sentence that the defendant is guilty as charged.

COOPERATIVE - A cooperative is a voluntary organization of persons with a common interest, formed and operated along democratic lines for the purpose of supplying services at cost to its members and other patrons, who contribute both capital and business.
CORPUS DELICTI - The body of a crime; the crime itself.
CORROBORATE - To strengthen; to add weight by additional evidence.
COUNTERCLAIM - A claim presented by a defendant in opposition to or deduction from the claim of the plaintiff.
COUNTY - Political subdivision of a state.
COVENANT - Agreement.
CREDIBLE - Worthy of belief.
CREDITOR - A person to whom a debt is owing by another person, called the "debtor."
CRIMINAL ACTION - Includes criminal proceedings.
CRIMINAL INFORMATION - Same as complaint.
CRITERION (sing.)
CRITERIA (plural) - A means or tests for judging; a standard or standards.
CROSS-EXAMINATION - Examination of a witness by a party other than the direct examiner upon a matter that is within the scope of the direct examination of the witness.
CULPABLE - Blamable.
CY-PRES - As near as (possible). The rule of *cy-pres* is a rule for the construction of instruments in equity by which the intention of the party is carried out *as near as may be*, when it would be impossible or illegal to give it literal effect.

D

DAMAGES - A monetary compensation, which may be recovered in the courts by any person who has suffered loss, or injury, whether to his person, property or rights through the unlawful act or omission or negligence of another.
DECLARANT - A person who makes a statement.
DE FACTO - In fact; actually but without legal authority.
DE JURE - Of right; legitimate; lawful.
DE MINIMIS - Very small or trifling.
DE NOVO - Anew; afresh; a second time.
DEBT - A specified sum of money owing to one person from another, including not only the obligation of the debtor to pay, but the right of the creditor to receive and enforce payment.
DECEDENT - A dead person.
DECISION - A judgment or decree pronounced by a court in determination of a case.
DECREE - An order of the court, determining the rights of all parties to a suit.
DEED - A writing containing a contract sealed and delivered; particularly to convey real property.
DEFALCATION - Misappropriation of funds.
DEFAMATION - Injuring one's reputation by false statements.
DEFAULT - The failure to fulfill a duty, observe a promise, discharge an obligation, or perform an agreement.
DEFENDANT - The person defending or denying; the party against whom relief or recovery is sought in an action or suit.
DEFRAUD - To practice fraud; to cheat or trick.
DELEGATE (v.)- To entrust to the care or management of another.
DELICTUS - A crime.
DEMUR (v.) - To dispute the sufficiency in law of the pleading of the other side.

DEMURRAGE - In maritime law, it means, the sum fixed or allowed as remuneration to the owners of a ship for the detention of their vessel beyond the number of days allowed for loading and unloading or for sailing; also used in railroad terminology.
DENIAL - A form of pleading; refusing to admit the truth of a statement, charge, etc.
DEPONENT - One who gives testimony under oath reduced to writing.
DEPOSITION - Testimony given under oath outside of court for use in court or for the purpose of obtaining information in preparation for trial of a case.
DETERIORATION - A degeneration such as from decay, corrosion or disintegration.
DETRIMENT - Any loss or harm to person or property.
DEVIATION - A turning aside.
DEVISE - A gift of real property by the last will and testament of the donor.
DICTUM (sing.)
DICTA (plural) - Any statements made by the court in an opinion concerning some rule of law not necessarily involved nor essential to the determination of the case.
DIRECT EVIDENCE - Evidence that directly proves a fact, without an inference or presumption, and which in itself if true, conclusively establishes that fact.
DIRECT EXAMINATION - The first examination of a witness upon a matter that is not within the scope of a previous examination of the witness.
DISAFFIRM - To repudiate.
DISMISS - In an action or suit, it means to dispose of the case without any further consideration or hearing.
DISSENT - To denote disagreement of one or more judges of a court with the decision passed by the majority upon a case before them.
DOCKET (n.) - A formal record, entered in brief, of the proceedings in a court.
DOCTRINE - A rule, principle, theory of law.
DOMICILE - That place where a man has his true, fixed and permanent home to which whenever he is absent he has the intention of returning.
DRAFT (n.) - A commercial paper ordering payment of money drawn by one person on another.
DRAWEE - The person who is requested to pay the money.
DRAWER - The person who draws the commercial paper and addresses it to the drawee.
DUPLICATE - A counterpart produced by the same impression as the original enlargements and miniatures, or by mechanical or electronic re-recording, or by chemical reproduction, or by other equivalent technique which accurately reproduces the original.
DURESS - Use of force to compel performance or non-performance of an act.

E

EASEMENT - A liberty, privilege, or advantage without profit, in the lands of another.
EGRESS - Act or right of going out or leaving; emergence.
EIUSDEM GENERIS - Of the same kind, class or nature. A rule used in the construction of language in a legal document.
EMBEZZLEMENT - To steal; to appropriate fraudulently to one's own use property entrusted to one's care.
EMBRACERY - Unlawful attempt to influence jurors, etc., but not by offering value.
EMINENT DOMAIN - The right of a state to take private property for public use.
ENACT - To make into a law.
ENDORSEMENT - Act of writing one's name on the back of a note, bill or similar written instrument.

ENJOIN - To require a person, by writ of injunction from a court of equity, to perform or to abstain or desist from some act.
ENTIRETY - The whole; that which the law considers as one whole, and not capable of being divided into parts.
ENTRAPMENT - Inducing one to commit a crime so as to arrest him.
ENUMERATED - Mentioned specifically; designated.
ENURE - To operate or take effect.
EQUITY - In its broadest sense, this term denotes the spirit and the habit of fairness, justness, and right dealing which regulate the conduct of men.
ERROR - A mistake of law, or the false or irregular application of law as will nullify the judicial proceedings.
ESCROW - A deed, bond or other written engagement, delivered to a third person, to be delivered by him only upon the performance or fulfillment of some condition.
ESTATE - The interest which any one has in lands, or in any other subject of property.
ESTOP - To stop, bar, or impede.
ESTOPPEL - A rule of law which prevents a man from alleging or denying a fact, because of his own previous act.
ET AL. (alii) - And others.
ET SEQ. (sequential) - And the following.
ET UX. (uxor) - And wife.
EVIDENCE - Testimony, writings, material objects, or other things presented to the senses that are offered to prove the existence or non-existence of a fact.
    Means from which inferences may be drawn as a basis of proof in duly constituted judicial or fact finding tribunals, and includes testimony in the form of opinion and hearsay.
EX CONTRACTU
EX DELICTO - In law, rights and causes of action are divided into two classes, those arising *ex contractu* (from a contract) and those arising *ex delicto* (from a delict or tort).
EX OFFICIO - From office; by virtue of the office.
EX PARTE - On one side only; by or for one.
EX POST FACTO - After the fact.
EX POST FACTO LAW - A law passed after an act was done which retroactively makes such act a crime.
EX REL. (relations) - Upon relation or information.
EXCEPTION - An objection upon a matter of law to a decision made, either before or after judgment by a court.
EXECUTOR (male)
EXECUTRIX (female) - A person who has been appointed by will to execute the will.
EXECUTORY - That which is yet to be executed or performed.
EXEMPT - To release from some liability to which others are subject.
EXONERATION - The removal of a burden, charge or duty.
EXTRADITION - Surrender of a fugitive from one nation to another.

F

F.A.S.- "Free alongside ship"; delivery at dock for ship named.
F.O.B.- "Free on board"; seller will deliver to car, truck, vessel, or other conveyance by which goods are to be transported, without expense or risk of loss to the buyer or consignee.
FABRICATE - To construct; to invent a false story.
FACSIMILE - An exact or accurate copy of an original instrument.

FACTOR - A commercial agent.
FEASANCE - The doing of an act.
FELONIOUS - Criminal, malicious.
FELONY - Generally, a criminal offense that may be punished by death or imprisonment for more than one year as differentiated from a misdemeanor.
FEME SOLE - A single woman.
FIDUCIARY - A person who is invested with rights and powers to be exercised for the benefit of another person.
FIERI FACIAS - A writ of execution commanding the sheriff to levy and collect the amount of a judgment from the goods and chattels of the judgment debtor.
FINDING OF FACT - Determination from proof or judicial notice of the existence of a fact. A ruling implies a supporting finding of fact; no separate or formal finding is required unless required by a statute of this state.
FISCAL - Relating to accounts or the management of revenue.
FORECLOSURE (sale) - A sale of mortgaged property to obtain satisfaction of the mortgage out of the sale proceeds.
FORFEITURE - A penalty, a fine.
FORGERY - Fabricating or producing falsely, counterfeited.
FORTUITOUS - Accidental.
FORUM - A court of justice; a place of jurisdiction.
FRAUD - Deception; trickery.
FREEHOLDER - One who owns real property.
FUNGIBLE - Of such kind or nature that one specimen or part may be used in the place of another.

G

GARNISHEE - Person garnished.
GARNISHMENT - A legal process to reach the money or effects of a defendant, in the possession or control of a third person.
GRAND JURY - Not less than 16, not more than 23 citizens of a county sworn to inquire into crimes committed or triable in the county.
GRANT - To agree to; convey, especially real property.
GRANTEE - The person to whom a grant is made.
GRANTOR - The person by whom a grant is made.
GRATUITOUS - Given without a return, compensation or consideration.
GRAVAMEN - The grievance complained of or the substantial cause of a criminal action.
GUARANTY (n.) - A promise to answer for the payment of some debt, or the performance of some duty, in case of the failure of another person, who, in the first instance, is liable for such payment or performance.
GUARDIAN - The person, committee, or other representative authorized by law to protect the person or estate or both of an incompetent (or of a *sui juris* person having a guardian) and to act for him in matters affecting his person or property or both. An incompetent is a person under disability imposed by law.
GUILTY - Establishment of the fact that one has committed a breach of conduct; especially, a violation of law.

H

HABEAS CORPUS - You have the body; the name given to a variety of writs, having for their object to bring a party before a court or judge for decision as to whether such person is being lawfully held prisoner.

HABENDUM - In conveyancing; it is the clause in a deed conveying land which defines the extent of ownership to be held by the grantee.

HEARING - A proceeding whereby the arguments of the interested parties are heared.

HEARSAY - A type of testimony given by a witness who relates, not what he knows personally, but what others have told hi, or what he has heard said by others.

HEARSAY RULE, THE - (a) "Hearsay evidence" is evidence of a statement that was made other than by a witness while testifying at the hearing and that is offered to prove the truth of the matter stated; (b) Except as provided by law, hearsay evidence is inadmissible; (c) This section shall be known and may be cited as the hearsay rule.

HEIR - Generally, one who inherits property, real or personal.

HOLDER OF THE PRIVILEGE - (a) The client when he has no guardian or conservator; (b) A guardian or conservator of the client when the client has a guardian or conservator; (c) The personal representative of the client if the client is dead; (d) A successor, assign, trustee in dissolution, or any similar representative of a firm, association, organization, partnership, business trust, corporation, or public entity that is no longer in existence.

HUNG JURY - One so divided that they can't agree on a verdict.

HUSBAND-WIFE PRIVILEGE - An accused in a criminal proceeding has a privilege to prevent his spouse from testifying against him.

HYPOTHECATE - To pledge a thing without delivering it to the pledgee.

HYPOTHESIS - A supposition, assumption, or toehry.

I

I.E. (id est) - That is.

IB., OR IBID.(ibidem) - In the same place; used to refer to a legal reference previously cited to avoid repeating the entire citation.

ILLICIT - Prohibited; unlawful.

ILLUSORY - Deceiving by false appearance.

IMMUNITY - Exemption.

IMPEACH - To accuse, to dispute.

IMPEDIMENTS - Disabilities, or hindrances.

IMPLEAD - To sue or prosecute by due course of law.

IMPUTED - Attributed or charged to.

IN LOCO PARENTIS - In place of parent, a guardian.

IN TOTO - In the whole; completely.

INCHOATE - Imperfect; unfinished.

INCOMMUNICADO - Denial of the right of a prisoner to communicate with friends or relatives.

INCOMPETENT - One who is incapable of caring for his own affairs because he is mentally deficient or undeveloped.

INCRIMINATION - A matter will incriminate a person if it constitutes, or forms an essential part of, or, taken in connection with other matters disclosed, is a basis for a reasonable inference of such a violation of the laws of this State as to subject him to liability to punishment therefor, unless he has become for any reason permanently immune from punishment for such violation.

INCUMBRANCE - Generally a claim, lien, charge or liability attached to and binding real property.

INDEMNIFY - To secure against loss or damage; also, to make reimbursement to one for a loss already incurred by him.
INDEMNITY - An agreement to reimburse another person in case of an anticipated loss falling upon him.
INDICIA - Signs; indications.
INDICTMENT - An accusation in writing found and presented by a grand jury charging that a person has committed a crime.
INDORSE - To write a name on the back of a legal paper or document, generally, a negotiable instrument
INDUCEMENT - Cause or reason why a thing is done or that which incites the person to do the act or commit a crime; the motive for the criminal act.
INFANT - In civil cases one under 21 years of age.
INFORMATION - A formal accusation of crime made by a prosecuting attorney.
INFRA - Below, under; this word occurring by itself in a publication refers the reader to a future part of the publication.
INGRESS - The act of going into.
INJUNCTION - A writ or order by the court requiring a person, generally, to do or to refrain from doing an act.
INSOLVENT - The condition of a person who is unable to pay his debts.
INSTRUCTION - A direction given by the judge to the jury concerning the law of the case.
INTERIM - In the meantime; time intervening.
INTERLOCUTORY - Temporary, not final; something intervening between the commencement and the end of a suit which decides some point or matter, but is not a final decision of the whole controversy.
INTERROGATORIES - A series of formal written questions used in the examination of a party or a witness usually prior to a trial.
INTESTATE - A person who dies without a will.
INURE - To result, to take effect.
IPSO FACTO - By the fact iself; by the mere fact.
ISSUE (n.) The disputed point or question in a case,

J

JEOPARDY - Danger, hazard, peril.
JOINDER - Joining; uniting with another person in some legal steps or proceeding.
JOINT - United; combined.
JUDGE - Member or members or representative or representatives of a court conducting a trial or hearing at which evidence is introduced.
JUDGMENT - The official decision of a court of justice.
JUDICIAL OR JUDICIARY - Relating to or connected with the administration of justice.
JURAT - The clause written at the foot of an affidavit, stating when, where and before whom such affidavit was sworn.
JURISDICTION - The authority to hear and determine controversies between parties.
JURISPRUDENCE - The philosophy of law.
JURY - A body of persons legally selected to inquire into any matter of fact, and to render their verdict according to the evidence.

L

LACHES - The failure to diligently assert a right, which results in a refusal to allow relief.

LANDLORD AND TENANT - A phrase used to denote the legal relation existing between the owner and occupant of real estate.

LARCENY - Stealing personal property belonging to another.

LATENT - Hidden; that which does not appear on the face of a thing.

LAW - Includes constitutional, statutory, and decisional law.

LAWYER-CLIENT PRIVILEGE - (1) A "client" is a person, public officer, or corporation, association, or other organization or entity, either public or private, who is rendered professional legal services by a lawyer, or who consults a lawyer with a view to obtaining professional legal services from him; (2) A "lawyer" is a person authorized, or reasonably believed by the client to be authorized, to practice law in any state or nation; (3) A "representative of the lawyer" is one employed to assist the lawyer in the rendition of professional legal services; (4) A communication is "confidential" if not intended to be disclosed to third persons other than those to whom disclosure is in furtherance of the rendition of professional legal services to the client or those reasonably necessary for the transmission of the communication.

General rule of privilege - A client has a privilege to refuse to disclose and to prevent any other person from disclosing confidential communications made for the purpose of facilitating the rendition of professional legal services to the client, (1) between himself or his representative and his lawyer or his lawyer's representative, or (2) between his lawyer and the lawyer's representative, or (3) by him or his lawyer to a lawyer representing another in a matter of common interest, or (4) between representatives of the client or between the client and a representative of the client, or (5) between lawyers representing the client.

LEADING QUESTION - Question that suggests to the witness the answer that the examining party desires.

LEASE - A contract by which one conveys real estate for a limited time usually for a specified rent; personal property also may be leased.

LEGISLATION - The act of enacting laws.

LEGITIMATE - Lawful.

LESSEE - One to whom a lease is given.

LESSOR - One who grants a lease

LEVY - A collecting or exacting by authority.

LIABLE - Responsible; bound or obligated in law or equity.

LIBEL (v.) - To defame or injure a person's reputation by a published writing.

(n.) - The initial pleading on the part of the plaintiff in an admiralty proceeding.

LIEN - A hold or claim which one person has upon the property of another as a security for some debt or charge.

LIQUIDATED - Fixed; settled.

LIS PENDENS - A pending civil or criminal action.

LITERAL - According to the language.

LITIGANT - A party to a lawsuit.

LITATION - A judicial controversy.

LOCUS - A place.

LOCUS DELICTI - Place of the crime.

LOCUS POENITENTIAE - The abandoning or giving up of one's intention to commit some crime before it is fully completed or abandoning a conspiracy before its purpose is accomplished.

M

MALFEASANCE - To do a wrongful act.

MALICE - The doing of a wrongful act Intentionally without just cause or excuse.

MANDAMUS - The name of a writ issued by a court to enforce the performance of some public duty.
MANDATORY (adj.) Containing a command.
MARITIME - Pertaining to the sea or to commerce thereon.
MARSHALING - Arranging or disposing of in order.
MAXIM - An established principle or proposition.
MINISTERIAL - That which involves obedience to instruction, but demands no special discretion, judgment or skill.
MISAPPROPRIATE - Dealing fraudulently with property entrusted to one.
MISDEMEANOR - A crime less than a felony and punishable by a fine or imprisonment for less than one year.
MISFEASANCE - Improper performance of a lawful act.
MISREPRESENTATION - An untrue representation of facts.
MITIGATE - To make or become less severe, harsh.
MITTIMUS - A warrant of commitment to prison.
MOOT (adj.) Unsettled, undecided, not necessary to be decided.
MORTGAGE - A conveyance of property upon condition, as security for the payment of a debt or the performance of a duty, and to become void upon payment or performance according to the stipulated terms.
MORTGAGEE - A person to whom property is mortgaged.
MORTGAGOR - One who gives a mortgage.
MOTION - In legal proceedings, a "motion" is an application, either written or oral, addressed to the court by a party to an action or a suit requesting the ruling of the court on a matter of law.
MUTUALITY - Reciprocation.

N

NEGLIGENCE - The failure to exercise that degree of care which an ordinarily prudent person would exercise under like circumstances.
NEGOTIABLE (instrument) - Any instrument obligating the payment of money which is transferable from one person to another by endorsement and delivery or by delivery only.
NEGOTIATE - To transact business; to transfer a negotiable instrument; to seek agreement for the amicable disposition of a controversy or case.
NOLLE PROSEQUI - A formal entry upon the record, by the plaintiff in a civil suit or the prosecuting officer in a criminal action, by which he declares that he "will no further prosecute" the case.
NOLO CONTENDERE - The name of a plea in a criminal action, having the same effect as a plea of guilty; but not constituting a direct admission of guilt.
NOMINAL - Not real or substantial.
NOMINAL DAMAGES - Award of a trifling sum where no substantial injury is proved to have been sustained.
NONFEASANCE - Neglect of duty.
NOVATION - The substitution of a new debt or obligation for an existing one.
NUNC PRO TUNC - A phrase applied to acts allowed to be done after the time when they should be done, with a retroactive effect.("Now for then.")

O

OATH - Oath includes affirmation or declaration under penalty of perjury.
OBITER DICTUM - Opinion expressed by a court on a matter not essentially involved in a case and hence not a decision; also called dicta, if plural.

OBJECT (v.) - To oppose as improper or illegal and referring the question of its propriety or legality to the court.
OBLIGATION - A legal duty, by which a person is bound to do or not to do a certain thing.
OBLIGEE - The person to whom an obligation is owed.
OBLIGOR - The person who is to perform the obligation.
OFFER (v.) - To present for acceptance or rejection.
    (n.) - A proposal to do a thing, usually a proposal to make a contract.
OFFICIAL INFORMATION - Information within the custody or control of a department or agency of the government the disclosure of which is shown to be contrary to the public interest.
OFFSET - A deduction.
ONUS PROBANDI - Burden of proof.
OPINION - The statement by a judge of the decision reached in a case, giving the law as applied to the case and giving reasons for the judgment; also a belief or view.
OPTION - The exercise of the power of choice; also a privilege existing in one person, for which he has paid money, which gives him the right to buy or sell real or personal property at a given price within a specified time.
ORDER - A rule or regulation; every direction of a court or judge made or entered in writing but not including a judgment.
ORDINANCE - Generally, a rule established by authority; also commonly used to designate the legislative acts of a municipal corporation.
ORIGINAL - Writing or recording itself or any counterpart intended to have the same effect by a person executing or issuing it. An "original" of a photograph includes the negative or any print therefrom. If data are stored in a computer or similar device, any printout or other output readable by sight, shown to reflect the data accurately, is an "original."
OVERT - Open, manifest.

P

PANEL - A group of jurors selected to serve during a term of the court.
PARENS PATRIAE - Sovereign power of a state to protect or be a guardian over children and incompetents.
PAROL - Oral or verbal.
PAROLE - To release one in prison before the expiration of his sentence, conditionally.
PARITY - Equality in purchasing power between the farmer and other segments of the economy.
PARTITION - A legal division of real or personal property between one or more owners.
PARTNERSHIP - An association of two or more persons to carry on as co-owners a business for profit.
PATENT (adj.) - Evident.
    (n.) - A grant of some privilege, property, or authority, made by the government or sovereign of a country to one or more individuals.
PECULATION - Stealing.
PECUNIARY - Monetary.
PENULTIMATE - Next to the last.
PER CURIAM - A phrase used in the report of a decision to distinguish an opinion of the whole court from an opinion written by any one judge.
PER SE - In itself; taken alone.
PERCEIVE - To acquire knowledge through one's senses.
PEREMPTORY - Imperative; absolute.
PERJURY - To lie or state falsely under oath.

PERPETUITY - Perpetual existence; also the quality or condition of an estate limited so that it will not take effect or vest within the period fixed by law.
PERSON - Includes a natural person, firm, association, organization, partnership, business trust, corporation, or public entity.
PERSONAL PROPERTY - Includes money, goods, chattels, things in action, and evidences of debt.
PERSONALTY - Short term for personal property.
PETITION - An application in writing for an order of the court, stating the circumstances upon which it is founded and requesting any order or other relief from a court.
PLAINTIFF - A person who brings a court action.
PLEA - A pleading in a suit or action.
PLEADINGS - Formal allegations made by the parties of their respective claims and defenses, for the judgment of the court.
PLEDGE - A deposit of personal property as a security for the performance of an act.
PLEDGEE - The party to whom goods are delivered in pledge.
PLEDGOR - The party delivering goods in pledge.
PLENARY - Full; complete.
POLICE POWER - Inherent power of the state or its political subdivisions to enact laws within constitutional limits to promote the general welfare of society or the community.
POLLING THE JURY - Call the names of persons on a jury and requiring each juror to declare what his verdict is before it is legally recorded.
POST MORTEM - After death.
POWER OF ATTORNEY - A writing authorizing one to act for another.
PRECEPT - An order, warrant, or writ issued to an officer or body of officers, commanding him or them to do some act within the scope of his or their powers.
PRELIMINARY FACT - Fact upon the existence or nonexistence of which depends the admissibility or inadmissibility of evidence. The phrase "the admissibility or inadmissibility of evidence" includes the qualification or disqualification of a person to be a witness and the existence or nonexistence of a privilege.
PREPONDERANCE - Outweighing.
PRESENTMENT - A report by a grand jury on something they have investigated on their own knowledge.
PRESUMPTION - An assumption of fact resulting from a rule of law which requires such fact to be assumed from another fact or group of facts found or otherwise established in the action.
PRIMA FACUE - At first sight.
PRIMA FACIE CASE - A case where the evidence is very patent against the defendant.
PRINCIPAL - The source of authority or rights; a person primarily liable as differentiated from "principle" as a primary or basic doctrine.
PRO AND CON - For and against.
PRO RATA - Proportionally.
PROBATE - Relating to proof, especially to the proof of wills.
PROBATIVE - Tending to prove.
PROCEDURE - In law, this term generally denotes rules which are established by the Federal, State, or local Governments regarding the types of pleading and courtroom practice which must be followed by the parties involved in a criminal or civil case.
PROCLAMATION - A public notice by an official of some order, intended action, or state of facts.

PROFFERED EVIDENCE - The admissibility or inadmissibility of which is dependent upon the existence or nonexistence of a preliminary fact.
PROMISSORY (NOTE) - A promise in writing to pay a specified sum at an expressed time, or on demand, or at sight, to a named person, or to his order, or bearer.
PROOF - The establishment by evidence of a requisite degree of belief concerning a fact in the mind of the trier of fact or the court.
PROPERTY - Includes both real and personal property.
PROPRIETARY (adj.) - Relating or pertaining to ownership; usually a single owner.
PROSECUTE - To carry on an action or other judicial proceeding; to proceed against a person criminally.
PROVISO - A limitation or condition in a legal instrument.
PROXIMATE - Immediate; nearest
PUBLIC EMPLOYEE - An officer, agent, or employee of a public entity.
PUBLIC ENTITY - Includes a national, state, county, city and county, city, district, public authority, public agency, or any other political subdivision or public corporation, whether foreign or domestic.
PUBLIC OFFICIAL - Includes an official of a political dubdivision of such state or territory and of a municipality.
PUNITIVE - Relating to punishment.

Q

QUASH - To make void.
QUASI - As if; as it were.
QUID PRO QUO - Something for something; the giving of one valuable thing for another.
QUITCLAIM (v.) - To release or relinquish claim or title to, especially in deeds to realty.
QUO WARRANTO - A legal procedure to test an official's right to a public office or the right to hold a franchise, or to hold an office in a domestic corporation.

R

RATIFY - To approve and sanction.
REAL PROPERTY - Includes lands, tenements, and hereditaments.
REALTY - A brief term for real property.
REBUT - To contradict; to refute, especially by evidence and arguments.
RECEIVER - A person who is appointed by the court to receive, and hold in trust property in litigation.
RECIDIVIST - Habitual criminal.
RECIPROCAL - Mutual.
RECOUPMENT - To keep back or get something which is due; also, it is the right of a defendant to have a deduction from the amount of the plaintiff's damages because the plaintiff has not fulfilled his part of the same contract.
RECROSS EXAMINATION - Examination of a witness by a cross-examiner subsequent to a redirect examination of the witness.
REDEEM - To release an estate or article from mortgage or pledge by paying the debt for which it stood as security.
REDIRECT EXAMINATION - Examination of a witness by the direct examiner subsequent to the cross-examination of the witness.
REFEREE - A person to whom a cause pending in a court is referred by the court, to take testimony, hear the parties, and report thereon to the court.

REFERENDUM - A method of submitting an important legislative or administrative matter to a direct vote of the people.
RELEVANT EVIDENCE - Evidence including evidence relevant to the credulity of a witness or hearsay declarant, having any tendency in reason to prove or disprove any disputed fact that is of consequence to the determination of the action.
REMAND - To send a case back to the lower court from which it came, for further proceedings.
REPLEVIN - An action to recover goods or chattels wrongfully taken or detained.
REPLY (REPLICATION) - Generally, a reply is what the plaintiff or other person who has instituted proceedings says in answer to the defendant's case.
RE JUDICATA - A thing judicially acted upon or decided.
RES ADJUDICATA - Doctrine that an issue or dispute litigated and determined in a case between the opposing parties is deemed permanently decided between these parties.
RESCIND (RECISSION) - To avoid or cancel a contract.
RESPONDENT - A defendant in a proceeding in chancery or admiralty; also, the person who contends against the appeal in a case.
RESTITUTION - In equity, it is the restoration of both parties to their original condition (when practicable), upon the rescission of a contract for fraud or similar cause.
RETROACTIVE (RETROSPECTIVE) - Looking back; effective as of a prior time.
REVERSED - A term used by appellate courts to indicate that the decision of the lower court in the case before it has been set aside.
REVOKE - To recall or cancel.
RIPARIAN (RIGHTS) - The rights of a person owning land containing or bordering on a water course or other body of water, such as lakes and rivers.

S

SALE - A contract whereby the ownership of property is transferred from one person to another for a sum of money or for any consideration.
SANCTION - A penalty or punishment provided as a means of enforcing obedience to a law; also, an authorization.
SATISFACTION - The discharge of an obligation by paying a party what is due to him; or what is awarded to him by the judgment of a court or otherwise.
SCIENTER - Knowingly; also, it is used in pleading to denote the defendant's guilty knowledge.
SCINTILLA - A spark; also the least particle.
SECRET OF STATE - Governmental secret relating to the national defense or the international relations of the United States.
SECURITY - Indemnification; the term is applied to an obligation, such as a mortgage or deed of trust, given by a debtor to insure the payment or performance of his debt, by furnishing the creditor with a resource to be used in case of the debtor's failure to fulfill the principal obligation.
SENTENCE - The judgment formally pronounced by the court or judge upon the defendant after his conviction in a criminal prosecution.
SET-OFF - A claim or demand which one party in an action credits against the claim of the opposing party.
SHALL and MAY - "Shall" is mandatory and "may" is permissive.
SITUS - Location.
SOVEREIGN - A person, body or state in which independent and supreme authority is vested.
STARE DECISIS - To follow decided cases.

STATE - "State" means this State, unless applied to the different parts of the United States. In the latter case, it includes any state, district, commonwealth, territory or insular possession of the United States, including the District of Columbia.

STATEMENT - (a) Oral or written verbal expression or (b) nonverbal conduct of a person intended by him as a substitute for oral or written verbal expression.

STATUTE - An act of the legislature. Includes a treaty.

STATUTE OF LIMITATION - A statute limiting the time to bring an action after the right of action has arisen.

STAY - To hold in abeyance an order of a court.

STIPULATION - Any agreement made by opposing attorneys regulating any matter incidental to the proceedings or trial.

SUBORDINATION (AGREEMENT) - An agreement making one's rights inferior to or of a lower rank than another's.

SUBORNATION - The crime of procuring a person to lie or to make false statements to a court.

SUBPOENA - A writ or order directed to a person, and requiring his attendance at a particular time and place to testify as a witness.

SUBPOENA DUCES TECUM - A subpoena used, not only for the purpose of compelling witnesses to attend in court, but also requiring them to bring with them books or documents which may be in their possession, and which may tend to elucidate the subject matter of the trial.

SUBROGATION - The substituting of one for another as a creditor, the new creditor succeeding to the former's rights.

SUBSIDY - A government grant to assist a private enterprise deemed advantageous to the public.

SUI GENERIS - Of the same kind.

SUIT - Any civil proceeding by a person or persons against another or others in a court of justice by which the plaintiff pursues the remedies afforded him by law.

SUMMONS - A notice to a defendant that an action against him has been commenced and requiring him to appear in court and answer the complaint.

SUPRA - Above; this word occurring by itself in a book refers the reader to a previous part of the book.

SURETY - A person who binds himself for the payment of a sum of money, or for the performance of something else, for another.

SURPLUSAGE - Extraneous or unnecessary matter.

SURVIVORSHIP - A term used when a person becomes entitled to property by reason of his having survived another person who had an interest in the property.

SUSPEND SENTENCE - Hold back a sentence pending good behavior of prisoner.

SYLLABUS - A note prefixed to a report, especially a case, giving a brief statement of the court's ruling on different issues of the case.

T

TALESMAN - Person summoned to fill a panel of jurors.

TENANT - One who holds or possesses lands by any kind of right or title; also, one who has the temporary use and occupation of real property owned by another person (landlord), the duration and terms of his tenancy being usually fixed by an instrument called "a lease."

TENDER - An offer of money; an expression of willingness to perform a contract according to its terms.

TERM - When used with reference to a court, it signifies the period of time during which the court holds a session, usually of several weeks or months duration.

TESTAMENTARY - Pertaining to a will or the administration of a will.
TESTATOR (male)
TESTATRIX (female) - One who makes or has made a testament or will.
TESTIFY (TESTIMONY) - To give evidence under oath as a witness.
TO WIT - That is to say; namely.
TORT - Wrong; injury to the person.
TRANSITORY - Passing from place to place.
TRESPASS - Entry into another's ground, illegally.
TRIAL - The examination of a cause, civil or criminal, before a judge who has jurisdiction over it, according to the laws of the land.
TRIER OF FACT - Includes (a) the jury and (b) the court when the court is trying an issue of fact other than one relating to the admissibility of evidence.
TRUST - A right of property, real or personal, held by one party for the benefit of another.
TRUSTEE - One who lawfully holds property in custody for the benefit of another.

U

UNAVAILABLE AS A WITNESS - The declarant is (1) Exempted or precluded on the ground of privilege from testifying concerning the matter to which his statement is relevant; (2) Disqualified from testifying to the matter; (3) Dead or unable to attend or to testify at the hearing because of then existing physical or mental illness or infirmity; (4) Absent from the hearing and the court is unable to compel his attendance by its process; or (5) Absent from the hearing and the proponent of his statement has exercised reasonable diligence but has been unable to procure his attendance by the court's process.
ULTRA VIRES - Acts beyond the scope and power of a corporation, association, etc.
UNILATERAL - One-sided; obligation upon, or act of one party.
USURY - Unlawful interest on a loan.

V

VACATE - To set aside; to move out.
VARIANCE - A discrepancy or disagreement between two instruments or two aspects of the same case, which by law should be consistent.
VENDEE - A purchaser or buyer.
VENDOR - The person who transfers property by sale, particularly real estate; the term "seller" is used more commonly for one who sells personal property.
VENIREMEN - Persons ordered to appear to serve on a jury or composing a panel of jurors.
VENUE - The place at which an action is tried, generally based on locality or judicial district in which an injury occurred or a material fact happened.
VERDICT - The formal decision or finding of a jury.
VERIFY - To confirm or substantiate by oath.
VEST - To accrue to.
VOID - Having no legal force or binding effect.
VOIR DIRE - Preliminary examination of a witness or a juror to test competence, interest, prejudice, etc.

W

WAIVE - To give up a right.
WAIVER - The intentional or voluntary relinquishment of a known right.
WARRANT (WARRANTY) (v.) - To promise that a certain fact or state of facts, in relation to the subject matter, is, or shall be, as it is represented to be.

WARRANT (n.) - A writ issued by a judge, or other competent authority, addressed to a sheriff, or other officer, requiring him to arrest the person therein named, and bring him before the judge or court to answer or be examined regarding the offense with which he is charged.

WRIT - An order or process issued in the name of the sovereign or in the name of a court or judicial officer, commanding the performance or nonperformance of some act.

WRITING - Handwriting, typewriting, printing, photostating, photographing and every other means of recording upon any tangible thing any form of communication or representation, including letters, words, pictures, sounds, or symbols, or combinations thereof.

WRITINGS AND RECORDINGS - Consists of letters, words, or numbers, or their equivalent, set down by handwriting, typewriting, printing, photostating, photographing, magnetic impulse, mechanical or electronic recording, or other form of data compilation.

Y

YEA AND NAY - Yes and no.

YELLOW DOG CONTRACT - A contract by which employer requires employee to sign an instrument promising as condition that he will not join a union during its continuance, and will be discharged if he does join.

Z

ZONING - The division of a city by legislative regulation into districts and the prescription and application in each district of regulations having to do with structural and architectural designs of buildings and of regulations prescribing use to which buildings within designated districts may be put.

www.ingramcontent.com/pod-product-compliance
Lightning Source LLC
Chambersburg PA
CBHW082034300426
44117CB00015B/2478